DATE DUE		

FROM ————————————★
WHISTLE STOP
TO
SOUND BITE ——★

FROM ———————————————★

WHISTLE STOP

TO

SOUND BITE

Four Decades of Politics and Television

SIG
MICKELSON

PRAEGER

New York
Westport, Connecticut
London

Library of Congress Cataloging-in-Publication Data

Mickelson, Sig.
    From whistle stop to sound bite : four decades of politics and
television / Sig Mickelson.
        p.   cm.
    Bibliography: p.
    Includes index.
    ISBN 0–275–92351–7 : (alk. paper). — ISBN 0–275–92632–X (pbk. :
alk. paper)
    1. Television in politics—United States.   2. United States—
Politics and government—1945–   I. Title.
HE8700.76.U6M54   1989
324.7'3'0973—dc19   89–3554

Library of Congress Catalog Card Number: 89–3554
ISBN: 0–275–92351–7
      0–275–92632–X

First published in 1989

Praeger Publishers, One Madison Avenue, New York, NY 10010
An imprint of Greenwood Publishing Group, Inc.

Printed in the United States of America

The paper used in this book complies with the
Permanent Paper Standard issued by the National
Information Standards Organization (Z39.48–1984).

10 9 8 7 6 5 4 3

To Elena

Contents

Contents

Acknowledgments

The largest share of the raw material on which this volume is based came either from extensive files I have retained from the early days of television's uneasy romance with politics or from miscellaneous bits and pieces of flotsam and jetsam that have been floating around in my mind. It was my custom after an event of importance to dictate a memorandum to the files describing our strengths and weaknesses and recommending specific steps to do better in the future. In some cases I thought a specific experience was so interesting it was worth preserving on paper. A score of speeches written on various facets of the topic and preserved in my library also helped jog my memory and fill in details.

For getting the filing process under way in an orderly manner and establishing a pattern that I could later follow, I must give full credit to Helen Anderson, who was my secretary at both CBS and Time, Inc. in the 1950s and 1960s.

John Chancellor, who has covered politics for NBC for three decades, furnished a thoughtful analysis of the evolution in coverage by both networks and local stations. He was particularly helpful in calling attention to the enormous impact of increasingly sophisticated telecommunications technology not only on reporting but also on the substance of the final on-the-air output.

David Buksbaum of CBS News added specific details on the deployment of both production personnel and technological facilities for CBS's coverage of the 1988 primaries, including a description of the satellite services the network made available for scores of affiliated local stations. David Poltrack, who directs CBS's audience research facilities, and members of his staff cheerfully researched their files and produced detailed evidence of the breathtaking growth of viewership for politics in the 1950s and 1960s and the subsequent leveling off.

Additional useful background and a personal chronicle of the swiftly evolving methods used by both candidates and television reporting teams came from Herbert A. Klein. Klein was deeply involved at the very beginning of television's immersion in politics. He was director of media in California for the Eisenhower-Nixon team in 1952 and served as a key media aid to Nixon during both his vice presidency and presidency. As editor of the Copley Press he is still an avid observer of the political scene and of the relationship between politics and the media.

I have been able to reminisce and recheck my memory from time to time over the years with Walter Cronkite and Don Hewitt, who were so deeply involved with me during the 1950s. I am also deeply indebted to James A. Hagerty, who was President Eisenhower's press secretary and later president of ABC News; to Abbott Washburn, a key member of the Eisenhower staff during the 1952 election and later a member of the Federal Communications Commission; to Carroll Newton, Batten Barton Durstine and Osborn's key political operative in the 1940s and 1950s; to Robert Mullen, who handled the press at the beginning of the Eisenhower campaign; and to a host of other party officials, advertising agency political specialists, political scientists, and experts on political financing such as Herbert Alexander of the Citizen's Research Foundation.

One other person deserves mention, but for a different reason. Merrill J. Lessley, vice chancellor of the University of Colorado at Colorado Springs and formerly dean of the College of Professional Studies and Fine Arts as San Diego State University, on numerous occasions helped harness a balky computer that often stubbornly refused to do my bidding. This unusual role for a university dean and vice chancellor merits attention if only for the frustration it spared me.

FROM ──────────★
WHISTLE STOP
TO
SOUND BITE ──★

Introduction

In 1974, television station WTTW, the public broadcasting outlet in Chicago, produced a program for the national Public Broadcasting Service entitled "The Selling of Abraham Lincoln." The program raised three provocative questions: First, would Lincoln be comfortable in using commercial television spot announcements to support his candidacy? Second, would he permit their use? Third, could he be elected in a society dominated by television?

The program concluded that Lincoln could not be elected in the 1970s because he either would not or could not adapt to television. It also was concluded that the new medium would prevent an able citizen from running for and winning the office of president. The requirements of television, it was implied, would distort the process of selecting the most competent candidate for public office. The camera would demand that the office seeker be telegenic. He could not win if he rebelled at selling himself or his ideas in spot commercials. By inference, the program suggested that the influence of television has been negative, if not dangerous, to traditional American democratic institutions.

This conclusion raises some disturbing questions: Has television so altered the process of electing public officials that an entire class of able potential candidates is automatically excluded from winning elections or even being nominated? How many superior candidates would we lose this way? Has television so degraded the electoral process that running for public office has become unattractive to able candidates? Or has it become so infused with advertising techniques that only hard sell can win?

Or, conversely, while it may be flawed, does television promise a more effective and democratic electoral system by opening channels for communicating more directly and more personally with large segments of the public?

The fact is that Lincoln probably could be elected president in the 1990s. It is unlikely that television would keep him out of the race. He had learned the secret of communicating, which is the essence of successful performance on the screen. The skinny body and the scratchy voice would be no deterrent to winning popular support. If he had the talent for winning over voters in person, there is no reason why he could not do it by electronic campaigning.

Lincoln's problem would not be a lack of talent for adapting to television. That he could acquire. Rather, it would be lack of the patience and endurance to devote two years or more of his life to the seemingly endless campaign grind required to win the nomination. The long and tortuous road to the nomination that presidential candidates must now travel is in many respects a legacy of television.

It is probably more than coincidental that public fascination with the presidential primary developed in 1952, the first year that television discovered the primaries as a great story for its evening news.

Prior to 1952, when television first immersed itself fully in covering politics, primaries were only marginally important. With few exceptions, the decisions that counted were made on the convention floor or in the "smoke-filled rooms." Most convention delegates came unencumbered by pledges to support the winners of primaries.

Then came 1952 and television. The number of homes with receivers was still low by present standards. Evening news programs on the networks were just beginning to catch hold. But news executives were beginning to sense some of the power that the medium would eventually demonstrate. They deployed their limited but inexhaustible forces on the campaign trail in New Hampshire and later in Wisconsin. Candidates could hardly move without being pursued by television reporting teams with cameras at the ready. Scenes from the campaign trail showing candidates shaking hands at factory gates, speaking to rallies, and responding to questions asked by television reporters were a staple on the evening news.

Senator Robert Taft of Ohio looked dyspeptic on television and bored by the endless lines of hands he had to shake. This inability to adapt to the new medium may have cost him his chance of winning the Republican nomination even before New Hampshire Republicans went to the polls. Conversely, Senator Estes Kefauver of Tennessee, running for the Democratic presidential nomination, was able to capitalize on the reputation he had gained on national TV. Senate hearings on organized crime that he chaired had been given nationwide television exposure, making something of a national cult hero out of the Tennessean, a reputation he richly capitalized on.

As television cameras were shut down and studio lights went out after a night of ballot counting in New Hampshire election headquarters, the results were not nearly as decisive as the conclusion that anyone running for public office thereafter had better reckon with television. Wisconsin's primary, which followed only a few weeks later, reinforced the conclusion and added emphasis. Television was clearly a force to be reckoned with.

Once television had discovered the lure of the early skirmishing, the primary became a standing item on the nightly news menu. Candidates and their managers, in turn, soon recognized that here was a cheap and easy method of getting national exposure. Some didn't realize, however, that it wasn't all the bargain it seemed. Television could create winners, but it could also condemn contenders to defeat. It was exhilarating if appearance on the screen could serve to energize campaigns and win over neutral or even hostile voters, but disaster if the screen did not treat the candidate well or the candidate was unable to master its eccentricities.

Apart from its effect on the candidate, moreover, television began to show signs that it would likely have a profound effect on the whole electoral process. And not all the effects would be to the good.

With some four decades of hindsight, it is now possible to survey some of the wreckage strewn along the way. Party structures have been weakened. Nominees are usually selected on the basis of popularity polls called primaries or of caucuses, rather than by political professionals seeking the candidate most able to win and, more important, to govern. Small states easily covered by television frequently exercise preponderant weight in the final selection despite the fact that they are small, simply because they ballot early. Set responses to questions and stunts performed for the camera are replacing serious discussion of issues. The insatiable need for money to produce and buy more television spot commercials has become a serious handicap to candidates lacking big bankrolls. Candidates, in order to make credible showings in primaries, must invest vastly increased amounts of both time and money long before the fall campaign begins.

Politics, however, has been good to television. Local stations are reaping a bonanza from the increased volume of spot commercials. Both networks and local news departments have a nearly inexhaustible fund of potential big-name interviewees for their news and discussion programs. The excitement of the political horse race keeps ratings high, and the quadrennial national political conventions have given the networks an opportunity to test their mettle in direct combat with each other.

To the candidates, television was clearly a mixed blessing. It created a new platform from which they could reach voters more directly and more personally than ever before. But they ran the risk that those additional voters would either dislike or distrust them. And an unfavorable reaction could spell instant disaster.

Television enabled candidates to use appeals, devices, and campaign methods that had never previously been possible. But they had to know what they were doing and plan well in advance, or their brilliant strategies could backfire. An unfavorable impression on the television screen could undo weeks of handshaking and cartons of direct mail.

Television would open new avenues to getting elected and would be a helpful device for holding office once there, but it would take new strategies, new plans, new techniques, new support personnel, and a lot of money to exploit it.

And who was there to anticipate what turns and twists television would take as it grew from its infancy in 1952 to full maturity within two or three decades?

It is too easy to credit television with all the changes in political methodology that have occurred in the last four decades. It has been the center of attention because it brings the excitement of the race directly into the home, in a format that is doubly attractive because its principal ingredient is entertainment. It permits vicarious participation in highly newsworthy events that most persons never have the slightest hope of seeing in person. On broadcast television it is free. And it is all there without leaving the confines of the home.

The press was equally fascinated with the upstart medium, perhaps partly out of fear of new competition, partly out of jealousy, and partly because the newspaper-reading public, stimulated by television coverage, was giving it so much attention. It was a beguiling new phenomenon opening up limitless new vistas to the viewer, who never had to leave the living room.

Eager television news teams were inescapable during the 1952 campaign. The portable film camera with its station or network call letters boldly displayed on its side doggedly pursued candidates as long as they were in search of votes. One night in Wisconsin, CBS even trailed Estes Kefauver to his bedroom and got one of its most memorable interviews. The Tennessee senator, his shoes off and half lying across the bed, shook off his weariness and answered a reporter's questions for nearly half an hour.

When the candidate or his aides plead for more funding, the reason is frequently the need to buy more television commercials. In short, television dominates the campaign. Trips are planned around television opportunities. Direct mail calls attention to television appearances. Campaign statements are timed to coincide with television deadlines.

It is a mistake to credit television with sole responsibility for changing the political campaign. No one who has lived through the latter half of the twentieth century, though, can have failed to recognize that it has been a driving and motivating force. It has hastened the adoption of other technologies. It has compelled campaign managements to devote more care to strategic planning and more attention to budgets. It has put a premium on fund raising. And it has affected the choice of candidates, who increasingly are being selected on the basis of their skills in performing before the camera. The complexities of its most effective use in the campaign have led candidates to rely to an increasing degree on "handlers" who specialize in planning campaigns that will achieve maximum favorable exposure on television.

Some of the technologies that are now commonplace in the campaign would have appeared on the scene with or without television. And they would have had a solid impact on their own. The airplane gave the campaign flexibility and ended its reliance on whistle-stopping. The computer enormously expanded capabilities for processing information. It permitted quick storage of research materials and ready access to them. It also simplified and speeded fund raising by facilitating use of direct mail. Electrostatic copying released the organization from relying on the slow and messy mimeograph or on a limited number of carbons in a typewriter. Facsimile made it possible to transmit documents or speeches across the country in minutes or even seconds, rather than wait for days for the mails to move the copy. The videotape recorder enabled campaign management to record speeches made by opposing candidates in order to prepare responses or attack the opponent's position, and to use the device as an indispensable tool in training office seekers for television interviews, news conferences, and campaign speeches.

These new technologies contributed in their own way to dramatic transformation of political campaign methodology. It was television, however, that sparked the revolution. It was television that captured the public attention, convinced political leaders to revamp their tactics to conform to what they assumed were television's requirements. Television was closer to the individual than jet aircraft, computers, or xerographic copiers. It was the source of entertainment, diversion, and information. It was always in its place, ready to open up a window on the world. It may not be solely responsible for dramatic changes in political campaigning, but no individual in his right mind could deny its compelling influence. The transformation in political methodology, whether good or bad, is largely television's doing. Whether the political system profits or loses is a separate question.

Television, therefore, is the logical takeoff point for an examination of changes in political methodology. It was out front. It was in the living rooms, the dens, and the bedrooms of increasing numbers of American voters. It was the device that caught the attention of candidates and their managers, and led to a dramatic transformation in the way they managed their campaigns.

It is my intention to recount the events of some of those early days when television was testing the water of politics and eventually opting for full immersion. It was a period of trial and error, of boundless enthusiasm and nearly unlimited energy. Patterns were established then that still prevail, although some of them, in retrospect, would have been better left undiscovered.

Only with some historical perspective is it possible to note how dramatic some of the changes in political methodology have been. Whether television is solely responsible, a major contributor, or a partial contributor is not important. The changes occurred, and television was there. It was the center of attention; if not the sole cause for change, at least the excuse. And the change has been profound.

Since 1952, national political conventions, except for ceremonial functions, have done little but ratify decisions previously made in primary elections or caucuses.

The power of the political party has eroded almost to the point where it is irrelevant to the election.

The national committee, while it is doubtful that it ever had much real power, has now been relegated to being largely a social club. Its principal responsibility, aside from raising money, is to arrange and produce a gigantic pageant and social gathering every four years that is called a political convention, an event that once served as a mechanism for carrying on party business but now has become largely bait to attract television coverage.

The party boss's power has evaporated. While this may make for intraparty democracy, it can also lead to sailing without a rudder. With the demise of the political boss and the erosion of the power of the party, we have witnessed a corrosion of continuity in policies and organizational structure. The Democrats have been amending their delegate eligibility rules almost quadrennially since the 1972 convention. Creating a favorable image on television was one excuse.

Traditional procedures for dispensing patronage have also come unhinged. The candidate or potential candidate who prefers not to submit to party discipline is now in a position to use television to go over the head of the party organization and appeal directly to voters. If elected, he can handle his own patronage and cut his ties to party leadership. Consequently, party power erodes further.

While the influence of the party and the leadership has been declining, the role of the advertising agency and the political consultant has risen sharply. Hardly a candidate down to the level of alderman dares to face the electorate in the television age without engaging the services of a consultant, an advertising agency, or both.

All of this has led to placing a premium on new talents, new techniques for approaching the electorate, new skills, and new processes for analysis of voter interests, whims, shifts in attitude, and responses to candidate appeals.

The old party "pol" operated from experience and intuition. His computer was his brain, where he stored data, organized it, massaged it, and from it drew his intuitive conclusions. Now it takes a staff of data gatherers and computer programmers backed up by high-powered, high-speed computers to perform the same job. The results are surely more accurate and provide almost limitless additional information, but they consume large cadres of additional personnel and cause budgets to skyrocket.

How much of the change in party structure and influence, and the party's declining influence with voters, results from the presence of television and how much would have come about in any event is probably a question without an answer. It is clear, however, that the bulk of the transformation has occurred since 1952, the year when television first burst onto the political scene. It is also possible to draw direct causal relationships between the efforts of political leaders to restructure their campaign methods in an effort to cater to television and the changes in tactics and methodologies that followed.

It is hardly necessary to look very hard to detect television's very considerable influence on the manner in which we select candidates, choose among them in elections, and support them once they are elected. It takes a little more effort, however, to piece together the story of television's entry onto the political scene and to note the ad hoc decisions made along the way that have since become standard operating procedure. By placing the origins of television's relationships with politics and politicians under close surveillance, we may equip ourselves with better tools to assess the merits and weaknesses of the present system and to better analyze proposed remedial measures.

In doing so, though, some reasonable limitations have to be imposed. How government, once elected, relates to the electorate and builds support for its policies is directly related to the matter of winning elections, but is peripheral to a study of the campaign. Likewise, the role of various pressure groups and quasi–political organizations would constitute a fascinating study in itself but is somewhat beyond the scope contemplated here.

Since some limits have to be imposed, it seems only reasonable to confine the project to direct relationships between television and the process of getting nominated and elected, and to focus largely on presidential campaigns. The election year 1952 is a logical starting point. Many of the techniques in use now and many of the recent changes in methodology have their origins in the relationships between politics and television that developed in the 1950s. Since that is the period in which I participated directly as a television news executive and as frequent spokesman for the combined television networks, much of what follows will be based on those years. There will be no hesitation, though, about commenting on developments that have taken place since nor in tracing present methods to their origins.

While it is intended that the focus be fixed largely on the campaign, doing so assumes that we could decide what constitutes the campaign and what is peripheral to it. Such a decision would be unrealistic. Voters do not approach the campaign with minds that are clean slates. They slip into it with a heavy load of mental baggage acquired from a broad variety of sources—personal conversations, radio, television, newspapers, news magazines, books, long-held personal prejudices, religious influences, family attitudes, and an intellectual or emotional response to events. The effort during the campaign to elicit their support must recognize that winning them over demands rearranging old attitudes and prejudices, reinforcing some and suppressing others—not creating entirely new ones. It would be a gross error, therefore, for either television personnel or candidates to assume that television can work miracles. It clearly has to be looked at in conjunction with other influences on voters and as a shaper of attitudes, not as a creator of new ones.

Rather than undertake the production of a definitive history of the first four decades of the relationship of politics and television, I have decided that I can more effectively fill a niche in that story by recounting some of my own experiences. During the 1950s, when the relationship first jelled, I was personally involved in nearly all facets of the negotiations between the networks and the national parties, and in the establishment of policies for political coverage. For example, I chaired the all-network committee that planned network coverage of the 1952 national political conventions and supervised the CBS network coverage. Many of the practices and procedures that we developed then are still standard operating procedure today. In my view, an eyewitness and personalized account of television's efforts to deliver a new type of coverage of American politics will do much to enrich and amplify our knowledge of recent American political history.

The emphasis will be on campaign coverage generated within the networks. It would not be reasonable, however, to overlook completely the efforts of the campaign organizations or the national parties to use television to their own ends. Commercial spot announcements, convention planning, and publicity stunts as produced within campaign organizations are significant elements of the campaign and deserve mention, but the emphasis will remain on network election campaign programming efforts and the influence they have exerted on politics.

Public television cannot be entirely neglected, nor can cable, specifically the Cable News Network and C-SPAN; but this is a story largely about commercial network television, and the spotlight will be focused there. Local television will be included insofar as local stations are network affiliates and their programming practices have influenced both networks and campaign organizations. The emphasis will be directed toward national presidential campaigns. It is not that campaigns for county sheriff or city alderman are not important and interesting, but inclusion of all races for all offices would scatter the shots and dilute the end product.

The enormous and growing burden of mushrooming campaign costs is another topic of immense concern and is generally considered to involve television directly, but it is my decision to concentrate on what is now called "free media" and leave the matter of burgeoning costs to others. The news and informational broadcasting departments of the networks are paying their own way and impose no burden on national parties or candidates.

It is with these reservations in mind that we look at television as a relatively new vehicle for delivering the diverse stimuli that we hope will draw the voters to the polls and encourage them to vote for one candidate over another, or one party or policy over another.

1

The Dream and the Reality

Euphoria almost thick enough to displace the heavy fog of cigarette smoke that had been accumulating since late afternoon the day before permeated CBS Television studio 41 during the early morning hours of November 7, 1952. The studio, on the third floor of New York City's Grand Central Station, had been converted for the night of November 6 into CBS Television's 1952 national election headquarters. Tally boards, painted in shades of gray, black, and white that registered effectively on television screens, were arranged to form a gigantic letter U around the studio's perimeter. Correspondents, assisted by writers, producers, and statistical analysts, sat at desks in front of the tally boards. In the center were Teletype printers clacking out wire service returns from across the country. Alongside them were network news personnel wearing headphones. They were using telephones to obtain additional returns directly from state election headquarters, thus bypassing the wire services. In some cases they were placing calls directly to key precincts or wards. Another corps of network staffers sat at adding machines, totaling up results and handling them to page boys for posting on the tally boards. Copies were delivered to the anchor position, where Walter Cronkite presided over the proceedings, and to the desk occupied by senior news executives who were coordinating and supervising the seemingly disorderly process. Television cameras deployed throughout the center of the studio roamed about, focusing on the tally boards, on the correspondents reporting and analyzing the returns, and on Cronkite, who served as ringmaster.

Television had covered elections before, but only as a little-observed sideshow to radio. In 1948 homes with TV sets were too few to justify elaborate coverage. Resources were too limited to support it financially.

AT&T lines capable of carrying television signals from city to city restricted coverage to the northeastern states.

The seemingly disorganized and chaotic but bustling scene in studio 41 represented the climax to more than a year and a half of intensive preparation to cover the election of a president of the United States and the attendant races for the Senate, the House of Representatives and state governorships. This was an assignment never before undertaken on this scale by American television journalists. There were no guidelines, no precedents, no trained personnel, no experience to rely on. Everything was trial and error. It had been a trailblazing effort from the preplanning stage that had begun 18 months earlier, and it continued to be so all the way to the moment it was clear that Dwight Eisenhower had been elected the thirty-fourth president of the United States.

The euphoria that dominated studio 41 stemmed from elation that the job had been well done, that a new and infinitely complicated communications medium had been harnessed effectively to deliver an unprecedented communications service. Joyful news personnel were confident that a new era in the American political process had begun.

Literally millions of American citizens had sat at their receivers through the night, watching an election night story unfold for the first time. They had been able to observe the tally boards as the vote totals grew. They had seen and heard network correspondents relating and interpreting results. And their range of vision was not confined to the studio. They saw, as it happened, the happy scene in the Commodore Hotel ballroom, only a few hundred yards from the CBS television studio, as exultant Republicans celebrated their first presidential election victory in 24 years. When Ike and Mamie Eisenhower stood on a raised platform in that ballroom a little before midnight and acknowledged the cheers of several hundred ecstatic supporters, not only had the military hero won election to the presidency of the United States, but there were clear signs that American political campaigning was entering a new era.

The scene that night in the Commodore ballroom was different only in minor detail from previous presidential victory celebrations. There was a little more enthusiasm. It had been 24 years since the Republican party had fielded a winner. The outsized blackboard at the rear of the platform was a little larger, and the figures a little bolder, than they had been previously. Eisenhower's campaign organization not only had smelled the sweet scent of victory and wanted no one to mistake the results, but they were also aware that television would show the festivities to millions of viewers across the country.

There was no mistaking television's presence. The unblinking eyes of a battery of cameras ranged over the crowd, zooming in on the Eisenhowers, panning the celebrators, and zeroing in on the big tally board behind them. As the board showed a mounting lead and an inevitable Republican victory, the cameras dollied through the crowd to catch exuberant individuals before returning to the platform to report the general's victory speech.

What the cameras showed was not too different from previous victory celebrations. The usual army of joyful campaign workers and national party officials crowded around the platform. Fred Waring's big band, a special favorite of the president-elect, ground out the victor's favorite tunes in a style that was familiar to millions of Americans as a result of Waring's heavy exposure on the concert stage and, more recently, as a featured attraction on a popular Sunday night television program. Except for the presence of the cameras, there was only one major change from previous elections: The whole nation was able to watch.

Cameras were also present on the grounds of the Illinois state capitol in Springfield. They captured an eerie scene about midnight when they followed the defeated governor, Adlai Stevenson, as he strolled across the wide and dimly lighted lawn to his office in the capitol building, where he delivered his speech conceding Eisenhower's election and congratulating the victorious general. In his talk the governor used an example that is remembered almost four decades later. He felt, he said, something like the little boy who, when he stubbed his toe, didn't know whether to cry because it hurt so much or to laugh because he was so clumsy.

Television viewers were treated to another example of television's newly discovered muscle. Following the Eisenhower victory speech, the networks cut to the Ambassador Hotel in Los Angeles, where Richard Nixon thanked the nation for his election to the vice-presidency. Since there was only a single microwave circuit able to carry a television signal from coast to coast, the networks were forced to order separate audio lines in order to broadcast commentary from their own correspondents.[1]

What seemed so miraculous to television viewers that night has since become so commonplace that no one now gives it a second thought. But this was television's first nationwide election coverage. The evidence seemed beyond dispute that the mixture of picture, sound, and motion relayed live to a fascinated public was capable of revolutionizing the traditional political process. Television news personnel had proved to their own satisfaction that they had mastered the art of using the new and highly complicated tool. Candidates and their supporters had generally been responsive to the new opportunities that television created, and had adapted their campaigning to maximize the effect of the medium, the Republicans more than the Democrats. Ratings surveys that were released later demonstrated that the public responded by watching in numbers exceeding the most optimistic expectations.

Eisenhower managers had been aware of the potential of television from the beginning, in early February, of the campaign in the New Hampshire primaries, even though their candidate was then undeclared. Largely influenced by New York Governor Thomas E. Dewey, who had made extensive use of the new medium in his 1950 campaign for the governorship, they had designed a campaign with cameras in mind. Their first and immediate objective was to block what seemed to be the inevitable nomination of the front-running Senator Robert Taft and then, after winning nomination, to defeat the Democratic nominee.

Stevenson, on the other hand, was a late starter. He was not a factor in the primaries and was considered an unlikely possibility for the nomination as the convention opened. Television, however, enabled him to enlarge his sphere from middle western governor to national presidential candidate before the convention was finished. It was his welcoming speech to convention delegates that made him a national figure, and his speech accepting the nomination that made him a viable candidate. Both were carried on television.

Leaders of the hastily recruited Stevenson campaign organization likewise recognized the part television could play in the campaign. A number of experienced broadcast executives assumed prominent positions in the Illinois governor's inner circle of campaign advisers. Their financial resources, though, couldn't match those available to the Republicans, and the governor didn't exude the easy charm and confidence before the camera demonstrated by the genial five-star general. And even though experienced broadcast personnel helped plan the governor's campaign, they apparently lacked the courage to experiment that was demonstrated by Eisenhower supporters. The governor could never become comfortable with the unfamiliar medium or responsive to its rigid time demands. Time limitations were a particular bane to him. Time after time he paced himself so badly in his major speeches that his punch line came after his time had expired, the cameras were capped, and the microphones were turned off.[2]

The elation demonstrated by television executives could easily be justified. Election news had been featured prominently almost every night on television news programs ever since coverage of the New Hampshire primary began in early February. Ratings for the conventions in Chicago in July exceeded all expectations. Some 55 million persons tuned in to at least some part of the two conventions. This was a remarkable figure in view of the fact that there were only some 18 million homes with TV sets in the entire country.

During the campaign that followed, it was to television that Richard Nixon turned when he was in danger of being ousted from his spot on the Republican ticket. It was his "Checkers" speech that turned the tide and kept his place on the ticket secure.

And now television had, for the first time, chronicled the drama of an election night for millions of viewers in all 48 states. No one knew at this point exactly how large the audience had been—the ratings would not be available for several days—but broadcast executives were confident that the totals would be mind-boggling, and they were jubilant that the medium had come so far in so short a time.

They were more than jubilant. They boasted confidently that the nation was at the dawn of a new day in political campaigning, a new day that would inevitably bring better candidates, better-informed voters, greater voter participation in the electoral process, the end of sham and charlatanism in campaigning. The camera's X-ray eye would expose fraudulent candidates. Campaigns would be shorter. Travel would be drastically reduced. Sloganeering would soon be a lost art. There would be no more "Keep Cool with Coolidge," "He Has Kept Us out of War," or "Rum, Romanism and Rebellion." From now on, reason would prevail over emotion.[3]

The strategies underlying the political campaign, it was proclaimed, would undergo dramatic revisions. There would be less personal contact, handshaking with individual voters, appearances before small meetings. Several nationwide television addresses would replace whistle-stopping across the country. No longer would it be necessary to wear out the candidate's lungs as he shouted to supporters or curious onlookers from the rear platform of a Pullman car. The whistle-stop would be a relic of the past. All this would make for a more flexible campaign. Themes for the main addresses could be changed to conform to changing circumstances. Approaches could be altered.

Television viewers would become better-informed voters. They would better understand issues and feel closer to candidates. Candidates, too, would change and inevitably for the better. Costs would be less because of reduced travel; thus, having access to wealth would not be as high a priority. The X-ray eye of the camera would expose charlatans and lay them bare for the voters to observe their weaknesses. Only the pure in mind and spirit would be able to conquer the all-seeing eye of the image orthicon tube. In short, the political millennium was fast approaching.

That was the dream as CBS election headquarters went dark on the morning of November 7, 1952. It was difficult then to perceive reality. So much had been accomplished, so many improbable results achieved, that it seemed there was nothing television could not do.

CBS Chairman William S. Paley was still mesmerized by the astonishing performance of the fledgling medium when he spoke to the Poor Richard Club in Philadelphia early the next year.[4] He advocated legislation limiting future presidential campaigns to a maximum length of eight or nine weeks. With television, he argued, a campaign longer than that was no longer necessary. Travel could be drastically reduced, personal contacts limited, and the television studio used as a stage from which millions of voters could be reached simultaneously.

There were only a few questioning voices. Senator William Benton of Connecticut, one of the founders of the highly successful Benton and Bowles advertising agency, had spent heavily to hold the seat in the Senate that he had won in a special election in 1950. In 1952 he lost to Prescott Bush (George Bush's father) in a high-budget campaign. Benton warned that the high cost of television might distort the political process.

Some newspaper analysts were beginning to question whether emphasis on television as a campaign tool might place excessive stress on show business at the expense of rational, issue-oriented campaigning. Some losing candidates complained that they had been done in by the power of the picture tube. Some eyebrows were raised at General Eisenhower's use of spot announcements, a technique borrowed from commercial advertisers, to supplement the traditional campaign speeches. Some Democrats questioned whether the price of campaigning on television might not be creating a new built-in advantage for their consistently wealthier Republican opponents.

Some skeptics wondered whether television would not require that candidates be selected for appearance, round and well-modulated voices, strong camera personalities, and what later came to be known as charisma. One obscure novelist, a refugee from the advertising business named John G. Schneider, speculated in an equally obscure piece of fiction called *The Golden Kazoo* whether it might be possible for an advertising agency to package a total nonentity in such a way as to win the presidency.[5] All that was needed, according to the theme developed in the book, was the application of principles of packaging that are normally used by advertising agencies. This would assure election.

Despite the desultory critical voices, skeptics were few. Their complaints had not yet begun to carry much weight. Television was still too new to have acquired a large body of detractors. The popularity of Milton Berle and "I Love Lucy" was contributing to rapidly increasing receiver sales. The number of TV sets in homes was increasing so rapidly that most set owners had not had enough time nor seen enough programs to become critical.

By the end of the 1950s, however, the number of sets began to stabilize, and with stability critics began to become more voluble. Some of the easy generalizations of late 1952 and early 1953 came under sharp questioning. Television increasingly had to run on its record rather than on the brilliant successes scored during its first outing. And the record began to show structural weaknesses.

Four decades of experience have exploded many of the myths that were accepted as reality in 1952. Campaigns are not shorter. They are longer, much longer. John F. Kennedy began his run for the presidency in 1960 almost as soon as the 1956 convention adjourned. Announcing for the presidency two years before the election has now become commonplace. The crucial Iowa caucuses, coming in early February of election year, demand that candidates begin their campaigns months earlier. The Federal Election Campaign Act of 1973 adds further incentive for an early start. It grants matching funds to candidates on the basis of their success, prior to December 31 of the year before the election, in having raised $5,000 in each of 20 states through contributions of no more than $250 each. Travel has not been reduced. In fact, it has increased almost exponentially. William Jennings Bryan traveled 18,000 miles during his 1896 campaign for the presidency. Since television, 100,000 miles is common. Richard Nixon campaigned in all 50 states during his 1960 run for the White House. One trip to Hawaii or Alaska would record almost half as many miles as Bryan's whole campaign.

Whether candidates are of higher or lower caliber than before television is debatable. We have no foolproof gauge that measures presidents or presidential candidates with respect to their qualifications or prospects for governing successfully. History, however, will not credit television with having helped a Washington, Jefferson, Lincoln, or FDR win the presidency since it moved center stage.

Voter participation, contrary to my bold forecast in Texas in 1961, has dropped to new lows. From the high of 62.8 percent of the eligible voters going to the polls in 1960, the percentage has dropped steadily to the 53.3 percent who voted in 1984. In the last 60 years only the 1932 and 1948 elections registered lower turnouts and that was only by minute margins.

Costs, contrary to bold predictions, are several times higher. Total expenditures on the campaign for all candidates at all levels totaled $140 million in 1952. By 1984 they had risen to $1.8 billion. Even allowing for inflation, the increase is astronomical.[6]

Rather than expose charlatans through an X-ray eye, television may have created a new soapbox for them. There is little evidence that voters are better informed. Judging by campaign tactics, the opposite may be true.

Contrary to predictions that it would improve the political system, television may be doing serious damage. It may be trivializing the process. It may be diverting attention from substance and fixing it on stunts designed to attract the attention of the camera.

Television news may be encouraging candidates to grant interviews filled with short, punchy, emotional assertions rather than reasoned comment on the major issues of the day. It may be that the art of campaigning for public office is abandoning any pretense of voter education in favor of going all out for show business, contrived events, and stunts calculated to attract the television camera.

Sloganeering is hardly dead. Since the birth of television we have had Kennedy's "New Frontier" and Johnson's "Square Deal." In 1988 slogans and catchwords proliferated. We heard Michael Dukakis's "I'm on your side," and George Bush's "No new taxes. Read my lips" and "A kinder, gentler nation." There is only one difference. The slogans in the days before television were designed for posters and print advertising. They are now created as "sound bites" for television.

Television is not solely responsible for the radical transformation in campaign tactics, but it does not require a Sherlock Holmes to discover that political strategists are not oblivious of its power to sway voters. Some were slow to grasp its significance, but once they caught on, they embraced it whole wholeheartedly. Television personnel are not entirely blameless, but it is the managers of the campaigns, the "handlers" of the candidates, who must assume the largest share of the blame for subverting political tactics to cater to the whims of the camera. Television created the environment for them to practice their black art and is responsible for letting them get away with it. The ease with which a campaign aide can bait the hook with fluff to capture a spot on a television news program is sure proof that the politicians have discovered either a willing or an unsophisticated target for their wares.

The performance in television's first election campaign was given high marks in part because there was no benchmark against which to measure it. In the excitement of watching dramatic events unfold live on the screen, a privilege that had never before been possible, errors or weaknesses were overlooked. No one seemed to notice, for example, that the screen creates remarkable images but in the process of selection can distort meaning and the relative importance of objects it photographs. The lens is rigid compared with the highly flexible human eye. It records only what the cameraman asks it to, without tempering its effect by showing the environment surrounding the object appearing in the camera's viewfinder. It lacks the synthesizing capability that is brought to the observation of the event by the reporter. No one commented on the fact that the television camera was constantly searching for the dramatic picture and that editors seemed loath to report events that had no pictorial value.

If any visionary in the studio on that election night had possessed the clairvoyance to read the implications for the future, he or she might have been less exuberant. Like so many strokes of good fortune, this one, too, would extract its penalties. With fame and fortune, not to mention high ratings, would come pressures: pressures to outrate the competition, to raise the income level even higher, to please the audience at almost any cost— in short, to use any devices within reason to build and hold audiences and attract sponsors.

The prophet who could have then foretold the future would have foreseen the inevitability of conflict between maintenance of judgment, journalistic standards, and a reverential approach to news, on the one hand, and succumbing to the siren song of ratings, on the other. As it finally developed, television's astonishing grip on the viewing public turned out to be a virus weakening it from within.

The evidence that television has left an unmistakable mark on the process of getting elected is clear enough not to need a battery of scholars to prove the point. More than four decades of TV have thoroughly shaken up political parties and campaign methods. If candidates are unchanged, at least their tactics are dramatically different. But what about the voters? Have they also succumbed to the lure of the TV screen?

The odds are that voters continue to vote their emotions and prejudices rather than their intellect, just as they always have. Their eyes and ears are bombarded more frequently and intensively than before television. They may feel they know candidates a little more personally by having seen them on the screen as frequently as they have over the protracted campaign. They may have been exposed more to both personalities and issues than in the past, and certainly to more skillfully crafted appeals.

Has it all, though, had any real effect? While the turbulence generated by politics on television swirls all about them, it appears very much as if the voters sit quietly in the eye of the campaign hurricane and feel only an occasional draft. There is no discernible evidence that the voters are any better informed than they ever were. By and large, it seems that they assimilate a great number of diverse impressions into their mental computers and go behind the curtain in the voting booth to vote their convictions about as they always did. If, in fact, they go to the polls at all.

The dream on election night 1952 was one of better candidates, a more informed electorate, wiser decisions, all at less cost and taking less time. Television was the prime force that would make it all possible. The reality is like the cold, gray dawn after a binge. Many of the wildest fantasies have proved illusory, but there has been change and perhaps, on balance, the nation is better off for having access to television's contributions, even though they are somewhat less grandiose than we dreamed on that early morning of November 7, 1952.

NOTES

1. Transcontinental television was still in a very primitive stage. The AT&T circuit could carry only one signal. In an effort to make it possible for each network to have its own personnel describe the scene and introduce the newly elected vice-president, each of the three networks contracted for its own audio circuit separate from the video signal. The sound circuit obtained by CBS traveled from Los Angeles to Seattle and Vancouver, then across Canada to Toronto and Montreal. From Montreal it reentered the United States and terminated at CBS studio 41 in the Grand Central Terminal building. There was a sufficient gap in time between the arrival of the picture, which took a direct route, and the sound that followed the roundabout path, that Nixon's lips, as seen on the screen, moved slightly before the sound caught up. This led Don Hewitt, who was directing the program, to observe irreverently that the vice-president was "out of synch."

2. One of the memorable shots of the campaign was caught by cameramen

covering Governor Stevenson's opening campaign speech at Cadillac Square in Detroit on Labor Day. As the governor sat on the platform waiting to be called on, he crossed his legs. Cameras caught a close-up shot of the sole of the governor's shoe, revealing a hole large enough to expose his sock.

3. I was still arguing as late as February 1961 that television had had a marked effect on increasing the percentage of Americans going to the polls. In a speech entitled "The Impact of the Media upon Political Procedures," delivered at a conference convened by the University of Texas at Austin on February 6, I referred to "... the consistent growth of the voter turnout in the era of television." I called attention to the fact that early estimates indicated some some 64.3 percent of eligible American voters had gone to the polls on Election Day. This was the highest level ever achieved in the nation's history. The speech was reprinted in *The Role of Mass Media in American Society*, ed. Dewitt C. Reddick (Austin: University of Texas Press, 1961).

4. The Paley speech was printed by CBS and is in the company's archives. I have a copy in my files.

5. John G. Schneider, *The Golden Kazoo* (New York: Rinehart and Co., 1956).

6. Herbert E. Alexander and Brian A. Haggerty, *Financing the 1984 Election* (Lexington, Mass.: Lexington Books/D.C. Heath, 1986). This volume contains a wealth of information regarding campaign costs since the advent of television.

2

In the Beginning

It was obvious as early as the winter of 1951 that the presidential election of 1952 would be an old-fashioned donnybrook. The country was in an ugly mood. The Korean war had created deep divisions not only between the two major parties but also among factions within those parties. McCarthyism was running rampant and compounding the disharmony. The China lobby was stirring up dissension by its unyielding support for Chiang Kai-shek and its scattershot denunciations of anyone suspected of opposing him. Inside the White House there were signs of scandal within President Truman's personal staff. The president himself was suffering a steep decline in personal popularity. Much of the respect and even affection that had been showered on him after his hairline victory over Governor Dewey in the November 1948 election had evaporated. Distrust was replacing admiration, and the truculent mood across the nation engendered by the Korean war was deepening.

It was in this contentious atmosphere that attention turned to the presidential election of 1952. It was probably going to be an unusual election in another sense. Unlike the previous five national elections, this time there was not likely to be an incumbent running. There was skepticism about whether Truman would try for another term. Even if he were to try, there was speculation whether he could win the nomination. If there were no incumbent in the race, both parties would face long and acrimonious contests for the nomination. Both national conventions would likely be torn by bitter intraparty conflict.

Then there was a new factor, one that had the professional politicians curious as to what role it would play. The new factor was television. As 1951 opened, it still didn't amount to much. As of January 1, there were television receivers in only 7.2 million homes, less than 10 percent of all the homes in the country. But a year earlier the count was a bare 3.2 million. And in 1948, the year of the previous national conventions, the total set count was a meager 400,000. It seemed not unreasonable, at the rate buyers were snapping up available sets, that the 7.2 million would at least double by the time the race for the presidential nomination began in earnest in 1952.[1]

The dramatic increase in the set count was being fueled by public fascination with the rising new stars of television. Milton Berle had been a superstar almost from the beginning. Now "I Love Lucy" was starting a move that would take it to the top, even outrating Berle. Sid Caesar and Imogene Coca were must viewing on Saturday night, as were Jerry Lewis and Dean Martin. Arthur Godfrey, Jackie Gleason, Perry Como, and Bishop Sheen were all becoming national stars. Later in the year, on November 19, Edward R. Murrow would make his debut with "See It Now." Television was also beginning to show strength as a news medium. John Cameron Swazey and the "Camel News Caravan" on NBC and "Douglas Edwards with the Evening News" on CBS were beginning to build national followings even though the facilities with which they had to work were primitive by present standards and the number of markets they could reach was limited.

There was no reason to doubt that television would be a factor in the impending political campaign, but just what it would do or how effective it would be was puzzling. Governor Dewey of New York had demonstrated in his successful run for reelection in 1950 that television could be a powerful campaign tool. Supported by a knowledgeable and media-wise staff that was backed up by some of the best creative advertising personnel in New York, Dewey used a number of innovative techniques. One of the most notable was a variation of the man-in-the-street format. The governor sat in his office, answering questions put to him by New Yorkers interviewed on busy street corners in the city. A popular television personality, Happy Felton, was recruited to attract crowds and introduce the questioners. Cameras caught both ends of the interviews. The format served to humanize the governor, caused enough commotion on street corners to compel the attention of the print media, and served as a mechanism permitting the candidate to address concerns of voters directly. Perhaps more important, it stimulated interest among political professionals and potential candidates in the 1952 national elections. If television could work so effectively for Governor Dewey, it stood to reason that it could succeed equally well elsewhere, particularly in view of the medium's incredibly rapid growth.

During the 1950 fall campaign, I had only a peripheral involvement in political coverage. My assignment at CBS was to direct what was then called "public affairs," a hodgepodge of nonentertainment programming for both radio and television that included documentaries, discussion programs, talks, education, religion, and sports. Politics was an important component in the discussion and talk programs and in some documentaries, notably the "Hear It Now" series on the radio network, produced by Ed Murrow and Fred Friendly, that we initiated in the fall of 1950. Otherwise, politics was largely a fiefdom of the news department, which jealously protected its turf from incursions by public affairs people.

The cool relations between news and public affairs heightened my surprise when I received a call in late spring 1951 from the president-designate of a soon-to-be-created CBS Television Network division. The president-to-be, Jack van Volkenburg, asked that I undertake negotiations with the leadership of the two political parties regarding the possibility of obtaining commercial sponsorship of the 1952 political conventions. Previous broadcast convention coverage dating back to 1936 had been totally free of advertising. Radio networks—there was little television before 1948—had accepted the responsibility of furnishing coverage and assuming the costs without complaint. The expenses involved in covering by radio, however, were only a pittance compared with the anticipated budgets that would face television.

Television was so inconsequential in 1948, at the time of its one effort at convention coverage, that apparently no thought had been given to attempting commercial sponsorship. Prospects for 1952 promised an entirely different set of problems. There were not only the costs of moving crews and equipment from New York to the convention site, installing intricate electronic gear, leasing transmission facilities from the telephone companies, and feeding and housing personnel to be considered. The loss of revenue from preempting programs already on the schedule promised almost to equal program costs.

Television had progressed sufficiently that its nighttime schedules were nearly sold out. Substituting sustaining programs for those commercially supported not only would mean loss of income for both time and talent but also could mean the scrapping of programs already paid for. An occasional preemption was acceptable, but mass preemptions extending over the better part of a week constituted a frightening prospect for a fledgling industry. On the other hand, a regulated industry, one that prided itself on the public service it delivered, could hardly afford to overlook an event as vital and as potentially attractive as a political convention, particularly in an era as turbulent as the early 1950s. Executives of the corporations that owned the television networks could not afford to overlook the enormous boost that hard-fought conventions might give to set sales.

There were two aspects to the job I set out to do. The first was to project, as well as possible, how the conventions would be covered, how much personnel it would take, how many hours of coverage would be devoted to each, and how much revenue would be lost as convention coverage replaced regularly scheduled programs. The bottom line was how much it would cost CBS. The second objective was to gather as much evidence as possible to convince party officials it would be in their best interests to encourage massive coverage. Agreeing to permit commercial sponsorship would clearly be an attractive inducement.

Since the Republicans planned to meet two weeks before the Democrats, it seemed sensible to approach Republican National Chairman Guy Gabrielson before requesting an appointment with Democrat Frank McKinney. Early in June, accompanied by CBS Washington vice-president Earl Gammons, I was in Gabrielson's office with my charts and statistical data. The total out-of-pocket cost for complete convention coverage, I predicted, would be a minimum of $5 million, an astronomical figure for that era.

What caught the attention of the GOP chairman and the party's national publicity director, William Mylander, was the audience projections that I had been able to develop with the help of the CBS research department. Our most conservative estimate predicted that approximately 17.2 million American homes, representing about a 25 percent saturation, would be equipped with television receivers by July 1, 1952. As many as 50 million Americans would probably look in on some part of the convention coverage, and as many as 10 million would watch the most dramatic episodes. Television was clearly a resource to be encouraged. In contrast with prospects for the massive television audience, the Chicago Stadium, the larger of the two facilities in Chicago being considered as a convention site, would accommodate approximately 18,000; the International Amphitheater, about 14,000. The contrast did not need any amplification.

Gabrielson and Mylander were not as adamant on commercials as we had expected. They expressed reservations about the type of sponsor to whom we might be able to sell the package, and they were concerned that too many commercial interruptions might destroy the mood and clutter up the proceedings. They were particularly worried about interrupting key speeches that would be delivered by such notables as President Eisenhower, former President Herbert Hoover, and General Douglas MacArthur, all of whom were expected to be on the program. Otherwise they seemed quite relaxed at the prospect

We had no objections to their reservations. It seemed unlikely that a manufacturer of packaged goods who depends on hard sell would be a reasonable prospect. We pointed out that it was unlikely that we could be dissuaded from selling to a sponsor they disliked for frivolous reasons, but we offered to consult with them before contracting with any given prospect. As to interruptions, we insisted that we were as interested as they in maintaining program flow and avoiding breaks in continuity. It was agreed that Gabrielson and Mylander would meet with their Democratic counterparts and draft a suggested code. Once drafted, it would be relayed to us for our agreement or suggested revisions. Copies also would go to the other networks. Before the end of the summer, following some gentle prodding, the code arrived. We had no problem accepting it.

By mid-July the reorganization at CBS was a fait accompli. Television and radio had been set up as separate, autonomous operating divisions of CBS, Inc. My radio public affairs responsibilities were transferred to a new news and public affairs department of the radio network, and I was made director of news and public affairs for television. This new assignment cleared up the mystery of why I was asked two months earlier by Jack van Volkenburg, now officially president of CBS Television, to enter into negotiations with the national committees regarding commercial sponsorship of television coverage of the conventions.

We were now in a position to put our convention coverage on the market, but not much could be done about creating a sales package until we could draw up a budget, and budgeting was not possible until the two parties made their final selection of a convention site. We knew that Chicago was to be the city, that the Republicans would meet on July 7 and the Democrats two weeks later. No decision had been made, however, as to which of the two available sites, the Chicago Stadium or the International Amphitheater, would be selected. In early October, executives from the network news departments, accompanied by technical operations personnel, boarded the Twentieth Century Limited for the overnight train trip from New York to Chicago. The purpose: to inspect both sites, to make recommendations to the national committees regarding their preference, and to begin the complicated specific planning procedure. Without the plans, no budget could be drafted and no sales effort undertaken.

The national parties were partial to Chicago Stadium. They coveted those 4,000 additional seats for faithful party followers. The networks concluded that it would be virtually impossible to deliver anything but a bare bones program from a cavernous building that was designed to be a sports arena. Even that would be costly and cumbersome. There was room for more spectators than at the amphitheater, but no support space for constructing studios, control rooms, equipment storage space, and offices. Television personnel wanted to cover the conventions as major news events, not simply turn the cameras on the rostrum and leave them there. They wanted to show their muscle, to demonstrate the wizardry of which their electronic equipment was capable in the process of reporting a complicated and critically important news story. It would not be possible at the stadium. On the other hand, the International Amphitheater had auxiliary space to spare. Except for the odor from the nearby stockyards, it was almost an ideal choice.

The two national chairmen dodged the issue. They deferred the decision until some vague later date. Thus the issue was drawn for the first confrontation between television and political leadership. The question now was how far the party executives would go in yielding to the demands of the new medium. Defeat could mean a serious setback in TV's effort to establish parity with other media. Victory would mark one crucial step toward parity with print and radio.

In the meantime, network planning, limited as it was by failure of the parties to select a site, continued. I was selected to head the network pool committee representing the four television networks (ABC, CBS, Dumont, and NBC) and the four radio networks (ABC, CBS, Mutual, and NBC). CBS won the draw to construct and manage the television pool and NBC the radio pool. General planning could go on, but specifics had to await a decision on the convention site.

In mid-November word came from our Washington office that the two national chairmen would meet two days later in the office of Werner Schroeder, arrangements chairman for the Republican convention, at 1 North La Salle Street in Chicago. A hurried conference call to the other networks resulted in a recommendation that I go to Chicago to present the case for network television.

The party executives agreed to hear me, so I made reservations to fly to Chicago the afternoon before the meeting and to appear at 10 o'clock the next morning. There was only one hitch in my plans. A severe blizzard was sweeping across the entire Midwest. I called an acquaintance at the National Weather Service in Washington to ask what the odds were on getting to Chicago on time.

The reply was disheartening at best. I had a much better chance of winding up in Kansas City than in Chicago. The Twentieth Century Limited was fully booked, but the CBS transportation office found me space on the Pennsylvania Railroad's Broadway Limited, scheduled to arrive in Chicago at 9:30 A.M. This would give me half an hour to get to the La Salle Street address, a tight schedule but with luck achievable. Luck, however, had deserted me. I awoke in my berth at about 8 o'clock the next morning, noted that the train was not moving, and opened the shade to look out. All I could see was snow. A porter told we were near Lima, Ohio, and would be at least two hours late into Chicago.

Fortunately, others who were scheduled to appear also were delayed. The meeting was under way when I arrived. William Wood Prince, president of the company that owned the Chicago stockyards and the International Amphitheater, was testifying. I was next. I presented revised figures indicating that there would be approximately 18 million homes with TV sets in the United States by July 1, and repeated the prediction made in Gabrielson's office in June that some 50 million viewers would see some parts of the two conventions. Attracting this large an audience, I added, was predicated on obtaining the space required to install and operate our equipment. I reiterated that we simply could not do an adequate job in the Chicago Stadium.

After approximately half an hour I was dismissed, and started off for the

New York Central station to catch the Twentieth Century Limited back to New York. As the train left the station, the party leaders still had not announced a decision. The next morning, as the train stopped in Harmon, New York, to switch to the electric engines required to make the run into the city, I was able to pick up a copy of the *New York Times*. The story I was looking for was there. The chairmen had voted to hold the conventions at the International Amphitheater. Television had won its fight to book the meetings into an auditorium that favored the medium at the expense of some party supporters who would be unable to get seats in the hall. Coupled with winning the right to offer the conventions for commercial sale, the score was now 2 to 0 in television's favor.

It was particularly gratifying to me, while attending a meeting of the arrangements committee of the Republican National Committee in San Francisco in early January 1952, to hear Werner Schroeder reporting in precise detail to the committee the projections I had made at the meeting two months earlier. Apparently he had listened carefully.

With the convention venue firmly set, it was now possible to begin definitive planning sessions. The process was greatly helped by some useful experience gained in covering the five-day Japanese peace conference at San Francisco in September 1951. The peace conference was, from our point of view, a political convention in microcosm.

In retrospect, that event itself did not make much of a mark on history. At the time, however, it drew the attention of much of the world. All of the countries that had been allies of the United States were still technically at war with the Japanese when the conference was convened on September 4. Japan was quiescent, but the Korean war threatened to spread to other areas in the Far East, in which case Japan could hardly have avoided deep involvement. The White House and the State Department had been working for months to bring the official state of war to a close. John Foster Dulles, a New York lawyer and diplomat who was later secretary of state, had been dispatched as a special envoy to negotiate the terms of a treaty as expeditiously as possible.

From the television perspective, coverage of the peace conference at the San Francisco Opera House yielded rich dividends. It demonstrated that the infant medium was capable of faithfully reporting a complicated event running over several days by delivering colorful pictures backed up by meaningful commentary. Two by-products may have been less significant, but they left a solid impact. One was the transmission of the peace conference proceedings live across the country, the first time the feat had ever been accomplished. The other was the introduction of Walter Cronkite to a national television audience as an "anchorman."

Prior to the peace conference, the only television programs to be seen on both coasts were either kinescopes or motion picture films. There were no live, simultaneous transmissions. AT&T had been working for several months to complete a circuit with sufficient band width to transmit a television signal. The job was completed in late summer 1951, but the new facility needed several months of testing before it could be put into commercial use. Knowing that it was nearing completion, the network news chiefs approached the telephone company's long lines officials in early August to determine whether it might be made available for transmitting peace conference coverage across the continent. Permission was granted, but only on the basis that use of the circuit was to be designated as "experimental." It would be withdrawn from use once the event was over and not put into commercial use until November.

Since the new circuit would accommodate only one television signal, pooling of the coverage was essential. This meant drawing lots to determine which network would take the responsibility for managing the pool. I drew the short straw. That meant it was my assignment to establish a plan of coverage; select a San Francisco station to furnish cameras, switching facilities, and technical operations crews; and pick a broadcaster to serve as the central figure for our coverage, the ringmaster who would do the running story and fit all the elements into their proper places—in other words, the "anchorman."

My choice was somewhat limited. All the reporter-broadcasters on the CBS news staff were on the radio payroll. Television could obtain access to them only by begging for their release from radio. There was one, however, who had no ongoing radio commitments. His name was Walter Cronkite. He had joined the CBS staff during the summer of 1950, shortly after the outbreak of the Korean war, ostensibly as a reinforcement for the team stationed in Korea. Before he was shipped out, however, there was a change in plans and he was assigned to broadcast the 11 o'clock nightly television news on channel 9, the CBS affiliate in Washington, D.C., in which CBS held a minority ownership position.

Since I had known both the Cronkites in Kansas City, where Walter was filing a wire for the United Press before being transferred to England to cover the European war, I was delighted to renew an old acquaintanceship. As a frequent Washington visitor, I had many occasions to watch the 11 o'clock news. I was impressed by the strength of the performance, by his skill at communicating, and by his ability to make complicated news events easily comprehensible. I discovered that Walter and his assistant, Neal Strawser, who later achieved correspondent status, clipped photographs, charts, and maps wherever they could find them, placed them on an easel, and used them in the broadcast to illustrate military movements and political events. Parts of the broadcast were ad-libbed.

Even if I had had the pick of the whole correspondent crop to handle the central narrator's chore in San Francisco, I would have selected Walter. I thought that, more than any other staff member, he had the strength of personality, the ability to ad-lib, and the background and communications skills to do the kind of job I wanted done. He exuded confidence and, from the viewer's standpoint, reflected believability.

It was not easy to free Walter from his nightly duties in Washington. The station manager was less than enthusiastic about releasing the rising star of a high-visibility time period for nearly two weeks. After applying some leverage from senior CBS corporate management, the release was grudgingly given, and Walter and I set out for San Francisco to blaze new television trails. It was Walter's first national exposure and, judging from comments by television critics, a smashing success.

I was not satisfied, however, to send him back to Washington and permit him to make a permanent career as a local news broadcaster. I had a larger role in mind. His success in San Francisco convinced me that in Walter we had an invaluable resource who could play a key role in the upcoming conventions. In my view, we needed a strong, even dominant, figure at a central location who could drive our coverage along. For some reason I used the term "anchorman" to describe the position. The term stuck. I visualized the "anchorman" as the best-informed person at the convention. All our communications lines would terminate with him. Reporters on the floor, in the wings, or in downtown hotels would transmit to a desk that would screen information to be relayed to him. The studio where we stationed him would be the heart and brain of our coverage.

I had seen enough in San Francisco to be convinced that Cronkite was our man. Others in the CBS hierarchy were less enthusiastic. They were infected with the notion that dictated that one goes only with a sure thing. Cronkite was new. He had no national reputation. He had never broadcast a national political convention. Bob Trout, on the other hand, was a superb ad-libber. He had covered political conventions since 1936. The public knew him and respected him. He would be easy to promote and would probably be attractive to potential sponsors.

It took several weeks to win my way. I argued that Trout was a superb craftsman with an unsurpassed skill at creating word pictures, but television already had pictures. What we needed was someone who could interpret pictures, give them meaning, and relate them to other pictures. It would be a waste of valuable time on television to describe scenes. The viewer could see for himself. It was our intention to cover the conventions as a news story, and to do so, we needed a genuine journalist who could put disparate scenes in perspective and produce a running story. Mindful of the intense rivalry between radio and television that was preventing genuine cooperation, I suggested that Trout was ideally suited for radio, and that it would be a mistake to transfer him to television. It took several weeks, but eventually opposition evaporated and I won my point. Cronkite was to be the anchorman.

Finding a sponsor took less effort. I returned to my office one day in mid-November 1951 to find Jack van Volkenburg, the CBS Television network president, and two guests awaiting my return. He introduced the two as John M. McKibbin, vice-president of the white goods division of Westinghouse Electric, and Edward Parrack, executive vice-president of the Ketchum, McCleod and Grove advertising agency in Pittsburgh. The topic of our conversation was the political conventions. Although all our internal planning to this point had been general, I proceeded to describe as specifically as I could what we intended to do and answered their questions positively.

It developed that McKibbin and Parrack had spent the morning at NBC and were dissatisfied with the responses they got. They came to CBS as an afterthought. As they left, they expressed deep interest in our plans and suggested that as soon as we were ready, they would like to see a specific proposal. Since the International Amphitheater had finally been designated as the site, it was now possible to begin the budgeting process. A specific proposal was shipped to Pittsburgh by mid-December, and the wait to see whether we would have our sponsor began.

Two days before Christmas, word came that they wanted to see us in Pittsburgh on the morning of December 26. William Hylan, assistant director of sales, and I were designated to make the trip. We left Westport, Connecticut, in a heavy snow storm on Christmas night for New York, where we transferred to the Pittsburgher for the overnight train trip to Pittsburgh.

The meeting in Pittsburgh took the full day. Most of the points of disagreement were relatively minor. We were offering 15 hours of coverage of each convention. They wanted a guarantee of 20 hours but would pay for only 15. They insisted that radio be included in the package. They also wanted to sponsor election night coverage on both radio and television, and additionally wanted a "bridge series" to maintain interest between the conventions and the election. None of the points of contention seemed insuperable, so we went back to New York optimistic that we had an order. It came through a couple of days later, so before the end of the year television had passed another milestone. NBC immediately went into forced draft sessions to duplicate our success and wound up with an order from Philco. ABC then went after Admiral Radio and received its order. With that, three of the television networks had nailed down their commercial sponsorship. The fourth network, Dumont, seemed ambivalent. That was of little significance, however, since it later abandoned any plans to cover the events. Sponsorship was no longer taboo. Commercials would become almost as prevalent for political conventions as for football games.

The most challenging problem facing the all-network planning committee as plans for operating the convention pool progressed related to access to stations. A Federal Communications Commission order imposed in 1949 had frozen the license-granting process. At the time of the imposition of the freeze, there were only 107 stations on the air in the entire country. NBC had been far more aggressive than the other networks in signing up affiliates before the freeze, and consequently had primary affiliations in many large single-station markets. If the network wished to exercise its contractual rights to the hilt, ABC and CBS would have been frozen out of major markets including Buffalo, St. Louis, Indianapolis, Milwaukee, Grand Rapids, New Orleans, and Houston. This would have spelled disaster for any hope of achieving ratings comparability. There were signs in the winter of 1952 that the freeze would soon be lifted, but it was doubtful that many licenses could be granted and stations built in time to go on the air before the July 7 opening of the Republican convention.

The second quandary developed out of the shortage of telephone company microwave or coaxial cable links to many sections of the country. The television signal demanded too much band width to be transmitted on ordinary telephone lines. AT&T had opened service to the West Coast in November 1951, but on July 7 when the Republicans convened, only that one original link would be in place. Additional service was still several months away. Florida, the Gulf states, Texas, Oklahoma, Kansas, and all areas west of Omaha were limited to one service.

It was agreed that some equitable solution would have to be found that would permit each network equal access to the available facilities, but only for actual convention coverage. This meant that "convention coverage" must be defined. Only then could there be agreement on what was being divided. The solution—designate the convention as running officially from "gavel to gavel." Sessions were then allocated by lot: network A feeding the single-station markets and the single-circuit links the first session, network B the second, and network C the third. The rotation resumed with the fourth session.

None of us who were involved in making that decision had any notion that the networks would still be clinging to the "gavel to gavel" principle four decades later. We confidently felt that as early as 1956 we would become much more discriminating, and pick and choose among the items offered on the party's bill of fare, as radio had at previous conventions.

The reason for the perpetuation of a practice designed to solve problems existing in 1952 is rooted in the competitive instincts and the overwhelming desire to whip the opposition. Only at the conventions and on election night did the networks fight it out head to head on the same terms and with the same ground rules. No one wanted to let go while the others were still grinding out the coverage on the "gavel to gavel" basis. ABC finally broke the pattern in 1976, but the drain on manpower and facilities was just as great. The network tape-recorded what it did not cover live, and fed much of it on a delayed basis after some editing.

The pool system devised for 1952 has undergone only minor adjustments since that time. Cameras at fixed positions inside the hall are still maintained and operated by a pool staff. Hand-held portable cameras and those in the network booths above the floor remain outside pool control. The most significant change has been the relaxing and enlarging of the pool to accommodate additional local stations and newly emerging services including Cable News Network, C-SPAN, and public broadcasting stations. In 1952 we were able to tell independent services we would provide coverage, for a price. But then the networks held a virtual monopoly. That monopoly has long since vanished.

By mid-June plans had progressed to the stage where not much more could be done. How those plans were implemented would depend on how the story developed. Whether they were adequate, no one would know until the first crisis arose.

At CBS we were still concerned about how we would squeeze out the 20 hours of coverage that Westinghouse had insisted on before the contract was signed. We need not have worried. Before we were finished with the Republicans, we had carried very nearly 60 hours. The Democratic event added about another 60. And political convention coverage had become a national television staple, to be repeated every four years.

NOTE

1. These statistics were compiled by the CBS research department in 1952. I used them frequently in presentations to the national political committees, to the sponsor, and in public speeches. They are now in my files.

3

Television's Great Leap Forward

The nation's attention was riveted so intently on television in the summer of 1952 that it surprised even the experts. The reason: the two national political conventions that dominated most of the month of July. All four networks covered the conventions from gavel to gavel, some 150 hours in all. More than 55 million persons, in excess of 61 percent of the nation's population, watched some part of the two meetings. At peak periods, more than 60 percent of American homes with televisions tuned in.

Only a few were fully prepared for the phenomenal response to television's first full effort at covering national politics. Political leaders, while giving lip service, were totally unprepared for the public's mass fascination with the new medium. They had only grudgingly acceded to network demands for suitable camera locations adjacent to the floor. They were fearful that giving up the space would deprive loyal party members of choice seats. The Republicans even refused permission to build a camera platform on the arena floor for head-on shots of the rostrum, a decision that was reversed in subsequent years after party leaders had an opportunity to note how much better Democrats looked when photographed from the camera platform they had refused to sanction.

Even those of us who had been preparing for more than 18 months for the biggest enterprise television had ever undertaken did not fully believe our confident boasts that we were on the threshold of a revolution in communications and politics. We knew the conventions would be big and exciting, but not many of us fully anticipated the enormity of the public response. Part of the surprising response rose out of the fact that most of the nation would have its first chance to look in on the quadrennial extravaganza. In 1948, the last time that the parties had met to select presidential and vice-presidential candidates, only a handful of viewers in the Northeast had been able to tune in any part. Only 400,000 homes in the entire country then had receivers, and only 9 cities could receive signals on existing network lines. When the gavel fell to open the Republican convention on July 7, 1952, 18 million homes in 62 interconnected cities across the country would be able to receive the network broadcasts.

Campaign managers for the principal candidates were certain that television was a force they could not overlook, but only the Eisenhower staff came near to fully estimating the power the medium would demonstrate. The Eisenhower campaign leadership realized that it would take an uphill battle to wrest the presidential nomination away from the more solidly entrenched Senator Taft from Ohio. They concluded that if they played it right, television would give them the magic weapon that would enable them to mobilize public opinion sufficiently to override the control of the political machinery maintained by the Taft forces.

The Taft campaign management was aware of the potential power of television. It had mounted an aggressive television campaign in the 1950 Ohio Senate race, which the senator had won handily. Television liaison personnel were on the job, but they did not show the imagination or enthusiasm of the Eisenhower forces. They were anxious to get their story on the air, but there was no evidence that we could detect of any television-based overall strategy.

Newspapers, news magazines, and radio and television had been haranguing the public for months about the impending spectacle. Those of us directly involved in planning had made scores of speeches and answered countless questions from media reporters. The public was well aware that hundreds of reporters and technicians, and thousands of pounds of electronic hardware were being shipped to Chicago for an unprecedented spectacle. But we were so preoccupied with preparations that we had no notion how massive the reaction would be.

Jack Gould, the broadcast critic of the *New York Times*, had a hunch that, in retrospect, makes him seem positively clairvoyant. On June 22, two weeks before the Republican convention opened, Gould wrote, "Television is going to wield a major and perhaps determining influence this year over both the conventions and the campaign to follow. This year, the 18 million receivers installed in homes will turn the nation into a gigantic town meeting. . . . "[1]

There was a vague feeling that Gould was right. All available evidence pointed to a phenomenal escalation of interest in both television and the conventions. But it was almost impossible to visualize just how explosive that new attention to the video screen would be. Those of us in the front lines were too busy preparing for an event for which there were no guidelines to contemplate more than what the next task on our checklists might be.

President Harry Truman removed the last doubt that both the conventions would be no-holds-barred donnybrooks when he withdrew his name from the list of Democratic contenders. At the conclusion of a televised address on March 30, he startled everyone by adding a line to his prepared script announcing that he would not be a candidate. For the first time since 1928, there would be no incumbent in the race. The winners would be decided on the convention floor.

There were no odds-on favorites in either party. Senator Taft of Ohio had an edge over other Republican contenders, but some of his support depended on winning a number of critical contests to be fought out in the party's credentials committee. General Eisenhower was coming on fast, but as the convention date approached, he still lagged behind the Ohio senator. Governor Earl Warren of California and Harold Stassen were still in the running. General Douglas MacArthur was scheduled to deliver the keynote address. There was speculation that he might ignite the convention with his dramatic oratory and run off with the nomination.

On June 22, two weeks before the GOP's opening date and one week before the credentials committee was scheduled to meet, Senator Taft was easily the front-runner, with 454 of the 604 votes needed to nominate, but a number of these, notably some of the 38 in Texas, were shaky. They were being contested by the Eisenhower forces. If some could be dislodged from the Taft column and moved to Ike, the Taft margin would be razor thin. The count of committed Eisenhower delegates on June 22 stood at 390. Governor Warren at that stage could count on 76, Stassen on 26, and Governor Theodore McKeldin of Maryland on 24. Only three were formally committed to General MacArthur, but 147 were still uncommitted and 13 were still to be chosen. There was also believed to be considerable underlying support for MacArthur among delegates already committed to other candidates.

The critical question was whose delegates would be seated as a result of the sparring over credentials, particularly in the delegations from Texas and Georgia. If Taft were to hold his strength, he still would not be assured the 604 votes necessary to nominate but would be close. If he were to lose some to Eisenhower, a deadlocked convention was a distinct possibility. In that event, a dedicated band of MacArthur supporters was counting on an emotional and melodramatic burst of patriotic oratory in the keynote speech to swing the convention, in a frenzied patriotic orgy, to the general.

The credentials committee was scheduled to begin its deliberations on Monday, June 30. The all-network pool committee begged party officials to open the hearing room to microphones and cameras. The answer was a resounding negative. The Taft forces, in command of the national party machinery, wanted to fight the battle in private. Cameras and microphones would be an intrusion, and they might show a dark side of the party that the Taft leaders preferred to keep undercover. Those of us representing television suspected that there was little enthusiasm for revealing how Republican delegates were selected in a state that had been overwhelmingly Democratic since the Civil War.

Business scheduled for Monday would be largely organizational. Hearings were to start on Tuesday, July 1. I had been under so much pressure from management to hold down costs that I had decided to gamble that we could arrive Tuesday morning without losing anything. Even then, we would bring only a skeleton production and broadcasting crew. The main force would not arrive until Friday and Saturday. CBS technical operations, however, had been on the scene for several weeks, installing facilities so that cameras and microphones were in position and ready to go as soon as broadcast personnel appeared.

When Walter Cronkite and I stepped off the Twentieth Century Limited on Tuesday morning at 9:30, the decisive battle had already started. Worse than that, NBC, anticipating that the credentials committee would get off to a fast start, had a full staff in place and had actually been on the air from Chicago on Monday. We needed to get on the air to establish a competitive position, but we had no director. I had foolishly decided to let Don Hewitt remain in New York to direct the "Douglas Edwards Early Evening News" for another couple of days before reporting to Chicago. This left us with an anchorman, Cronkite, and full physical facilities but no director to call the shots. I asked the technical operations crew whether, if I could get television network headquarters in New York to release air time for a broadcast, they would take directions from me. This was a touchy point, since I was not a member of the directors' union. There were no objections, so our first broadcast from Chicago found me sitting in the director's chair. Our maiden effort was followed by an urgent call to Hewitt to come to Chicago immediately, to take over.

By Wednesday morning it was evident that the battle in the credentials committee was heating up. We begged once more for the right to bring in our cameras but again were rebuffed. The only alternative was to set up in the corridor just outside the door to the committee room. Eisenhower supporters who had resisted the ban on coverage were quick to note that we were giving them a channel for releasing their version of the proceedings. Whenever the tally lights on the cameras of one of the three networks flashed on, signifying that a picture was on the air, a steady procession of delegates supporting the general made their way to microphones to furnish their version of the debate inside. It was clear that the Eisenhower delegates had been carefully selected to represent a new breed of political leader: young, attractive, and telegenic, in contrast with the traditional old-line politicians who represented Taft. The contrast could not have been missed by television viewers. It was a credit to Eisenhower planners, who had anticipated that the fresh, young look would create an image that would rub off on their candidate. They were looking not only to jaded delegates in Chicago but also to television in the expectation that delegates could be influenced by pressure from home.

Except for our slow start, we thought we were doing relatively well with our cameras stationed outside the committee room door. We were, however, missing the essence of the debate. We missed the give and take, the clash between opposing viewpoints, the personalities of the combatants, the atmosphere in the meeting room. We petitioned again for access and again were rebuffed.

That night I was sound asleep when the telephone rang. It was Paul Levitan, our director of planning and facilities. Levitan had asked me during the afternoon whether I would object if he could find some way of planting a microphone in the room where the committee was meeting. Since it didn't seem a very reasonable possibility, I rather absentmindedly gave consent. When Levitan told me he had accomplished his mission, I quickly awoke. He described how he and the deputy director of technical operations had slipped into the committee room after the corridors were clear, with the intention of hiding a microphone behind a drape. They were astonished to discover that there was already a mike there, and assumed it belonged to NBC. Further examination revealed that it would be easy to tie into the committee's own sound system, thus delivering a far superior signal. They quickly completed a simple wire-splicing maneuver, bridged into a line that would carry the signal to our studios on the fifth floor, and for double protection arranged to have a duplicate signal delivered to network headquarters in New York. At that early period in television's history, ethical considerations did not deeply disturb us.

When Cronkite arrived at the fifth-floor headquarters the next morning, he was able to put on a headset and overhear the proceedings directly from the committee room. The signal was never used on the air, but it enriched the CBS coverage by permitting Cronkite to sense the tension and bitterness that characterized the debate on the floor. It thus added a new dimension to the reports received from Eisenhower supporters as they left the meeting room to give interviews in the corridors.[2]

The contest in the credentials committee was only a prelude to the main event, but it served to whet even more interest than had already been generated. By Saturday, July 5, Chicago's Loop area was swarming with boisterous Republicans, outfitted in hats, blazers, and buttons carrying the names of their favorite candidates and their campaign slogans.

We were still concerned—needlessly, as it turned out—with the Westinghouse requirement that we program 20 hours from each convention. We decided that we ought to stockpile as many hours as we could before the convention opened on Monday morning. Finding program material was no problem. Impromptu rallies were springing up in hotel lobbies and on Michigan Avenue. "I Like Ike" banners were everywhere.

We arranged with network headquarters to assign us an hour from 8 to

9 on Saturday night. Levitan promised to find exciting material to fill the time. He had discovered that public relations representatives of the various candidates had acquired such a voracious appetite for television time that they would deliver rallies, demonstrations, and parades to order. We had some reservations about broadcasting staged events, but in the interest of filling the time with exciting material, we stifled our reservations and went on to book demonstrations and rallies to fill the hour. It is obvious now that if we had had a little more concern about journalistic ethics, we would neither have bugged the credentials committee nor have encouraged staged news. But that was 1952. Television was still boisterous, immature, and competitive.

If television can be charged with immaturity, many delegates could be found guilty of the same charge. The stunts performed by normally dignified national leaders for the benefit of the television camera were ludicrous. For our purposes, though, they served to further whet the public appetite for the main event on Monday morning. Whether they did any good for the candidate they were supporting is open to question. The most memorable performance involved Senator George Bender of Ohio, one of the dominant Taft leaders, vigorously swinging a cowbell in the lobby of the Conrad Hilton Hotel and leading a boisterous rally in singing the Taft campaign song, "I'm Looking over a Four-Leaf Clover." Wherever a television camera appeared, a crowd was sure to gather, waving pennants and banners, and pushing and shoving to dominate the scene, sometimes to the point where police had to intervene.

When Republican Party Chairman Gabrielson rapped the gavel on Monday morning, July 7, to open officially the twenty-fifth Republican National Convention, the only noticeable difference from previous conventions was the presence of television cameras that displaced some seats in the front rows of the balcony. Otherwise, television at this stage was still relatively unobtrusive. Its operating personnel were mostly working from studios, control rooms, newsrooms, and offices in one of the wings of the International Amphitheater, where they occupied 35,000 square feet of space. It was not long, however, before the convention was fully aware of television's presence.

There were no concessions to television in the opening ceremony. There were the usual presentation of the colors, pledge of allegiance, national anthem, invocation, and official photograph of the convention. Then came the welcoming speeches by the mayor of Chicago and the Republican candidate for governor of Illinois, most of it dutifully covered by television.

What was happening on the rostrum at the convention hall obviously was purely ceremonial. The story was with the milling delegates on the floor and downtown in the Loop, at the Conrad Hilton and Blackstone hotels. There the committees, even though the convention was in session, were struggling to complete the business that was essential to beginning the real decision making. The critical impasse was caused by the credentials committee. No business could be conducted before delegates were certified and cleared to vote. That would require a report from the committee and its acceptance or modification by the full convention. Delegates whose names were on the official roll were entitled to vote on the credentials report, but only on that. So until that matter was disposed of, the convention would mark time.

We at CBS had decided months earlier that we would approach the conventions as a very large and complex news story. It was our intention that the ringmaster for our coverage, the "anchorman," should be the best-informed person in the city of Chicago, and that he should be able to interpret for the viewer the scenes portrayed on the screen. Pictures were to be used to supplement and explain the story, not stand alone for pictorial value.

An elaborate communications structure was designed to keep constant contact with reporter/correspondents. It included both strategically placed telephones and hand-held portable radio transmitters called walkie-talkies. Reports from correspondents were either to be accepted as background material for Cronkite's use or, sometimes, to go directly on the air. We were concerned with the background and interpretative information our correspondents could pick up on the convention floor, in the fringes of the hall, and in the downtown hotels. We expected the proceedings to be sufficiently complex, and many actions taken so obscure, that they would need explanation. The respected sociologists Kurt and Gladys Lang reflected the theory behind our planning when they wrote in a detailed study of the 1952 conventions, "CBS sought to cover the convention as a news service would."[3]

It became increasingly clear during the opening session that not much news was being made on the rostrum. The story, as we had expected, was on the floor or in the Loop. While speakers droned on from the platform, we interrupted with increasing frequency to report from both locations. Only by doing so could we make any sense out of what might have appeared to be inconsequential parliamentary maneuvering. The expectation of the leaders of the parties had been that television would be much more attentive to the formal program on the rostrum. Instead, a precedent was being set in which television executives made the decisions. They decided whether the speaker at the podium or the ceremony in progress should be interrupted or preempted for breaking news. In so doing, they were creating a pattern that would dominate in subsequent years.

The opening session passed quickly enough, without any fireworks. There was one disturbing note, however. NBC had appeared on the floor with hand-held portable cameras. We had heard rumors that this might happen and had looked into the possibility of obtaining one or more for ourselves, but abandoned the project because of uncertainty regarding the signal quality. The quality demonstrated by NBC was passable if not superior. It posed enough of a threat to make it imperative that we institute some countermeasure. In order to add any real meaning to the running story, we recognized that we must talk to delegates on the floor. Interviews would be immeasurably more effective if they were done on camera. We tried placing cameras on tripods on the periphery of the floor so they could be wheeled out on signal. The process, however, was too cumbersome. We needed a better solution.

Don Hewitt found the answer. He negotiated with the CBS radio network to place a camera in the CBS booth, high up against the wall behind the rostrum. From our control room we could direct our floor correspondents, who were equipped with portable transmitters, to potential sources of information or accept their offers of interviews or commentaries. The cameraman in the booth could overhear the instructions and keep a lens trained on the correspondent. Each reporter was given a flashlight to signal his position to the cameraman in the radio booth. The improvised system worked. The flashlight beams were easily visible, and a long lens on the camera enabled a tight focus on the reporter and his interviewee.[4]

There had been no intention as the convention opened to do this much reporting from the floor, but it was evident that the infighting would be so intense and the issues dividing the forces so complicated that they could be unraveled only by constant personal contact and interviews with participants who were plotting strategy or had a major stake in the outcome of the debate.

The result could have been expected. There was chaos on the floor as broadcast reporters elbowed their way through inattentive delegates, print reporters, political handymen, and sergeants at arms in pursuit of the story. To the home viewer, though, the end justified the turmoil. There was an important story to be told, and the floor reporting in this instance added an important dimension. In subsequent conventions, when there was either no story at all or only the thread of one, the search for morsels of information turned into a mad celebrity chase as reporters and cameramen churned about in pursuit of movie stars, daughters and wives of candidates, or anybody with a name and recognizable face. That was the unfortunate legacy we left from 1952.

Just prior to the Monday night session, which was to feature the keynote speech, I had my first (and last) unpleasant confrontation with Walter Cronkite. I had been under considerable pressure from senior management to give some significant exposure to Douglas Edwards, who was our principal news broadcaster and the occupant of the chair on our 7:30 evening news. I was very fond of Doug and regarded him highly for his work on his regular news broadcast, but I was convinced that for the strenuous and challenging task of making a complex political convention understandable to our viewers, Cronkite was a better choice. The Monday evening session seemed a likely spot to give Doug his chance. It was evident there would be very little business conducted from the rostrum. The only newsworthy item on the evening agenda was the keynote speech to be delivered by General MacArthur. If the general turned out to be so eloquent that he was able to start a stampede leading to his nomination, I saw an advantage in having my best and most politically knowledgeable reporter on the floor with a microphone. In short, this seemed the best opportunity we would have to give Doug the exposure, thus keeping the network sales department and his sponsors happy.

I have never seen Walter as angry as when I told him I wanted to put Doug in his chair for the evening session. He started to storm out of the studio. I stopped him by grabbing him by the coattails. I handed him a walkie-talkie and a flashlight, and told him to get down to the floor, where we badly needed him. He stomped off, obviously still burning with resentment, but there has probably never been as effective a job done by a television reporter in as turbulent a situation as Walter did that night.

The MacArthur speech was a typical MacArthurian spellbinder, charged with emotion and characterized by the rising and falling cadences that had become the general's trademark. The audience stomped, whistled, and cheered, but the speech failed to ignite the spark that would stampede delegates into handing the presidential nomination to the general, certainly a disappointing result for his loyal supporters and probably for the general himself.

Cronkite's goal on the floor was not only to assess the response to the keynote speech and the prospects for a MacArthur boom but also to learn what was holding up the credentials committee. There was still no definitive word when its deliberations might be finished. The committee's report would not necessarily decide the final outcome of the presidential nomination race, but it surely would bear heavily on it. And the convention was dead in the water until it reported. No business except voting on the credentials report could be conducted until delegates were formally seated by vote of the convention. Except during the keynote, Walter roamed the floor unceasingly, powering his way through knots of inattentive delegates, pouncing on key leaders who could help bring some understanding to the tangled affairs, waylaying others who might have something to add. It was a virtuoso performance. But the next morning we would be back in his anchor position. His competence there was too important to waste.

There was little the convention could do while it waited for the credentials committee other than bring a parade of loyal Republicans to the rostrum to address the convention and with it, even though bored stiff by the partisan oratory, a national television audience. It was a method of rewarding faithful party workers while simultaneously killing time.

One of the party faithful scheduled for air time was Senator Joseph McCarthy of Wisconsin. The timing could not have been worse for the networks. McCarthyism was at its crest across the nation. Fear was rampant in network corridors, where blacklists had abruptly ended the careers of widely known stars and were threatening the careers of some prominent television journalists and producers.

We had to answer several questions: Do we carry the senator's speech or disregard it? If we start, do we dare interrupt it for news from the floor or downtown? If we don't carry it or if we interrupt it, what outrageous charge will the senator make against us? And what damage would the charges do? None of three networks was courageous enough to incur the senator's wrath. McCarthy's reign of terror and the bullying tactics he had so successfully demonstrated brought the proud networks to their knees. He had his time to talk to the nation, and was virtually the only one of a long procession of speakers who did. It was not a proud day for television news.

As the Tuesday night session opened, there was still no indication from the credentials committee as to when its report would be ready. Former President Herbert Hoover, symbol of Republicanism and the last member of the party to hold the presidency, was to deliver the featured address. It was unlikely, in view of the prestige of the speaker, that television would interrupt for anything less than a cataclysm.

Something else happened, however, that left me distinctly uneasy. Lack of a camera platform on the center of the floor directly in front of the rostrum was severely interfering with efforts to deliver effective pictures. The only camera angles available were profiles from side positions in the balcony. The enterprising Don Hewitt found that he could deliver a striking picture by using the camera in the radio broadcast booth directly behind the rostrum and high above it. The shot of the former president from the rear, with his audience spread out before him, was a dramatic one. There was one aspect, though, that concerned me. While watching the back of the speaker's head, it was also possible to follow the text on the Tele-PrompTer directly in front of him. Hewitt was so fascinated by this unusual shot of a former president reading from a TelePrompTer that he was reluctant to abandon it. We finally decided that it was demeaning and reluctantly gave it up.

Late Wednesday afternoon the credentials committee finally informed the chairman that it was ready to report. The majority, as expected, favored the Taft delegations, but Eisenhower supporters submitted a minority report. The ensuing debate that continued until the early hours on Thursday demonstrated how carefully the Eisenhower strategists had planned for catering to the television audience. Their speakers were younger, relatively new to national politics, and virtually unknown nationally. They were the new wave, carefully recruited to build an image not only in the hall but also on television screens across the nation. This was in clear contrast with the Taft defenders, whose image was "old guard."

The delegates apparently noted the contrast. They were also under pressure from faithful party members at home who, impressed by what they saw on the screen, urged them to support the new wave.

Tensions ran high as the debate raged on. Donald Eastvold, the Washington state attorney general and floor leader for the Eisenhower forces, conceded all states except Georgia and Texas. For those two he offered substitute motions to seat the Eisenhower delegates. Georgia was the first to come to a vote. It was close, but the Eisenhower slate won by a vote of 607 to 531. Once the Eisenhower strength had been demonstrated, Texas fell into line. The general was now virtually certain of 14 of the 17 Georgia delegates and 33 of the 38 in Texas, not enough to assure him the nomination but sufficient to prevent a Taft runaway. It is clearly impossible to identify the number of delegates the skillfully crafted play for the television audience netted the Eisenhower effort, but in view of the closeness of the final vote, it was obvious that television and the Eisenhower team's use of it were decisive factors.

Once the delegates were seated, the business of the convention could proceed. By now Eisenhower was the favorite. At the end of the roll call of the states, he was only a handful of votes short of nomination. Minnesota asked to shift its votes from Harold Stassen to Ike, and the general was over the top, the Republican presidential candidate, nominated on the first ballot.

For television, the convention season was only half over. The Democrats were due to open at the International Amphitheater on July 21. Democratic officials had been painstakingly watching the Republican proceedings with particular reference to television. They were quick to approve a center platform for television cameras and redid the rostrum area to make it more attractive on the home screen. There was not much more that could be done at that late date, except to hope that they could adhere closely enough to schedule to assure that the party would look its best during prime television time.

While Dwight Eisenhower and Richard Nixon left Chicago as heroes of the Republican Party, the convention had been instrumental in elevating one other individual to star status—Walter Cronkite. Previously virtually unknown, Cronkite was now a familiar figure to millions. I became aware of just how great was his newly found fame as I walked along South Michigan Avenue with him en route to dinner one night between the two conventions. He told me he had been approached by a team of talent agents who were anxious to sign him to a contract. He wanted to know how I felt. I advised him to go ahead and sign. He was now an established television personality who would attract many high-paying assignments. I would be much more comfortable if we could negotiate through our respective representatives, his agent and my talent negotiator, rather than face to face. He subsequently signed with Stix and Gude, and as this is written, is still represented by the same firm.

The Democrats had no significant credentials contest to solve, but they had an equally sticky problem. The party had been rocked on its heels in 1948 when a number of Southern delegations walked out of the convention to protest a civil rights plank in the platform. The walkout almost cost the party the election. In 1952 the party leadership wanted delegations to sign a loyalty oath pledging to support the party and its nominees, no matter what action was taken by the convention. A number of Southern states bitterly resented this intrusion into their affairs. Some compromise would have to be reached before presidential and vice-presidential candidates were nominated. The alternative could be the loss of the election.

In contrast with the Republican convention, where there were two clear front-runners, there were at least five Democrats who came to Chicago with measurable support. The leader was Senator Estes Kefauver of Tennessee, who had made his reputation on television as chairman of a Senate committee investigating organized crime. But Kefauver arrived in Chicago with only about half the 604 delegates needed to nominate. Senator Richard Russell of Georgia, Senator Robert Kerr of Oklahoma, Averell Harriman of New York, and Senator G. Mennen Williams of Michigan all had sufficient strength to be considered in the running. Governor Adlai Stevenson of Illinois had no pledged delegates, but a number of dedicated workers, some of them influential in party affairs, were quietly building a sold base for a last-minute drive for his nomination. President Truman had carefully avoided committing himself, but his name was listed on the Missouri delegate roster and he was expected to attend. Unless he chose to announce his intentions earlier, he would have to reveal his choice when the Missouri delegation was polled. If he did not attend, his place would be taken by his alternate, Thomas Gavin. It was assumed that Gavin would reflect his position.

The convention started about as the Republicans' had. There were the usual opening ceremonies, but there was one noticeable difference. Adlai Stevenson electrified both the convention and the television audience with what normally would have been a purely ceremonial welcoming speech on behalf of the state of Illinois. Almost instantly he became a viable candidate. Enthusiastic endorsements from members of the television audience who had been impressed by the performance reinforced the reaction of delegates who witnessed the performance from the floor. The real battle for the nomination, however, was still four days away. Before calling for nominations, the convention had to settle the vexing loyalty oath problem and to find a way for loyal Democrats to parade to the rostrum to share some of the coveted television exposure. This led to a full quota of largely extraneous speeches. Some of the invited speakers took the trouble to gear themselves specifically to television.

One of the party faithful invited to address a daytime session while the convention was marking time was Georgia Neese Clark, treasurer of the

United States. Prior to making the trip to Chicago, Mrs. Clark attended a short course CBS Television conducted in Washington for convention participants. A CBS Television press release dated July 17 reports, "As a result of her tutoring, Mrs. Clark has decided to wear a gray shantung dress with pastel collars and cuffs for her speech next Tuesday. She made her selection after trying on several dresses before the school's television cameras." Mrs. Clark also was the first to take full advantage of television's capability of transmitting illustrative material. Prior to her speech she had arranged for delivery to television control rooms of visual aids that had been designed to illustrate her message.

The speaker of the House of Representatives, Sam Rayburn, who was to serve as permanent chairman, also went to school. The press release reports that he decided to "experiment with pancake and theatrical powder make-up (to reduce the reflection from his bald head) and was offered the services of a CBS make-up expert before he stepped up to the podium as permanent chairman." It would have been unthinkable before television to conceive of the dour speaker using the services of a theatrical makeup artist before assuming his duties in the chair.

Delegates, too, were making concessions to the new medium. "Already television has made one large contribution to the nation's taste," wrote John Crosby in his broadcast column in the *New York Herald Tribune* on July 7. "The Ladies are being asked to abandon, for God's sakes, those large floral print dresses which have been the tribal costume of the political committeewoman since forever. They look even worse on television."

The presence of television was largely forgotten on Thursday as the convention attacked the divisive issue of the loyalty oath. All intentions of maintaining reasonable decorum before the cameras were forgotten in the heat of the battle that did not end until after four o'clock Friday morning. Sandwich wrappers, paper coffee cups, and discarded newspapers were piled high on the floor as the angry debate went on. At one point a discarded match ignited a pile of debris. Flames shot high enough to be clearly visible on television cameras. Panic was avoided when a delegate took to a microphone near the swiftly spreading flames and shouted for calm. Other delegates stamped out the fire, and the debate proceeded.

Except for interviewing key floor leaders in an effort to interpret the ongoing debate for its viewers, television was an onlooker, not a participant. Its role was to report, not to influence. As time went on, it became more and more difficult to remain in this role. The medium soon became the message. It was too prominent, too obtrusive, too influential to remain wholly on the sidelines.

As the convention approached the call for nominations for the presidency, there was still no favorite. The nominating process would begin on Friday morning. Adlai Stevenson had been picking up support during the week following his welcoming speech, but Estes Kefauver was still in the lead in delegates committed. Attention now was focused on what President Truman would do. It was anticipated that even though he had not so far expressed support for any of the candidates, his opinion would carry substantial weight. It was now known that the president was definitely coming to Chicago. As a delegate he was eligible to vote, but he probably would not arrive until after the first ballot had been completed. His alternate, Thomas Gavin, was expected to be in the delegation when the first roll call began, and it was assumed that Gavin's vote would reflect the president's preference. It was still common practice in 1952 to call for a poll of a delegation in which each delegate would have to declare himself publicly. That meant he would have to announce his preference on television with the cameras focused tightly on him. It seemed inevitable that someone would call for such a poll to smoke Gavin out.

The president was booked to leave Washington National Airport about the time the polling would begin. We had scheduled a mobile unit to be at the airport for the departure, but I was not sure how we were to communicate with the Washington crew. Hewitt was so busy following action on the floor that I picked up the private-line phone to ask broadcast operations in New York how we were planning to coordinate the Washington cut-in. I was told that no cue line would be available to permit us to see what was happening in Washington. Broadcast operations personnel, though, would give us a play-by-play report by telephone. From the phoned descriptions we could decide when to call for the Washington picture. But I would have to keep the line open. Then there occurred a miraculous coincidence that was made to order for television.

When I placed the call to New York, the poll of the delegations was already under way. Within seconds Missouri would be called, so I asked whether the president had arrived at the airport. He had, I was told, and should be approaching the ramp in a few minutes. A camera would pick him up as soon as he came into view. I asked that I be warned as soon as he could be seen in a tight shot. The polling of the Missouri delegates had begun and by this time was nearing Gavin's name. New York told me that they had the tight shot I wanted. I said, "Take it."

Hewitt was baffled when he saw the picture of the smiling president come up on the screen. I had not had time to tell him what I was doing, so the picture was totally unexpected. As the president stepped out of his car, I shouted, "Take Chicago." Gavin's name was the next to be called. The president's alternate got to his feet, reached into a pocket, extracted a letter, and began to read an endorsement of Adlai Stevenson for the Democratic presidential nomination. The letter was signed "Harry S Truman."

As I heard the president's name, I almost screamed into the telephone, "Take Washington." In a fraction of a second, there on the screen was President Truman on the plane's ramp, smiling broadly and waving his hat. He turned, entered the aircraft, the door closed, and we returned to Chicago.

The timing was so perfect it could never have been planned. For television at that stage in its technological development, it was a case of outrageous good fortune. Only a few years later, it all could have been accomplished effortlessly, but only if the extraordinary coincidences in timing could be repeated.

The president's endorsement did not clinch the nomination for Stevenson, but it furnished a powerful boost. Coupled with the favorable impression that had been created by his welcoming speech, it moved him well into contention. The first ballot was indecisive. On the second, Stevenson moved within striking distance. By the third, the opposition was beginning to crumble, and before it was finished, Governor Adlai Stevenson of Illinois was officially declared the candidate of the Democratic Party for election to the presidency of the United States.

Would it have happened without television? That question obviously is impossible to answer. Some importance, however, has to be attached to the enthusiasm that Stevenson created with his brilliant speech at the opening session and to the spirited response from the television audience.

From television's point of view, the marriage of politics and television had been a smashing success. The medium had suddenly advanced from an intriguing curiosity to a virtual necessity. Politics would never be the same again. Doubters had been converted. Future conventions and campaigns, it was certain, would be built around television.

Some reservations, though, were voiced. Jack Gould of the *New York Times* raised one of the more pertinent ones:

It may be wise to temper some of the excitement over the role of television in politics and recognize that as the novelty of the marriage between the two fields wears off there will be a greater sense of perspective by both the broadcaster and the politician. A good rule of thumb for both would be that television's job is to report the show, not to produce it.[5]

Gould's advice would have been well taken if politicians in future convention years had not gotten so greedy that they began to look on the convention as the opportunity of a lifetime to "produce a show" that had more to do with selling the party than with selecting candidates—and if the television networks had not been so greedy for ratings that besting the competition became more important than reporting the story.

NOTES

1. Jack Gould, "The X of the Campaign—TV Personality," *New York Times*, June 22, 1952. In James Fixx, *The Mass Media and Politics* (New York: Arno Press, 1972), p. 22.

2. Several years later I discovered that the microphone behind the drape in the meeting room had not been placed there by NBC. At a news broadcasters' con-

vention I was introduced to a news director from a 250-watt radio station in Houston owned by Roy Hofheinz, one-time mayor of that city. He reminded me that we had met in the Conrad Hilton Hotel in Chicago during the 1952 Republican convention. Our rooms had been on the same corridor. I remembered that as I walked down the corridor, I had seen a man, sitting beside an open door, wearing a headset and listening intently to something I could not hear. I asked him if he happened to be the man with the headset. He replied affirmatively, so I went on to ask what he had been listening to so patiently for hours at a time. His answer: he had been monitoring the proceedings of the credentials committee through a microphone he had placed behind a drape in the committee room.

3. Kurt Lang and Gladys Lang, *Politics and Television* (Chicago: Quadrangle Books, 1968), p. 137.

4. The radio booth camera position was used for another purpose that might have been questioned for its propriety. During former President Herbert Hoover's formal speech to the delegates, the camera was sometimes used to shoot past the back of the former president's head to the TelePrompTer from which he was reading. Viewers could follow along word for word as he was reading the text. I was sufficiently embarrassed to ask that we discontinue.

5." After Chicago," *New York Times*, July 26, 1952. In Fixx, *The Mass Media and Politics*, p. 23.

4

The Struggle for Parity with Print

Television first achieved parity with the printed press in covering presidential elections in an improbable location. It happened in Abilene, Kansas, on June 5, 1952. The occasion was Dwight Eisenhower's first press conference as a candidate for the Republican nomination for the presidency. He had formally announced his candidacy in a major speech the night before. The speech, delivered in a park in Abilene, had been broadcast by both CBS and NBC. The press conference was to be an informal opportunity to meet with representatives of the press who would be following the campaign.

Prior to that date, television news personnel had been trailing along behind their more prestigious brethren and picking up the scraps. There had been extensive coverage of the primaries, principally those in New Hampshire and Wisconsin, but television journalists and their camera crews were not welcome in the elite circle of print regulars. They picked up their film stories mostly on their own initiative and notably not by covering press conferences.

Very few candidates for high state and national offices had demonstrated much interest in television as a campaign tool. The notable exceptions were Governor Dewey of New York, Senator Taft of Ohio, and former advertising agency executive William Benton of Connecticut. All three used television extensively in their 1950 campaigns, but it was mostly of the paid type: speeches, rallies, and, in Dewey's case, an innovative telethon. News on television was considered mostly as a bonus, hardly rejected but not particularly sought after. When a candidate wanted news coverage, he went to the newspaper. Television was still largely a fascinating toy.

It was no better than a stepchild when General Eisenhower returned to his hometown of Abilene on June 4 to make a formal announcement of his candidacy for the Republican nomination. Plans called for the general to fire his opening salvo in an open-air meeting on the night of June 4. He would hold a press conference in an Abilene movie theater the next morning. CBS and NBC, at a cost of $80,000, a sizable outlay at that time, had agreed to finance construction of a temporary microwave relay connecting Abilene with the transcontinental AT&T circuit at Omaha. This facility would enable them to deliver a pooled television signal to their respective networks, thus giving national exposure to the Eisenhower campaign kickoff, not as a paid commercial but as a news event.

The Eisenhower campaign staff, while obviously pleased with television coverage of the announcement ceremony, adamantly refused to give permission to television to cover the press conference. As reasons they cited the shape of the hall, which would complicate camera placement, and the general's sensitivity to television lights shining in his eyes. The real reason was never given: Representatives of the printed press had handed down an ultimatum that if television were permitted into the theater, they would boycott the event. To back up their ultimatum, they issued a threat. If the Eisenhower managers were insistent that television cameras be present, they would enlist teams of Boy Scouts to shuttle in and out, delivering short bulletins for release by telegraph to their home offices. It isn't difficult to visualize how all the hubbub would affect a five-star general accustomed to stern discipline and absolute decorum. Television would be left with nothing but chaos to transmit.

Robert Mullen, who had been assigned by the promoters of the Eisenhower candidacy to serve as the general's press and public relations secretary, was reluctant to provoke retaliatory action by the press, and he had the support of the senior campaign leadership.[1]

It was CBS Chairman William S. Paley who had first encouraged making a commitment of the rather substantial expenditure required to feed the signal out of Abilene. At the time he gave his approval, I made a strong plea for support in demanding access to the press conference, but there was not even a nod of approval from the chairman. On several subsequent occasions I reiterated my contention that television should be present. At some point, I argued, we must establish parity with the other media. Furthermore, it was an important news story, and we should be there. It was not enough just to cover the speech. The news would be made at the press conference. I added that I thought the Eisenhower campaign would profit from our coverage.

Still there was no encouragement, no offer to back us up if we carried the fight to the top of the Eisenhower command. Since I knew that Paley was close to leaders of the Eisenhower movement—among them was his brother-in-law Jock Whitney—I took that to mean we had better not force the issue. The problem was not solely Paley's brusque refusal to as much as discuss the issue. A more important concern related to preempting a sponsored program in order to open up a time period where we could schedule the press conference. This required getting the approval of the television network program plans board, of which Paley was chairman. I knew from experience that no move would be made without his support.

The general's speech, if not a disaster, was certainly a colossal bust. Mullen, against his better judgment (as he admitted to me subsequently), had agreed to schedule the event outdoors in an open park. There was no auditorium in Abilene large enough to accommodate the crowd expected. There was no consideration given to the millions who might watch the event on television, and none to the weather.

As the candidate mounted a roofless platform, a heavy rainstorm struck. A local volunteer held an umbrella over Eisenhower's head as he spoke, but the rain dripped off the umbrella onto his manuscript, thoroughly soaking it. On one occasion the umbrella was moved far enough so that the rain pelted him in the face and fogged up his glasses. It was obvious on the television screen that he was bored and irritated. To compound his discomfort, the speech was the first written for him by Bryce Harlow, later to become one of his favorite writers, but at this time Harlow was unfamiliar with the general's style. It was a dismal beginning for what was to have been the first big step in a whirlwind campaign leading to Chicago and the Republican nomination.

I watched the rain-soaked affair from my home in Westport, Connecticut. Following the conclusion I sent a telegram to our two executives on the scene, news director Fritz Littlejohn and facilities and planning director Paul Levitan. I complimented them on making the best of an impossible situation and urged them to be ready to move in the event there was any last-minute relaxation of the ban against our coverage of the press conference.

The next morning, having abandoned all hope, I was about to leave for the station to catch a train to New York when the phone rang. It was Bill Paley, calling from his home on Long Island.

"Oh, Sig," he opened, "don't you think it would be a good idea if we covered that press conference out in Abilene this morning?"

That was all the encouragement I needed. I told him that I would call Abilene immediately and set plans in motion.

Levitan answered the phone. We had only about 90 minutes before the conference started, but he assured me he would be ready. He had alerted his broadcast crew to the possibility there might be a change in plans and had prepared for quick action. After the speech the previous night, he had gambled on getting a last-minute approval and moved his cameras and microphones to the lobby of the theater. They were in position to be moved into the press conference site on a moment's notice. NBC was not so fortunate. Levitan's counterpart at NBC had loaded his equipment onto a truck and sent it back to Kansas City.

I then urged Levitan, as soon as he had moved his gear into the theater, to inform the Eisenhower campaign leadership that he would leave the theater only if forcibly ejected. It was easy for me to be courageous from a safe distance of 1,500 miles.

Mullen was on his way to Eisenhower's quarters to meet the general prior to accompanying him to the theater when he was told about Levitan's move. He was informed that the cameras were in the hall and that television was determined to stay. He reported that information to the general, expecting an outburst. The reaction, though, was mild. "If the cameras are in the theater," Eisenhower told him, "we had better leave them there."[2]

The Eisenhower press conference was a smashing success. There was none of the boredom and irritation of the previous evening. The general was confident, articulate, quick to respond to questions, and even jovial. Much of the damage from the night before was undone. And no Boy Scouts were running in and out of the hall with messages.

From the television point of view, the incident was equally significant. For the first time in its short life, television had insisted on equal rights with the printed press and had won. In its political coverage it had frequently been fed table scraps after the newspapers and wire services had gorged themselves on the main feast. It was common practice for television personnel to be permitted to attend press conferences, but only with pencil and paper. No cameras were allowed. Now the standard practice had been challenged, and by standing firm television had succeeded in breaking the traditional pattern. The new boy on the block had stood up to his peers and had signaled a demand for respect.

Victory in the battle of Abilene did not assure television that it had achieved full parity with print in all situations in all parts of the country. Skirmishing between video and print journalists continued in many areas for several years. It did, however, weaken the barriers in Washington. The Washington example in turn created leverage that could be used elsewhere. By 1960 many campaign planners were designing press conferences primarily for television exposure. Print in many cases was secondary, and the expression "news conference" was being used with increasing frequency as a substitute for "press conference." The televised news conference had become a campaign staple.

Television's first 1952 effort at covering politics was not undertaken without a number of important handicaps. There was no tradition for coverage by television, no precedents. To much of the printed press, it was an intruder with its roots in show business, not in journalism. Radio was generally accepted, but it had a longer history and was far less obtrusive. As television news crews pursued the candidates into New Hampshire in February, there was no warm welcome from newspaper correspondents, and mostly bewilderment from candidates and their staffs, who were baffled about how to treat the intruder. Television crews, in turn, had no patterns, no guidelines to follow in planning coverage. Every step broke new ground.

There was a shortage of experienced personnel. There had never been a significant effort to cover a national campaign. CBS was particularly restricted by the fact that all its corps of talented correspondents were assigned to the CBS Radio staff and could be pried loose to undertake television assignments only at the whim of radio executives. Camera crews, film editors, and field producers were just learning a new trade. They were additionally hampered by the inadequacy of the technology available for field coverage in 1952.

Those of us in management positions were still so enthralled by the awesome capabilities of the electronic television camera that we overlooked the deficiencies inherent in the film cameras that we had to use in the field. We knew the quality they delivered was inferior, but we were so impressed by the "gee whiz" aspect of our reporting that we hoped the viewers would forgive the gray and indistinct picture quality and the scratchy sound. The cameras we used, largely because there were no others on the market, were 16mm units designed for home movies. Sound, when we used it, was noisy and distorted. Videotape recording was still a dream for the future. It did not arrive until five years later. Film laboratories were few in number and were mostly concentrated in large cities. Film stories had to be shipped unprocessed and uncut to New York, for processing and editing there. Air service was slow and spotty. It was frequently more efficient to transport film from New Hampshire to New York by car or bus than to use what air service there was.

The coverage of the 1952 campaign had to be planned and executed within the constraints imposed by the inadequate technology. Same-day coverage was usually out of the question. Live electronic coverage could be scheduled only in major cities that had been interconnected by microwave or coaxial cable facilities, and New Hampshire had neither large cities nor a single television station on the air. Abilene was to be an exception, but only because Bill Paley had personally approved the expenditure of what was then considered a very large sum. The campaign coverage as seen on the air reflected the technology available. There were few, if any, live pickups from the field, few press conferences, a total absence of live appearances by candidates except in the major cities.

What we saw on the networks was candidates shaking hands at rallies or outside factory gates, footage of lunches or dinners at which candidates spoke, and some interviews that were not so perishable that they could not be held for up to 48 hours. Paid television in that era normally consisted of half-hour speeches delivered from a major city, but since there were no operating television stations in New Hampshire, commercial time was out of the question. It was in this trackless environment that pioneers from a new medium set out to earn a position of respect as legitimate partners with print and radio. Ironically, their efforts were destined to go unnoticed in New Hampshire, where there were no transmitters to broadcast their efforts.

Time constraints had a profound influence on the type of coverage delivered by television reporters. There couldn't be any of the breathless "I have just learned . . . " type of reporting. It would sound rather ridiculous 18 to 24 hours later. Since at CBS we had a limited number of reporters to send into the field, much of our political reporting was prepared by staff writers in our news headquarters and given to Douglas Edwards to read either on camera or as voice over film delivered from the field. When we did succeed in sending a reporter along with a camera crew, he prepared his report with full knowledge that it would not be seen and heard for many hours. The time lag called for a thoughtful, reflective, and analytical report rather than one designed for immediate release.

The coverage did not lack color. Scenes of California Governor Earl Warren sitting on the dais at a political rally in Wisconsin trying to eat his chicken dinner while being harangued by lady politicians on either side; of Senator Estes Kefauver half reclining on a bed in a dingy Wisconsin hotel room while answering a reporter's questions; or of Senator Robert Taft turning a mechanical smile on and off as he shook hands with followers in New Hampshire are memorable even though it may have taken 24 hours or more from the time the negative was exposed until the story was on the air. There was, however, an advantage. The narration that accompanied the film stories did more to add perspective to the campaign than the action-oriented coverage that followed the advent of satellites, videotape, electronic editing, and fiber optics.

Jack Gould of the *New York Times* was one critic who noted that television was more than an intruder on the political scene. He predicted that the concept regarding television held by most politicians would require substantial revision:

Up to now, they have thought of television primarily in terms of guest appearances or the purchase of time over which they would have control. . . . But the New Hampshire primary showed that television's complementary role of independent reporter may be of even greater significance. . . . The most rewarding and absorbing film "shots" from New Hampshire were the informal and unprepared scenes which caught the human equation in the raw and told their own stories in terms of character and personality.[3]

What Gould did not explain is that television covered New Hampshire and subsequent primaries in 1952 as it did because it did not have the technology to do anything else.

It is clear in retrospect that the evolution of political reporting on television, whether for better or for worse, has paralleled the advance of communications technology and is indelibly marked by it. The style of reporting, the nature of the coverage, and the contents of individual reports were all influenced by the equipment available. Speed, convenience, and improved quality all exerted their influence, and not always for the better. In retrospect, the television reporting that Gould saw in 1952 may have contributed more to public understanding than all of the electronic legerdemain and instant reports of the late 1980s.

The television of the 1950s, primitive as it was by present standards, began to reshape the entire process of campaigning for public office. It focused attention on the primaries, showed vast numbers of Americans how exciting a national political convention can be, and furnished close-ups of the fall campaign that brought a new dimension to politics. It further established that television could not be overlooked or disregarded in subsequent campaigns. For all its inexperience and technological deficiencies, television was creating a niche for itself in political coverage. Its role would grow with dazzling speed in subsequent years.

The campaign of 1952 was a campaign in transition. The traditional whistle-stop became virtually extinct. Television combined with the airplane offered a more efficient method for reaching masses of voters. The Eisenhower campaign demonstrated in late August how the two could be linked to reach thousands of voters quickly and economically. In two days the general was able to campaign in six cities in three states, an unheard-of feat even four years earlier. Each rally at a shopping center or downtown square was planned in advance, and local television was encouraged to cover. The possibility of coverage by local television stations was the new element that made the effort attractive. Thousands could see and hear the candidate, in contrast with the handful who could cluster around the rear platform of the candidate's private car on a whistle-stop tour.

Innovations, however, were still relatively few. Most candidates and campaign managers were still wedded to print as the only surefire medium for winning elections. Television was at best a fascinating toy. Even after the rousing success at the political conventions in midsummer, the staple for reaching the masses by television in the fall campaign was not the news broadcast. It was the half-hour speech delivered on paid time. Television correspondents on occasion traveled with the presidential and vice-presidential candidates, but as second-class citizens; and, as was true in the primaries, their reports were, for the most part, radio-type "think pieces." Sometimes they were done on camera with campaign activity in the background, and at other times they were submitted to New York as written copy for incorporation in "voice-over" reports. Press conferences were still off limits to television cameras in most parts of the country. The exceptions were Washington and New York, where television's right to be present had been fairly well established. Discrimination against television was particularly pronounced in California, where the normal practice called for three separate meetings with the media: the first for pencil-and-paper reporters, the second for radio, and the third for television.[4]

The one item during the campaign that, more than any other, focused the spotlight directly on television and in which TV was clearly the number one target, was the now famous "Checkers" speech. The use of television to reach a nationwide audience from a studio was not in itself innovative, but both the methods used and the results were, especially the results. A story had leaked to the media that Richard Nixon, the Republican vice-presidential candidate, was the possessor of a private expense fund totaling $18,235. The money had been donated by 76 California supporters. It was designated for the candidate's personal use, not as a contribution to the campaign.

The story was particularly embarrassing because one of the principal themes of the "Ike and Dick" campaign was a condemnation of "the mess in Washington." Nixon's "slush fund" undercut efforts to cast the Democrats in the role of villains and the Republicans as the knights in shining armor. There was a rising tide of demands that Nixon prevent any further embarrassment to Eisenhower by withdrawing from the ticket. Ike was said to be considering whether to ask for his withdrawal.

Rather than resign, Nixon started a counterattack. After meeting with his inner campaign staff, consisting of William Rogers (later attorney general); Ted Rogers, his television adviser; Jim Bassett, a print media adviser; Murray Chotiner, a close political adviser; and Herb Klein, it was decided to buy a half-hour of prime time on the NBC television network and the CBS and Mutual radio networks for a speech that would answer the charge. Total cost for the three networks was a meager $75,000.

Nixon, according to Klein, was his own writer, producer, director, and actor. The result was the now celebrated "Checkers" speech.[5]

The purchase of a half-hour of time for a political speech was no novelty, nor was origination from a studio. What was unusual was the style and content of the presentation and the response.[6]

The speech furnished a striking demonstration that under the right circumstances, television was capable of galvanizing a whole country. The reaction was not unanimously favorable. Critics scoffed at the mawkish sentimentalism displayed in Nixon's reference to Pat Nixon's "good Republican cloth coat," and to the little cocker spaniel, Checkers, that had been a gift to his children. The critics, however, could not laugh off the results. An avalanche of letters, telephone calls, and telegrams poured into Republican National Committee headquarters and into offices of newspapers. The committee reported that its count showed 350 to 1 support for keeping Nixon on the Republican ticket. Eisenhower invited Nixon to Wheeling, West Virginia, to reiterate his confidence in his running mate.

Television was present as Eisenhower patted Nixon on the shoulder and told him, "You're my boy, Dick." The Checkers speech had played to the largest audience ever tuned in to a political program. If doubters concerning television's role in politics needed further convincing, the Checkers speech was the clinching evidence.

By the fall of 1952, television had clearly made its mark. The conventions had drawn unexpectedly high ratings. The presidential candidates were booking time for televised formal speeches, and the "Checkers" performance had demonstrated how public opinion can be manipulated by effective use of the medium.

By 1956, campaign leaderships had learned their lesson. They were no longer skeptical about the newcomer. To the contrary, they were greedy for television exposure, but on their terms. Print was still the prime target, but television was an attractive bonus. It had progressed well beyond the haphazard experimentation of 1952 and had begun to formulate its own patterns for political coverage. It had the experience gained in 1952 and 1954 to build on. It had more and better-trained personnel. What it lacked was new technology that would simplify and speed the process. A prototype of a videotape recording and playback unit was demonstrated in April 1956, but no production units would be available until the winter of 1957. The jet airplane was still three years away; the first communications satellite, six. There were more 16mm film labs available, but cameras still delivered both sound and picture of inferior quality. The one area in which substantial progress had been made was the extension of two-way microwave and coaxial cable transmission to many areas from which feeding into network lines was impossible in 1952. This, in some cases, eliminated lead time and permitted more current reporting, but it was expensive and, except in unusually newsworthy situations, it was rarely resorted to. Even though there were more television reporters trailing the candidates, the emphasis was still on analytical think pieces rather than on breathless spot news.

Further attention was focused on television as a result of an innovation in the method of selling time for political speeches. The 30-minute purchase was costly, and audiences drawn were only a small fraction of those attracted to the entertainment programs displaced. Preemptions frequently irritated viewers, who resented missing their favorite programs. The networks were not enthusiastic about having their mood-sequence program flow interrupted by insertion of a political speech into the middle of a carefully crafted sequence of programs in which one leads into the next and holds viewers throughout the evening. Both networks and campaign staffs were aware of the meager ratings drawn by political speeches and of the annoyance of many viewers when their favorite programs were preempted for political oratory.

There was a possible solution to the dilemma. If candidates would be willing to limit their presentations to five minutes, and the regularly scheduled programs could be trimmed by that amount, viewers would be spared the irritation of missing their regular programs, the networks would save most of the program preemption costs, and the candidate would profit by retaining the lead-in from the regularly scheduled program. Defections to competing networks were less likely. The networks enthusiastically supported the suggestion. They agreed to charge only one-sixth of the rate card price for a half-hour program rather than the one-third that the rate cards called for. As a result, the public saw a great number of five-minute political speeches during the 1956 campaign and a diminishing number of half-hour ones.

There were a number of new techniques employed by candidates that demonstrated their swiftly developing interest in exploiting television's capabilities for winning over voters. In his second run for the vice-presidency, Nixon was again an innovator. He and his staff anticipated that there were votes to be won by catering to college audiences, and that television could be the device that would enable him to make an incursion into college student ranks. A televised appeal to college students would, in addition, certainly be of interest outside the college populations, thus giving him a novel approach to supplement his traditional campaign methods. With the help of the national Young Presidents Organization and the Junior Chambers of Commerce, he scheduled a televised college press conference on the campus of Cornell University shortly before the election. Even though the Eisenhower staff worried, according to Herb Klein, that the college press conference experiment might "blow the election," it turned out to be a considerable success and created a pattern that the vice-president would follow in his run for the presidency in 1960. Television again was the medium for which the program was designed, not a secondary target permitted to pick up scraps from print.

CBS formalized its participation as an equal partner with print by creating what it called a "campaign caravan." It was more gesture than substance, but it added a promotional twist. A station wagon painted with the CBS logo roamed through New Hampshire, Wisconsin, and later Illinois and California, carrying a CBS camera crew and correspondent. The caravan attracted attention from both candidates and voters, but it did not help the team expedite shipments of film and commentary to New York to get on the air. It traveled several thousand miles during the primary season and stayed on the heels of the presidential candidates. It trained its cameras on them as they pitched horseshoes in New Hampshire, attended lunches in Wisconsin, shook hands in Illinois, and kissed babies in California. Team members dozed in hotel lobbies all across the country, and in the process of their exhaustive travels helped establish television as a bona fide member of the club of political campaign reporters.

By 1956 many political managers were fully alert to television's influence on voters, some of them too alert. They had already begun to dream of themselves as show business entrepreneurs and of their candidates as potential stars. The medium that had had to fight for recognition four years earlier now had to put on the brakes in order to avoid becoming a tool of the political organizers. Technology at this stage, though, was not keeping pace. By 1960, however, videotape recording was finally a reality.

The introduction of videotape recording in the 1960 campaign further aided television in competing directly with print for campaign coverage. Picture quality was vastly better. Laboratory processing time was eliminated, and editing time was appreciably reduced. Film was still the standby for news coverage, but videotape was available for special programs. Otherwise, there were refinements that made both reporting campaigns and promoting candidates easier, but there was nothing dramatic. Jet planes flew to more airports, television programs or filmed material could be picked up and fed into network lines from many more points than in 1956, computers were faster and more powerful, the number of American homes having television receivers was approaching 75 percent, but, except for videotape, there was no genuine breakthrough. Even videotape was still in a primitive stage. Electronic editing was in the future, so cutting and splicing were done manually.

The John F. Kennedy campaign first demonstrated in a dramatic way how a combination of live television and videotape could be used by imaginative programmers for political advantage in a manner impossible for print to duplicate. Campaign advisers were convinced that Kennedy's adherence to the Roman Catholic faith had to be defused as an issue to assure his victory. In early September, Kennedy accepted an invitation to speak to the Houston, Texas, Protestant Ministerial Council. The Kennedy campaign managers decided this would present an opportunity to face the religious issue head-on. Accordingly, the candidate talked forthrightly for a few minutes about his attitudes regarding the relationship of church and state, then invited questions. The questions were pointed and demanding, and the answers were candid and blunt. The program was carried by channel 13 in Houston, which also videotaped it. Willard Walbridge, the channel 13 general manager, was so excited about the performance that he called the Kennedy campaign's advertising agency to urge that the agency buy the tape for network release. The Kennedy high command approved of reusing the tape, but not as Walbridge had recommended. They decided to target their audiences more narrowly. They would buy spot time in areas where the candidate intended to campaign, and saturate the community with the program immediately before his arrival. The technique demonstrated for the first time that television could be used as a rapier rather than as a blunderbuss.

It was the Nixon organization that wiped out the last traces of the separate but unequal press conference. It introduced the first live televised press conference to the art of presidential campaigning. Scheduled to take place in Peoria, Illinois, in mid–October, it almost turned into a disaster when the candidate got trapped in a crowd outside the studio and arrived three minutes late. Unfortunately for Nixon, it was Kennedy, as the winner of the election, who was able to introduce the live televised press conference as a function of the presidency.

By 1960 television had earned its stripes as a fully qualified equal of print and radio as a political reporting medium. Network reporting of the campaign was more thorough and intensive than it had been before. Network correspondents and camera crews traveled with the candidates during the entire period. They had made substantial progress toward achieving parity with their print counterparts. The separate press conference was largely a relic of the past. Reports from the field were carried regularly on an increasing number of network news programs.

I was less than enthusiastic, though, about the contents of the reporting. We were in a transitional era between the thoughtful and analytical pieces of 1952 and the hard-hitting, fast-paced instant news of the 1980s. The pace of the campaign, the increasing speed of communications, and the greater number of program outlets available called for reporting that probed more deeply into campaign developments and voter motivations, that sought to furnish more perspective on voter interests and candidate response. What I thought we were getting was too much "How is the candidate doing?" "Will he be able to carry the state?" "What are his prospects?" and not enough real reporting. Our correspondents seemed to be infected with the horse race syndrome. In retrospect, perhaps we were better off with the inferior technology and the more reflective pieces of 1952 than the more superficial content of 1960.

The two most conspicuous innovations of 1960 were the televised Kennedy-Nixon debates and the increasing employment of computers as aids in tracking public attitudes regarding the campaign. The debates, produced principally for television, drew audiences in excess of 70 million. There was no longer any doubt that the medium had outgrown second-class status. For the first time voters, thanks to television, were given the opportunity to see both candidates on one platform at the same time and on all three networks. Computers were used by both television networks and campaign organizations to track voter attitudes and shifts in preferences. (More about both debates and computers will appear in later chapters.)

The 1950s must seem like the Dark Ages in contrast with television's role in the election process in the 1980s and 1990s. The 16mm movie motion picture cameras used by the three networks in 1952 and 1956 have given way to lightweight, portable electronic units with their accompanying miniaturized three-quarter and half-inch videotape recorders. The tedious process of sitting at an editing table poring over reels of film has been replaced by electronic editing of tape. No longer is it necessary to ship film to New York for processing and editing. All that is required is to feed the signal to a satellite sending dish aimed at a geostationary satellite stationed 22.3 million miles above the equator. In a fraction of a second, the signal will be received in New York or the most convenient origination point, ready for air. Portable lap-top computers, tied into telephone lines, move script or background information into news headquarters at the speed of light. What muscle had failed to achieve in winning equal status with the press, technology was quickly accomplishing.

In the 1950s there was still very little political coverage by individual stations. Only the three television networks had both the resources and the desire to cover a full campaign. Since then there have been dramatic changes. Many network affiliates have become sufficiently strong financially to undertake extensive coverage at least in their own areas. Independent stations lacking network affiliation have become much more aggressive. In the early 1970s many public broadcasting stations began to produce political programs of their own, particularly of the debate variety. More recently the Cable News Network, C-SPAN, Conus, a number of station groups, and many independent stations are assigning reporting teams to political coverage.

The single crew that CBS sent to New Hampshire and Wisconsin in 1952 is dwarfed by the 140-man team it sent to New Hampshire and Iowa in 1988. In those states in 1988, CBS used eight satellite transmitting dishes, two of them belonging to CBS and the rest leased from other sources. They fed programming to transponders on three separate satellites. These communications facilities were not used exclusively by CBS. CBS News personnel furnished services to the 38 affiliated stations that sent representation to cover the stories. Similar services were performed for their affiliates by the other networks.

Photographs taken in Des Moines just before the Iowa caucuses show a forest of satellite transmitting dishes in an open area near a headquarters hotel. Some 3,500 news personnel swarmed all over the state during the campaign. It was obviously a case of overkill. Neither Iowa nor New Hampshire, in retrospect, was important enough in 1988 to justify the excessive deployment of money, manpower, and technical facilities that was so evident in both states. The networks, which had dominated television coverage in past elections, were now in the minority. Technology had made it possible and economically feasible for stations, groups, new cooperative news-gathering agencies, cable, and CNN all to cover the story from the scene. From its status 36 years earlier as a novelty, television not only had moved center stage but was almost upstaging the candidates.

The effect of new technology on the content of news coverage was equally disturbing. The 15-second sound bite became the most desired commodity. The electronic camera and the satellite made it possible to furnish almost instantaneous coverage to home stations. The easiest item to cover is the "sound bite" delivered by the candidate or extracted from an interview or press conference. Candidates developed expertise in formulating colorful 15-second statements that they could drop into answers to questions. In some cases they even bought "bites" from specialists who wrote them for a fee. Broadcast reporters became adept at looking for them. They wrapped a few descriptive sentences around the bite and zipped it off by satellite to their home stations. Gone was much of the reflective and thoughtful reporting of the earlier era. In its place was formula coverage, devoid of much interpretation or background but reeking of color and breathlessness. Campaign managers and candidates quickly adjusted to the new environment.

As television news has become more ratings-oriented, its content has been altered to emphasize entertainment values. It is succumbing to its own entertainment-oriented environment and the blandishments of political managers who have become infected with show business. There is a real question now whether the calm, reflective pieces of the 1950s could get on the air today. Television has, in only four decades, radically altered the process of running for political office. It not only has won the dubious distinction of becoming the most attractive target of campaign managers and their most desired medium for winning votes but also has remade the campaign, and with each new addition to the technological arsenal it continues to remake it. It changes not only the campaigning methods used by candidates but also revamps the style of reporting and the content of the coverage. It has moved in directions and at a pace that could never have been dreamed of as the first reporting teams left New York to cover the New Hampshire primary in February 1952.

For one who has followed politics, the changes are self-evident. The linear campaign of the first half of the century that followed railroad lines has given way to an ad hoc criss crossing of the country by plane, going where the needs of the moment call, putting out fires, snapping up opportunities to pick up a few votes, and standing for interviews with both network and local broadcast news personnel. The opportunity for additional television exposure is the lure that has attracted candidates from rear platforms of trains to shopping malls and downtown plazas.

The media coverage of the campaign has been democratized to the extent that the old political pundits, for the most part representing metropolitan newspapers or syndicates, no longer dominate coverage as they once did. Television ratings and voter polls are more highly regarded as measures of progress than columns written by old-time syndicated star reporters. Campaigns have been modified to cater to the camera and the television reporter.

There is a new emphasis on campaign methodology, largely stimulated by the increasing role played by television. Theodore H. White caught the spirit and in 1960 started the production of a quadrennial series of books documenting campaigns, their strategies, and their methodologies.

Finally, with the demise of the campaign train and its entourage of reporters, there has come a new phenomenon, the "boys on the bus" or, more properly, the "boys on the airplane." Many of the "boys" have come from television, and have brought with them cameras, lenses, tripods, sound recording equipment, and lights. Campaigning in the era of television has, in short, become as unrecognizable to the 1948 political reporter as it has to the voter. Television has clearly won the jackpot, but the question now is whether it is investing its winnings wisely.

NOTES

1. Mullen described the whole affair to me several years later, including his reluctance to incur the disfavor of the printed press. He was convinced that the threats were real, and wanted to take no chances that the campaign would get off to so chaotic a start. I recorded the conversation in January 1970 and have the cassette in my files.

2. Mullen cassette (see note 1).

3. Jack Gould, "Video and Politics," *New York Times*, March 16, 1952. In James Fixx, *The Mass Media and Politics* (New York: Arno, 1972), p. 17.

4. Herbert Klein, who directed media relations for the Eisenhower-Nixon campaign in California in 1952, told me that newspaper opposition to the presence of the camera was so unyielding that he made no effort to alter the pattern. The interview, conducted in February 1988, was recorded and is in my files.

5. Klein gave me a detailed account of preparations for the speech in the February 1988 interview (see note 4).

6. A full analysis of the content of the speech and an account of its impact on the Nixon image is in Kurt Lang and Gladys Engel Lang, *Politics and Television* (Chicago: Quadrangle, 1968), pp. 212–49.

5

Remaking the Campaign

Harold Stassen arrived at the last minute at the San Francisco airport one Sunday morning in mid-January 1952 to board a United Airlines plane bound for New York. One of the few seats left was on the aisle beside me. We had both come from a meeting of the Republican National Committee: he, to promote his candidacy for the Republican nomination to the presidency; I, to lobby for more consideration from the arrangements committee for the personnel and space that the television networks felt would be required for covering the party's national convention at Chicago in early July.

We were not total strangers. I had covered his campaign for the Republican presidential nomination in 1948 as news director at CBS-owned station WCCO in Minneapolis and St. Paul, and had even dined at his South St. Paul home. It was only minutes before the conversation turned to television and political campaigning. Stassen was acquainted with the medium, had appeared from time to time on interview programs, but had very little idea of how he should use television in the campaign for the Republican nomination. There were few guidelines available. Since I was one of the few executives in the medium with whom he was acquainted, apparently I seemed a logical person to turn to.

During the primary campaigns and the jockeying for delegates in the winter and spring of 1948, I had followed Stassen's almost successful campaign to win the nomination, but my work had been in radio, not television. In June I went to Philadelphia to watch his last-gasp effort at the Republican National Convention. As the convention was called to order, he was generally conceded to be Governor Dewey's principal opponent for the nomination, and at that point he was by no means a sure loser.[1]

We had met several times during the intervening years, and I had helped on occasion, when Stassen was serving as president of the University of Pennsylvania, to get air time for prominent guests of the university. We had not been seated long before he began asking pointed questions. He was eager to explore methods by which he could get maximum exposure for his campaign on television. He was curious about techniques he might be able to use. The relationship between politics and television was still so new at this point that there was very little I could offer.

Very few political advisers had gone much beyond the standard 30-minute speech either delivered to a large audience in an auditorium or to the cameras in a television studio. Governor Dewey had used the telethon to good advantage in running for governor of New York in 1950. Senator Taft had bought time for speeches in his Ohio Senate race the same year. Senator William Benton of Connecticut had made what were then novel plans for employing television in his campaign for reelection in 1952, but few others had more than a vague notion that television would probably be a valuable campaign tool.

There were still no spot commercials produced for television. Interview programs were largely the province of the networks and stations. NBC's "Meet the Press," a popular weekly interview program, would be skittish about inviting a declared candidate for fear of running afoul of Section 315 of the Federal Communications Act. The act mandates that any station giving time to one candidate must give equivalent time to all other candidates for the same office. Normally it could be expected that between 15 and 20 individuals would declare themselves candidates for the presidency. Under FCC interpretations of Section 315, each would be entitled to equivalent time.

Paid half-hours, not requiring much imagination, were the order of the day but were not entirely satisfactory. Audiences were small, and the candidate ran the risk of alienating viewers who were forced to miss their favorite programs. I suggested to Stassen that his best bet would be to make himself available for appearances on regular news broadcasts. In the late 1980s this would be described as "free media." He would have to have something newsworthy to say, and he would have to realize that his comments would be subject to severe editing, but he would reach a far larger audience than he could expect from a set speech. He would be guaranteed an audience with a demonstrated interest in public affairs. For longer segments of paid time, I suggested that he arrange to be interviewed rather than go it alone with a lengthy speech. If he were to buy the time, he could select his own interviewers and the topics to be covered. The interviewers would loosen up the content, add pace, and bring a variety of faces to the screen.

I did not have much more to offer. We had been far too busy preparing for convention coverage to give much thought to advising candidates how they might campaign on television. CBS had its own counterpart to "Meet the Press," a program called "Man of the Week," but in selecting guests we scrupulously avoided inviting declared candidates for office in order to remain clear of the Section 315 trap. We could not afford to run the risk of being forced to furnish time for each of the 15 to 20 individuals, some famous and some unknown, to appear on our program. It was obvious that six months before the convention, Stassen had no television strategy and was still groping for ideas. He could not turn to political consultants who specialized in media; they were still an unknown breed. He might have turned to advertising agencies, but those with experience in politics were pretty effectively tied up.

Stassen's lack of television sophistication seemed to characterize most of the other candidates for the nomination. There was surprisingly little evidence that any of the potential candidates or their supporters had devoted much attention to planning television strategies, or even knew where to begin. The only one of a half-dozen candidates for the Democratic nomination to take the trouble to inquire about campaigning on television was Senator Richard Russell of Georgia. Senator Russell invited the news directors of each of the television networks to join him for dinner in the Oak Room at the Plaza Hotel in New York City in mid-March for an informal conversation. He was interested in meeting executive television personnel, but the dinner turned out to be largely social.

In retrospect, the conversation with Stassen appears light-years in the past. It is inconceivable that four decades later anyone could be no naive as to ask how television could best be used to further the interests of a campaign for the presidency—or, for that matter, for any other political office. Since that time, candidates, political managers, consultants, and advertising agencies have sprung up like weeds with magic formulas to exploit television in the interests of winning elective office.

In 1952, though, their numbers were few. The specialists who had experience with television in political campaigns were largely limited to the New York advertising agency executives who had worked with Governor Dewey in the 1950 campaign in New York. A number of executives at other agencies were interested in politics and eager to become involved, but there was no reservoir of specialists competing for assignments.

At CBS we took the initiative in scheduling a series of programs that would introduce the major candidates to the medium. Starting in late winter, we assigned a weekly nighttime half-hour spot to the candidates of the two parties to program as they saw fit. Under the title "Bandwagon," the program ran from 10:30 to 11 P.M. on Friday nights until all major candidates had had a chance to make their appeals to the voters. We furnished a studio, production personnel, technical facilities, and a set. What they did was up to them. We saw no evidence of striking innovations or imaginative production. It was largely straight talk.[2]

There was very little about the programs that suggested much thought had been given to adapting standard vote-getting techniques to the requirements of television. The performances were notably lacking in any of the glitter that would become standard operating procedure in another decade. It began to become evident as spring progressed toward summer, however, that the movement to win the nomination for General Eisenhower would bring to bear a multiplicity of talents that could hardly overlook the special benefits that television might have to offer.

The formal announcement of Eisenhower's intention to run did not come until the June 4 ceremony in Abilene, Kansas. The small cadre of American journalists covering the general at SHAPE headquarters in Paris was certain, however, as early as mid-March that a decision to make the race had been made. While they could not get formal confirmation, every move they observed suggested to them that formal entry into the race was imminent. David Schoenbrun, the CBS correspondent in Paris, sent me a confidential memorandum, dated March 20, reporting on a meeting of a select group of the American press corps. At an informal luncheon Eisenhower had suggested he would probably write a letter of resignation to Secretary of Defense Robert Lovett with a request that Lovett relay it to President Truman.

The most disturbing information in the Schoenbrun memo was his implied prediction that television would have to be content with second-class status in an Eisenhower presidential campaign. In planning for a press conference celebrating the anniversary of NATO, the general insisted that there be three separate press conferences: the first at 10 A.M. for print media, the second at 10:30 for radio, and the third at 11 A.M. for television. He was adamant, according to Schoenbrun, and could not be dissuaded even by Schoenbrun's argument that he should do his television interview while he was fresh. The memo reflected pessimism that the NATO commander would be able to adapt himself to television well enough to wage a successful campaign.[3]

At this point the prognosis for a television-oriented campaign was something less than favorable. The general's key supporters in the United States, however, were especially well qualified to exploit the new medium to the hilt. The small group promoting the Eisenhower candidacy included an unusual wealth of political experience, but they had something more to offer. In their ranks were experienced users and producers of television. The top stratum of the inner circle included Governor Dewey, Senator Henry Cabot Lodge, Paul Hoffman, General Lucius Clay, John Hay Whitney, and Whitney associate Walter Thayer—hardly a blockbuster television lineup but men with finely tuned political instincts and a willingness to embrace new approaches.

On the periphery of the inner circle were two of the most television-minded advertising executives in the country: Sig Larmon, chief executive officer of Young and Rubicam, the advertising agency with more broadcast production experience than any other, and Ben Duffy, president of Batten, Barton Durstine and Osborn, another large agency with television experience, some of it acquired in political campaigns. Duffy's BBDO had served as Dewey's agency in the 1950 campaign and had been responsible for much of the imaginative approach that sealed the election for the New York governor.

Duffy brought to the group not only his Irish street fighter's instincts toward winning elections but also his experienced staff, including the men who had functioned so effectively in Dewey's smashing 1950 victory: Carroll Newton, Al Cantwell, and John Elliott. Larmon contributed his acute political sense and a host of experienced producers, directors, and account executives.

There was little specific that the Eisenhower group could do in the winter and early spring of 1952. Before starting an overt campaign, they had to await a formal announcement of the general's entry into the race. This could not come until he had resigned his post as commanding general of NATO. The time, however, was not wasted. It furnished an opportunity to develop a detailed strategy for winning the nomination. Television was certain to play a significant, if not dominant, role.

It was a situation made to order for the new medium. The Republican convention was scheduled to begin on July 7 in Chicago. Senator Taft would inevitably arrive in Chicago with a considerable lead in pledged delegates. Assuming that Eisenhower would not be free to declare his candidacy until early June, there would be barely a month to create an environment conducive to his selection. It could not be done on a state-by-state basis. Most of the delegates were already selected. It would have to be a national campaign designed to create a popular mood that would impose pressures on delegates to leave the candidate to whom they were pledged and join the Eisenhower bandwagon.

What was really required was not a traditional political campaign but a gigantic nationwide public relations effort. If public response to television coverage of the political conventions were to measure up to network predictions, a determined effort at national attitude manipulation might succeed. If the Eisenhower forces were made to look attractive, imaginative, and progressive, and the opponents stodgy, tradition-bound, and wedded to the past, an irresistible wave of pressure from the home constituencies might succeed in dislodging enough committed delegates and winning over enough uncommitted to pull off a triumph. It could be done, though, only by an astute use of television.

The key was new faces, new voices, new personalities, assuming that television viewers would note the contrast between the old wheelhorses who had dominated party councils for years and the fresh, young newcomers who represented a new generation of voters and leaders alike. The first test came in the credentials committee and the floor fight that followed the committee's report. (The victory of the Eisenhower forces was described in detail in Chapter 3, as was the ultimate victory over Senator Taft.) The strategy would never have paid off if the only media available had been print and radio. The distinction between the new force and the old guard could be made only visually. It took pictures to make the contrast clear. The Eisenhower high command gambled that viewers would turn out in the millions for their first opportunity to watch in person the selection of presidential candidates. And they did, some 55 million persons in all, up to 20 million for some key sessions.

Following the triumph at the convention, the Eisenhower team apparently let its guard down. BBDO, which had played a key role in the preconvention planning, was bypassed in favor of the Kudner agency, which had represented Senator Taft. The confusion in the Eisenhower ranks became startlingly apparent to me by early August. As part of its contract with Westinghouse, CBS was committed to produce a series of eight one-hour programs on the election campaign as a bridge between the conventions and the election, which Westinghouse was also committed to sponsor. Our plan was to arrange a series of eight debates, each to feature a supporter from the Stevenson camp lined up against one arguing the Eisenhower case. The program title was "Pick the Winner."

Only a short time after we started to line up talent, the program's producer told me he was surprised at some of the choices being made by the Eisenhower camp to present the general's case. It appeared to me that the preconvention strategy of featuring the new, fresh, and young faces had been abandoned in favor of relying on the old pros who had been in the Taft camp. I was sufficiently curious about this strange twist that I called Abbott Washburn, an old friend at the Eisenhower headquarters in Denver, to ask whether the names being proposed represented a change of policy—or might there be some mistake? I described our experience in some detail and asked whether he might be able to explain what had happened to change the pattern so drastically. He seemed surprised and promised to call back in a couple of hours, after checking the matter out with Ike's closest advisers. The reply confirmed our suspicion that there was some loose management in the Eisenhower command. Washburn asked that hereafter all calls regarding talent for "Pick the Winner" go directly to him. No one else would be authorized to make selections or recommend participants.

Within a few days it was announced that the Kudner Agency, while continuing to work on the campaign, would take a back seat to BBDO, which was being brought in as the senior agency. It seemed apparent that the Taft forces, after losing the nomination, had simply moved into the Eisenhower camp and were taking over as much of the leadership role as they could.

Young and Rubicam remained a significant factor in the campaign, but not at Eisenhower-Nixon central headquarters. Y and R was selected to represent Citizens for Eisenhower, an organization set up independently of the central campaign. Its assignment was to appeal to independents, Democrats, and all those potential voters who might feel uncomfortable in Republican ranks. Executives of two other agencies, Alfred Hollender of Grey Advertising and Rosser Reeves of Ted Bates and Company, played significant roles as individuals even though their agencies were not involved. Both volunteered to serve. Hollender had been on Eisenhower's staff in France during the war, and Reeves offered his services as a result of his enthusiasm for an Ike victory.[4]

The participation of advertising agencies in political campaigns was not a wholly new departure. The George H. Batten Company of Buffalo, New York, had been involved as early as 1916 in the campaign for the presidency by Charles Evans Hughes. The Alf Landon campaign in 1936 had been supported by radio spot commercials prepared on behalf of the Liberty League, a conservative, anti-Roosevelt citizens group. In 1948 the Ted Bates agency had prepared some sample radio spots in support of Governor Dewey's candidacy, but they were never used.[5]

Television added an entirely new dimension to the political scene. The spot commercial could, in effect, become a 60-second variation on the 30-minute speech. If the candidate recorded the spots in person, he could talk directly to an audience far larger than for the traditional 30-minute speech—an audience that tuned in not to see him but Milton Berle or "I Love Lucy" or one of the popular television programs of the day. If television could sell soap in a 60-second spot, why could it not sell a candidate and his ideas? It might have worked on radio, but it was not given a full trial. Television had the advantage, however, of presenting both the candidate and his voice, not his voice alone. There were some eyebrows raised at a CBS Television plans board meeting when we first heard that the Eisenhower campaign intended to use spot commercials. There were some who questioned the propriety. There was a real policy question involved. Our policy held that television commercials may be used to sell merchandise but not to sell ideas. Political spots, however, prevailed and are clearly the most conspicuous heritage of the marriage of politics and television.

There is some confusion concerning the identity of the first person to convince the Eisenhower campaign to use spot commercials. Martin Mayer says it was Alfred Hollender. Robert Mullen gives the credit to Rosser Reeves. It was Reeves who took a three-month leave of absence from his agency, prepared the first storyboards, received the go-ahead from the Eisenhower high command, and wrote the 60-second spots for the general to read. There was no fancy production involved, no film from the Korean war (which was one of the principal subjects attacked), no scenes from supermarkets showing housewives rebelling at high prices, and no shots of taxpayers protesting increasing tax rates. All one saw was the fatherly and sincere general patiently answering a question that was put to him by a concerned citizen.

The Eisenhower campaign staff also pioneered the use of the documentary format for creating public support. For some reason that defies explanation, I was invited by my old friend Abbott Washburn to sit in on a number of lunches with an informal Eisenhower support group. In the group were Elliott Bell, a McGraw-Hill executive and former member of Governor Dewey's staff; Gabriel Hauge, also of McGraw-Hill and later a key member of President Eisenhower's staff; and John Elliott of BBDO. At one of the sessions there was discussion of the possibility of producing a film documentary for television supporting the Eisenhower candidacy. The intention was to obtain film clips from widely scattered sections of the country in order to demonstrate the Republican candidate's widespread support. The weakness in the plan was the total lack of any notion as to where film clips of the type required might be obtained. Where could cameramen be found to deliver the required product? Did anyone have a list of free-lancers who might be able to deliver product to meet the specifications?

It so happened that I knew where such a list could be found. Our news staff had been screening both amateurs and professionals for months, trying to build a reliable list of competent camera operators who could be called on to deliver usable product when a news story developed in their areas. With some reluctance induced by a fear of showing favoritism in the campaign, I offered to make the list available. There was an advantage for us in assuring more work for independent contractors on our list, and I decided that I was aiding only in the mechanics, not in the program production. At my request our assignment desk sent Elliott the list he asked for.[6]

By 1956 the production of filmed biographies of candidates for showing on television had become standard operating procedure. The most dramatic use of film for television in the early television era was demonstrated at the Democratic National Convention in 1956. The Democratic National Committee had commissioned the production of a documentary extolling the virtues of the Democratic Party. It was shown to delegates following the conclusion of the keynote speech and was narrated by a young senator from Massachusetts, John F. Kennedy. (More of that in succeeding chapters.) It was clear from the manner in which the film was scheduled that the intended audience was not the 15,000 persons in the hall but the television audience of several million.

The Stevenson campaign in 1952 had been outmaneuvered in the use of spot commercials. Several members of the Stevenson inner circle, including then independent producer (later CBS Television president) Louis G. Cowan, Cox Broadcasting president Leonard Reinsch, and Victor A. Sholis, general manager of the Louisville, Kentucky, *Courier-Journal*'s station, WHAS-TV, were involved in television programming. Spots were not included in their original plans, however, and they reacted too late to the

Republican initiative. Their advertising representative, the Katz agency from Baltimore, made an effort to play catch up during the last few days of the campaign, but the money was gone. By Election Day the Republicans had spent $1.5 million on spots and the Democrats $77,000.[7]

The Democrats made another strategic error involving television almost two months before Stevenson was nominated. Under the erroneous assumption that larger segments of the public would be attracted to political speeches at set times than if the performances were scattered throughout the schedule, the national committee in May reserved the time period from 10:30 to 11 P.M. Tuesday and Thursday nights from September 2 through early November. This froze them into an inflexible position and made it easier for viewers who preferred entertainment programs to switch channels.[8]

The Republicans were not caught in the same trap. They bought time as required for specific objectives, kept their speeches as informal as possible to compensate for Eisenhower's stiff and cold demeanor on the platform, and interspersed formal talks with the spot commercial campaign. They obviously read television requirements and the public's response to TV better than their opponents.

By 1956, however, the pattern (at least regarding spots) had changed. Stevenson was now deeply involved in short commercials. "The Man from Libertyville" series of spots featuring the Illinois governor was a considerable artistic success even though it didn't help much in winning enough votes to dislodge a popular president. The technique employed was not very different from the Rosser Reeves-produced spots for Eisenhower four years earlier. In each Stevenson discussed a single issue in a chatty format. The difference was that the Stevenson spots were shot on location, not in a studio. The most used backdrop was the governor's farm near Libertyville, a northwestern Chicago suburb where the candidate had his home. Libertyville was far enough from the city to be genuinely rural but near enough to be easily accessible. One memorable shot showed the candidate sitting on a rail fence, calmly discussing farm issues.

One pioneer who fully understood the impact that television might have on politics but had little chance to use it himself was William Benton, cofounder of the Benton and Bowles advertising agency, one-time assistant secretary of state for information and cultural affairs, senator from Connecticut, and chairman of the board of Encyclopaedia Britannica. Benton had made a number of public speeches as early as mid–1950 arguing that TV "was about to become a critically important factor in American politics."[9]

In winning a Senate seat in 1950 Benton developed an innovative plan embracing seven basic formats for television, which later would be used widely. Among them were questioning by a group of college or high school youngsters, street corner interviews, reporters' panels, fireside chats, and set speeches by the candidate on the issues of the day. There was little chance, however, to implement his suggestions. There were no VHF television channels operating in Connecticut. Signals came into the state from New York, Massachusetts, and Rhode Island, but going outside the state to buy television time involved an economic waste. There was little virtue in spending money to win over voters who did not have the franchise in Connecticut.

The 1952 and 1956 campaigns represented an era of testing the water, trying out new ideas, experimenting with visual appeals, determining how best to exploit the power of the visual medium. The 18 million Americans who owned receivers had grown to approximately 35 million by 1956 and more than 46 million in 1960. The set count had risen to well over 50 percent of American households.

By 1960 whistle-stop campaigning, far from dominating, had become a novelty. Half-hour speeches that had been a staple in 1952 were retiring to secondary status and were being replaced by techniques with more visual appeal. The five-minute speech had been given a brief fling in 1956 but was now being cut back in favor of more spot television commercials. Film documentaries were becoming commonplace. No serious candidate would dream of running for the presidency without a film biography. The advertising agency was a necessity of life for the presidential candidate, and a new breed of specialist, the campaign consultant, was taking a position of importance alongside the agency. The jet airplane was an important factor in the changes that were occurring at an accelerating pace. Improved communications simplified a more complex campaign. But the critical force that motivated the change was television. The 107 television stations that had been on the air as the 1952 campaign opened had grown to more than 500. Networks that had difficulty interconnecting only 25 or 30 stations in 1952 could now serve 200 or more. Television had become a major factor in American life. The "CBS Early Evening News with Douglas Edwards" that was seen in only 18 to 20 cities prior to the lifting of the freeze was now a staple in nearly 200.

Along with the increasing size of station lineups came an increasing emphasis on news. More stations were broadcasting news and devoting more effort to it. NBC opened up a new block of time in January 1952 when, with great fanfare, it inaugurated its long-running "Today" program. The "Today" format allowed for two five-minute local news cut-ins in each of its two hours. Many affiliated stations built up their news staffs to fill the time and tap a new source of revenue. CBS followed several months later with its own counterpart, thus creating another opening for news broadcasts. In mid–1953, CBS had canceled news film service from a syndicator and built its own worldwide Newsfilm organization, including bureaus in Washington, Chicago, and Los Angeles. News had moved up from being a novelty add-on to the entertainment schedule to a status approaching equivalency.

The Federal Communications Commission freeze on granting new station licenses that was imposed in 1949 was lifted in May 1952. CBS Television promptly scheduled a meeting of its affiliates and prospective affiliates with the primary purpose of furnishing guidance on constructing, organizing, and programming a new television station. One of the primary topics was news: how to organize a news staff, what sources of film and still pictures were available, and what equipment would be required. Very few station operators were sufficiently acquainted with television to know how to proceed without help. I was given an hour of time to make a detailed presentation that four decades later reads like a primer. In the course of my lecture I even advised prospective owners and managers regarding types of rewinds for silent film, sound film readers, and film barrels they might buy. The interest of the managers was reflected in the lengthy question-and-answer session that followed. It was put into action within a few months in the rapidly increasing volume of news on the air on television stations.

The impact on political campaigning followed quickly. Political managers and advertising agencies noted the increasing volume of free time available in news broadcasts and discussion programs, and started making plans to capture it. Whereas in New Hampshire and Wisconsin in 1952 television had to force its way in, by 1956 advance men began to set up candidate appearances in venues most favorable to television film coverage and to set the stage by recruiting enthusiastic supporters to function as window dressing.

The attention paid by advance men to television was not entirely a new phenomenon. The Eisenhower campaign in 1952 planned in meticulous detail for each of the general's public appearances, all with a view to showing off the candidate in the most favorable light. The kickoff speech for the campaign was scheduled for September 4 at Independence Square in Philadelphia. Campaign workers scrupulously followed a 39-page blueprint in preparing for the candidate's performance. "It covered everything from how the candidate would place himself so that he could be photographed with his right hand on the Liberty Bell to the allocating of 25,000 fresh cut roses, 300 noise makers, 500 flags and 25,000 programs to the anticipated throng."[10]

As national television saturation deepened and campaign organizations became more comfortable in preparing for television appearances, the care exerted in preparations became more evident. No political rally would be complete without high school bands in uniform, pom-pom girls, cheerleaders, and a liberal representation of colorful citizens of the area. The John F. Kennedy campaign added "jumpers and screamers" to the format, girls in their upper teens and early twenties who jumped and screamed whenever the candidate came into sight.

So much attention was paid to appearing most attractive on the magic screen that wardrobes for television appearances came under intensive scrutiny. One of the eccentricities of the old three-inch black-and-white image-orthicon camera tube was its tendency to draw a black line around a white object. Men's white shirts were particularly subject to showing a black band around the neck. Blue, on the other hand, registered without any aberration. In preparing a speech to deliver at the University of Wisconsin in the spring of 1956, I borrowed a title from the "Tales of Paul Bunyan" and converted "Winter of the Blue Snow" to "Summer of the Blue Shirt." I called attention to the sea of blue shirts we would see on the floors and platforms of the two political conventions we would cover that summer.

Governor Frank Clement of Tennessee was scheduled to be keynote speaker at the Democratic convention. Approximately a month before going to Chicago, the Tennessee governor came to the CBS Building to lunch with a number of executives. During the luncheon he asked me about the wardrobe he should buy for his appearance. A couple of hours later I received a call from Saks Fifth Avenue. It was Governor Clement. He told me he had found a dark blue silk suit, a lighter blue shirt, and a dark blue tie. He asked whether I thought he should take them. I told him I thought the combination would be just right. The governor cut a very handsome figure on the platform as he delivered his speech. If he had not insisted on emulating the preacher at a revivalist meeting and loaded his message with hell and damnation and fire and brimstone, he might have achieved what appeared to be his ambition: to project himself into the presidential race. As it turned out, his Saks Fifth Avenue wardrobe could just well have stayed on the shelves. A black line around his neck would not have made much difference.

Efforts to call attention to the position of the candidate on specific issues also succumbed to the lure of the television photo opportunity. Candidates began to describe their stands on agricultural issues, for example, while sitting on a plow or watching a milking machine in action; on veterans' affairs by visiting a veterans' hospital; on Social Security by watching a horseshoe pitching contest in St. Petersburg, Florida; or on a labor matter by standing near an automobile assembly line or visiting a steel mill. All this in the interests of a television picture related to the subject at hand.

On some occasions candidates got carried away and went to extreme lengths. Richard Ottinger, a candidate for the Senate in New York in the early 1970s, jumped into the polluted East River in New York to demonstrate his concern for pollution. George Bush, in an apparent effort to downplay his "wimp" image, climbed into the cab of a snowplow and demonstrated his agility in running it following a snowstorm in New Hampshire just before the 1988 primary there. Television dutifully portrayed the smiling vice-president at the controls of the giant vehicle.

In 1956 Richard Nixon discovered the political value of appearing on a college campus, and accordingly scheduled his college press conference at Cornell. Political managers quickly noted that the college campus not only would provide an attractive backdrop but also would permit the candidate to surround himself with articulate and knowledgeable students. The campaign visit to the college campus soon became part of established operating procedure. It turned out to be an environment made to order for television.

In 1968 the Nixon organization discovered another innovative program form for exploiting television, a discussion format that soon was labeled an "arena" program. The presidential candidate sat in the middle of a group of presumably representative citizens and talked with them about the campaign issues that most concerned them. Very little was left to chance. The participants were carefully screened and knew in advance what was expected of them. The whole affair seemed quite spontaneous, and permitted Nixon to chat amiably about significant issues in an informal setting made to order for the television camera.

While the Nixon high command demonstrated well-honed skills in commanding television exposure when they wanted it, they also knew how to minimize access to the candidate when they considered it a disadvantage. In Nixon's run for reelection in 1972, every media appearance was tightly controlled. Television cameras were allowed into the White House rose garden for tightly disciplined ceremonies. On a trip to Independence Hall in Philadelphia, cameras were permitted to be close enough to photograph the president in the historic site, but reporters were kept at a discreet distance so that no embarrassing questions could be asked. Nixon was being presidential. He was not permitted to get into any unseemly situations with reporters in which the cameras would catch him in any role but that of the dignified president going about the business of state. It was a reverse twist on earlier television, when the medium was regarded largely as an opportunity to purvey ideas, not image, and when managers and consultants were constantly looking for exposure, not seeking to avoid it.

In a relatively short period of time, not more than two decades, the process of campaigning for public office had been totally revolutionized. The whistle-stop was almost as dead as the dodo. It was revived from time to time, but as a novelty, not as an authentic aid to winning elections. The spot commercial had become standard operating procedure, all the way down to the state legislature and county sheriff levels. Advertising agencies had become essential to making the race, but as advisers on tactics they were giving way to specialized consultants who had begun to dominate both strategy and tactics. Television had won parity with print at news conferences, and its news programs had elbowed out print as the prime target of the candidate, particularly with respect to timing. Prior to television, news releases were timed for either morning or evening newspapers. In the television era they were timed to coincide with established broadcast times. Attractive sites to illustrate the candidate's interest in specific issues replaced the auditorium platform as the venue for policy statements. The most important single influence on campaign planning became the television camera and the microphone that went along with it. Jet airplanes, computers, and facsimile transmission all contributed, but it was television that transformed the process of running for office.

The attitude of the candidate toward voters changed dramatically as media targets shifted. The infusion of show business into running for office introduced an entirely new set of objectives. It was no longer enough to explain stands on complicated issues. When political appeals were juxtaposed with entertainment programs, appeals to voters had to take on the cast of show business. The candidates began to treat the voters as audiences to be entertained, not as citizens to be convinced. Appeals to reason frequently became a secondary function. Since entertainment became a primary objective, all too frequently the man elected became the one who was the most skilled user of show business techniques, including superior production, staging, and on-the-air performance.

The evidence is overwhelming that the campaign has been remade to television specifications, and not all of those specifications are as much requirements of television as of methods campaign managers have devised to win elections in the television era. The question to be answered is whether that is in the best interests of democratic government.

The shorter campaigns that television could have made possible would surely have reduced time, expense, and wear and tear on the candidate. But the lure of the TV screen was too hard to resist, and the campaign went to new lengths.

With television receivers in 97 percent of American homes, achieving quick name recognition is not a problem. Nor is establishing a personality, setting out a program, attacking an opponent's position, activating supporters, and appealing for funds.

Candidates need not be in constant motion for two years or more, leaping from state to state in pursuit of delegates to caucuses or conventions. State officials, greedy for publicity (or notoriety), shuffle conventions and caucuses to the most favorable times to attract national attention. Television follows and so do newspapers, wire services, and news magazines. Television is a willing partner but not the originator. And it would do just as well if emphasis on the primaries were dampened and the convention were restored to its old position as the prime mechanism for selecting national candidates.

Many of the clichés concerning what makes one candidate a bright prospect and the other a doomed man are just that—clichés. Television didn't create the primary, the caucus, the spot commercial, or the "three day media tour." The people who manage parties and plan campaigns did. Television may have been too gullible to resist or too eager to participate to remain aloof.

Irrespective of how it all started, though, the business of running for national office has been dramatically altered.

A senator, because of his constant national exposure on the tube, has a much better chance than a congressman or governor to be nominated. Of the major party candidates for president or vice-president in the nine elections since television became a force in 1952, 20 were senators, eight were governors, and five were representatives. The eight count for former governors includes two runs each for Adlai Stevenson, Spiro Agnew, Jimmy Carter, and Ronald Reagan. The list from the House includes William Miller, Geraldine Ferraro, and Jerry Ford (who is counted twice, although on his try for the presidency he went from the vice-presidency). George Bush is counted although he served in a number of other senior government jobs after he left the House. The Senate, because of its continuing attention from television, is clearly the logical jumping-off point.

Costs have ballooned, but television is not solely responsible. Jet travel, computers, mailing lists, and enlarged staffs don't come cheap. And the lengthened campaign keeps the money raisers working longer to stop checks from bouncing.

The candidate who knows how to project to the camera has a better chance than the neophyte or the slow learner or the dull and spiritless plodder.

A combination of factors has surely caused profound changes in campaigning and electing. They have come about partly in response to the legitimate requirements for successful performance on television and partly from the perception of television's requirements held by candidates and their managers.

There is also a third factor. Modifications have been made in the campaign process in order to cater to what is perceived, either rightly or wrongly, to be the power of television to influence the electing of public officials. This may be the most telling, and even the most sinister, influence of the medium: its capacity to stimulate party leaders and campaign managers to change the established order to maximize use of television's capabilities.

NOTES

1. In order to get a better seat to watch the drama unfold, I had managed to talk the sergeants at arms guarding access to the floor to let me through the barricade, into the delegates-only section. I found a seat in the Minnesota delegation and wound up squarely in the middle of the Stassen high command. It was a strange blend of disparate personalities. The campaign manager was Warren Burger, later chief justice of the U.S. Supreme Court. Floor leader was Senator Joseph McCarthy, junior senator from Wisconsin, (later the discredited Communist witch-hunter). Governor Luther Youngdahl of Minnesota was leader of the state delegation, and the senior adviser was Minnesota's junior senator, Edward J. Thye. For several sessions I sat squarely in the middle of this high-level strategy group. When it was evident before the second ballot that a Dewey victory was inevitable, Youngdahl asked me what he should do about announcing a vote for the Minnesota delegation. It was committed to Stassen, with no provision for a release to another candidate. He had not

been able to find Stassen to ask permission to switch to Dewey. Before I had a chance to reply, Stassen appeared at the rostrum, surprising his high command by releasing his delegates to the New York governor.

2. We invited only major candidates, but one minor candidate slipped in by order of the FCC. A book salesman from St. Louis named William Schneider had on a number of occasions tried to get time on CBS Television to make a half-hour speech. On each occasion he was turned down. When he learned that we were scheduling the "Bandwagon" program, he promptly declared himself a candidate for the Republican nomination for the presidency and applied for time under Section 315. The FCC granted his appeal, so there was nothing for us to do but give him his time. It made for an odd lineup of speakers: Senator Robert Taft, Governor Earl Warren, former Governor Harold Stassen, former Senator Henry Cabot Lodge speaking for General Dwight Eisenhower, and William Schneider occupying the time in successive weeks. Ironically, Schneider failed to get credentials to attend the national convention.

3. The memo from Schoenbrun is in my private files. There is a clear suggestion in the memo that Eisenhower's ambivalent position between functioning as NATO commander and possible candidate for the presidency of the United States was beginning to get on his nerves. There was little doubt, though, that he intended to make the run.

4. A detailed description of the contributions of Hollender and Reeves is in Martin Mayer, *Madison Avenue, U.S.A.* (New York: Harper, 1958), pp. 293–97.

5. Ibid., p. 294.

6. There was one fascinating discussion that consumed most of one of the luncheon sessions. Even though it had nothing to do with television, I remember it vividly. A shipment of a book written by Kay Summersby, one of General Eisenhower's English wartime chauffeurs, that purportedly went into great detail concerning Miss Summersby's wartime relationship with the general was scheduled to arrive at Boston within a few days. The question was what, if anything, could be done about it. The final decision was to buy the entire shipment at the dock to prevent its distribution. What ultimately happened I have never heard, but I can't forget the conversation.

7. William Lee Miller, "Can Government Be Merchandised?" *The Reporter*, October 27, 1953, p. 13.

8. Edward M. Glick, *The New Methodology. A Study of Political Strategy and Tactics* (Washington, D.C.: American Institute for Political Communication, 1967), p. 17.

9. Sidney Hyman, *The Lives of William Benton* (Chicago: University of Chicago Press, 1969). Hyman describes the victorious 1950 campaign and Benton's defeat when he ran for reelection in 1952.

10. Glick, *The New Methodology*, p. 21.

6

What Hath Television Wrought?

When Democratic Chairman Paul Butler angrily strode to the rostrum toward the close of the opening night of the Democratic convention in 1956, he delivered the coup de grace to the national political convention as a legitimate news event. The convention thereafter would be a showplace for party functionaries, a stage for a quadrennial extravaganza extolling party virtues, a revival meeting designed to exhort parishioners to pledge their faith in the party of Thomas Jefferson, Andrew Jackson, Woodrow Wilson, and Franklin Roosevelt—but hardly a site for selecting candidates for the presidency. That would all be taken care of weeks earlier, in caucuses and primaries. Everyone in the hall knew that Adlai Stevenson would win the presidential nomination. The only remaining suspense surrounded the selection of a vice-presidential nominee.

Butler's fury was occasioned by the fact that one of the three networks (CBS) had failed to carry in its entirety a documentary film produced by the national committee. The film's purpose was clearly to praise the virtues of the Democratic Party and to arouse enthusiasm for the Democratic ticket. It was narrated by a young senator from Massachusetts, John F. Kennedy. Convention managers, arguing that it was mandatory that the networks carry it, insisted that the film was linked to the keynote speech. The two features were a single unit. Party leaders unmistakably hoped to create a mass outpouring of Democratic support across the nation.

As the house lights went up following completion of the film, Chairman Butler, trembling with rage, strode to the rostrum and bitterly charged that "one of the networks has failed to keep its commitment to present this documentary film to the American people." There was little doubt that the guilty "one of the networks" was CBS. Butler pointedly thanked both

ABC and NBC for their cooperation and public-spiritedness and never uttered the letters CBS.[1]

I had been informed at my post in the master control room that Butler was outraged, to the extent that he was likely to deliver a blast at us. We were hardly prepared, though, for the vehemence of his attack and for the violent reaction of the delegates in the hall. There were loud choruses of boos from the floor. Some delegates stood and shook their fists in the direction of the CBS radio booth, high above the floor behind the rostrum. There were shouts of "Throw them out!"[2] Reporters and cameramen on the floor were afraid their equipment would be wrenched from their hands and smashed before they were able to move to safer ground.

The decision not to carry the film was mine. I was never formally informed that a film was in production, although I had heard rumors that one was tentatively scheduled. While walking out of a CBS television studio one night a couple of weeks before the convention with CBS President Frank Stanton, I told him of the rumors I had heard. I informed him that if the film were to be scheduled as part of the convention program, I intended not to carry it. I would not, I told him, have it racked up on a projector and shown from beginning to end. We would treat the film as a news event. At some point we would show the darkened hall and the audience watching the documentary. We would focus in on the screen long enough to show what the delegates were looking at. But we would not bow to the party's wishes to the extent that we would obligate ourselves to carry the entire film.

"Why?" Stanton wanted to know. I explained that we intended to cover a political convention, not a party rally. Insofar as the film was news, we would cover it. But we should not get into a position where we became a vehicle to serve the party's interests by furnishing free time on the full network for party promotion. Our convention coverage should not be equated with a paid political commercial. There was no response. Our conversation moved on to other topics.[3]

The episode stirred up a minor flurry of media attention at the time but was quickly forgotten by the public. The influence on television coverage of political conventions in subsequent years was longer lasting. Paul Butler brought me a peace offering, a bottle of premium Scotch, several weeks later and apologized for his outburst, but in early 1960 we learned that the Democrats were again producing a film for showing on the convention floor. This time they were careful to inform us in advance and promised to arrange a screening prior to its scheduling. I went to the screening, saw the product, and agreed that it would not in itself be offensive in any way. The fight had gone out of me. I had been effectively defused. We accepted the film, racked it up on the projector, and dutifully showed it, as did the other networks. Even though we yielded on this issue, we were not wholly in the party's pocket. We still left the rostrum to go to the floor or to a downtown hotel when we thought the news was there. But we had shown the white flag on a major issue. The surrender would continue to haunt television in subsequent conventions.

With that concession the networks had lost their claim to be independent news-gathering agencies. They had compromised their standards and had become tools of the national political parties. The conventions had ceased to be legitimate news events and had evolved into party rallies that the networks willingly relayed to the public under the guise of legitimate ac-tuality coverage. They were not totally subservient, however. Their cameras cut in and out of the proceedings with abandon. Much of the pure fluff was carefully avoided, thus irritating party leaders who failed to understand why the networks would not show an attractive Republican woman presenting a gavel or the convention portable electronic pipe organ to a faithful party worker. When it came to a feature deemed significant by the party lead-ership, though, the networks knuckled under. There was one exception. At the Republican convention in 1984, CBS refused to show a party film. It was subjected to unmerciful criticism but held to its guns. Both CBS and NBC rejected films again in 1988, but by then the ground rules were changing. The networks were cutting back on coverage.

The significance is not so much that the networks are docile but that the party organizations have scored enough victories to assume the unrestricted right to demand network cooperation in carrying what they deem impor-tant. Party power prevailed so long as the networks maintained dominance as the only vehicle delivering live coverage. The introduction of new tech-nologies enabling local stations, the Cable News Network, C-SPAN, and the Public Broadcasting Service to compete on roughly equal ground has given the networks a little freedom to exercise discretion, but party leaders still feel they have a right to demand coverage. Local stations and CNN are likely to be more resilient and accept what the networks would be likely to reject.

Previous efforts by the parties to exploit television were frequently lu-dicrous. The Republicans established an all-time record for insensitivity to audience interests and the basic principles of showmanship in 1956 when the medium was still new. They were eager, perhaps too eager, to get on the bandwagon, and apparently failed to seek advice from television profes-sionals or to use common sense with regard to elementary principles of showmanship.

The first of the blunders involved a skit staged by Republican women. The participants employed an old elementary school stunt. Sixteen loyal party members each came center stage, one at a time, carrying a word representing a Republican accomplishment achieved during the Eisenhower administration. As the *Proceedings of the Twenty-sixth Republican National Convention* describes it, "When all the words had been given, the young ladies carrying the placards formed a line on the platform; then they showed the reverse side of the placards which carried the initial letter of each word. Thus the words 'Republican Women' were spelled out." Television cameras paid little attention to the charade, which may have been just as well for the planners.[4]

The convention arrangements committee scheduled another performance that could have been at least a moderate success if members had given any thought to timing. The intention was to provide each member of President Eisenhower's cabinet with five minutes of time to address the convention and, not incidentally, the television audience. Each member of the cabinet was present with the exception of Secretary of State John Foster Dulles, who was described as being out of the country on delicate national business. The secretary was represented by Under Secretary Herbert Hoover, Jr. It was a power-packed lineup and theoretically could have been effective in underscoring the strength of the Eisenhower administration.

Unfortunately, the convention planners had overlooked one essential element, timing. Would they be able to schedule it at a time when it was unlikely there would be competition for television's attention? Just as Under Secretary Hoover began his remarks, the television networks discovered that air traffic control had registered a blip on the radar screen from President Eisenhower's plane inbound from Washington, D.C. Network directors immediately switched to cameras at the airport control tower and on the landing ramp to await the president's arrival.

While cabinet members droned on before a rapidly emptying house, conveniently forgetting that they were to be limited to five minutes each, television long since had jumped ship. It was showing pictures of the president's plane approaching the airport, its landing, and of the president and his party boarding cars for the trip to their hotel in downtown San Francisco. When the entourage had been loaded into open limousines for the 15-mile trip to the city's center, television followed them virtually every foot of the way. Not until the president stepped into an elevator in the hotel lobby did the networks return to the Cow Palace. By that time the parade of cabinet members, mercifully, was just winding up. The third session was ready for adjournment.

The Democrats, even though CBS temporarily balked, had established a precedent that a filmed documentary was a legitimate feature of a convention program and that television had a responsibility to relay it to its audience. The Republicans had stubbed their toes in a futile attempt at big-time television production, but they had the winning candidate, so little else mattered. They could try again next time to exercise whatever show business talents they might have or be able to recruit. Since they would then have no incumbent to support, the stakes would be higher.

As the gavel fell, concluding the final session of the Republican convention on August 23, it did not take supernatural vision to note that television would no longer need to sell itself as it had had to do in 1952. To the contrary, it would henceforth have to fend off pressures to convert the convention process into a game designed to enable the political parties to exploit television.

The primary objective of political managers likewise underwent substantial change. Television was no longer a minor nuisance, to be accommodated without offending the newspapers and wire services or, more important, the big-name columnists who had traditionally received kid glove treatment. Television had become the number one target. The picture on the television screen now mattered more than the front page of the *New York Times* or an editorial page column in the *Washington Post*.

What appeared on the television screen had become the test of success or failure, almost as much as election results. The major objective of party leaders in 1964 was to create for the television screen a mood of unity, harmony, confidence, and serious devotion to the concerns of the public. Programs were carefully designed to ensure that dissent and controversy would be shunted off to periods when expected viewing would be at low levels. Prime time, particularly in the eastern time zone, would be reserved for the party stars. Every effort would be made to display a broad cross section of party supporters; blacks, Hispanics, Orientals, Native Americans, farmers, laborers, teachers, young party members, retired party leaders, and former presidents or presidential candidates.

Planning for the convention was a meticulous process involving months of effort calculated to exhibit the party's most attractive supporters in ways that would not look too contrived and would stand a reasonable chance of capturing television's attention.

In 1964 I was offered a chance to reverse roles and approach convention planning from the national party side rather than as executive in charge of network television coverage. In 1961 I had moved from CBS to Time, Inc. In the autumn of 1963 I was approached by the Republican National Committee to accept temporary appointment as executive program director for the 1964 convention in San Francisco. With the approval of senior Time executives, I accepted. Time granted me a leave of absence from April 1 through the end of the convention in mid-July.

I am still surprised at how unmanageable a political convention really is, how political expediency can upset the most carefully developed plans, how much effort must be devoted to placating various minority elements within the party, not to mention the deference that must be shown to aging party fat cats, and how brutal senior party leadership can be when some obstacle stands between the ruling clique and achieving its objectives. I was impressed by the minute detail, some of it appearing to be no more than trivia, that goes into serving up program fare that will cater to disparate party interests: young and old, moderates and conservatives, Wasps and minorities, political has-beens who still carry weight and up-and-coming young party members. Many fail to see a contradiction between finding a spot on the program for unknowns, for the purpose of placating potential dissidents, and building a program that will interest television program executives. One cannot fail to marvel at the naiveté of party officials who firmly believe that some of their contrived plans are surefire television programming.

I was so fascinated by the experience that I saved all my files, and consequently have in my possession a detailed record of correspondence, memoranda, minutes of planning sessions, and logs of convention proceedings. Among them there is a bulky file of letters and memos regarding selection of clergymen to give invocations and benedictions, vocalists to sing the national anthem, attractive lesser lights (with special attention to minorities) to lead the pledge of allegiance, drum and bugle corps to open each session, a color guard to march into the hall with the flag, and a host of introducers of principal speakers, givers of gavels and badges to outstanding party members, and entertainers to keep the delegates amused during long stage waits.

All must have impeccable credentials as faithful party members and should represent a wide diversity of races, creeds, and geographical areas. I quickly learned, for example, that the first invocation should be assigned to the highest-ranking member of the Roman Catholic hierarchy in the host diocese, that under no circumstances should we proceed without locking up a rabbi for one of the sessions, and that Protestants should be selected to represent a variety of faiths. We had considerable latitude to recruit a wide range, since we had five sessions to cover, with an invocation and a benediction for each.

Selecting the leaders for the pledge of allegiance gave us an opportunity to reach out to interesting personalities who were not necessarily in the party's mainstream. The high school student who had won the American Legion national oratorical prize was a natural. David Eisenhower was another. A prominent Armenian from San Francisco, George Mardikian, who had achieved a national reputation as a specialist in organizing food relief programs, permitted us to display a prominent representative from a country that is now a Soviet satellite.

Entertainers notably had to pass a Republican litmus test before being invited. Some members of the national committee thought that the Kingston Trio would be a popular entertainment feature. It turned out that two of them and their manager were rabid Democrats. They were dropped from the list of possible invitees. It is unlikely that they would have accepted anyway. Lloyd Nolan and Victor Jory were given a warm welcome, as was Art Linkletter. All three are enthusiastic Republicans. My files show that for some reason there was little enthusiasm for enlisting Ronald Reagan as a participant in a program featuring Nolan and Jory.

The most complicated problem turned out to be devising a process to give deserving Republicans who presumably had served the party well an opportunity to appear on the rostrum, no matter how menial the task.

There were several devices we could use: introductions of principal speakers and sometimes introductions of introducers, presentation of gavels to the temporary chairman and to the permanent chairman, and of medals to party leaders who for one reason or another were not scheduled to be on the program.

Selecting a theme and a slogan for the convention was a particularly vexing problem. The Leo Burnett advertising agency, under contract to the Republican National Committee but not to the convention arrangements committee, apparently under the false notion that you can sell ideas to voters the way you sell them breakfast cereals, proposed "Stand Straight, Stand Tall, Stand Proud—Go Republican." Robert Pierce, the arrangements committee vice-chairman, and as such the chief convention executive, wrote to the party's general counsel, Fred Scribner, "The individual who dreamed this up should also have added 'Stand Still' since the opposition would surely add it as this theme was made public." The theme ultimately accepted was a very simple "For the People." This brief phrase, although it did not reflect much imagination, enabled convention planners to invoke the name of Republican hero Abraham Lincoln.

The agency had some gaudy, Hollywood-type suggestions for spicing up the convention, all of which were lost somewhere along the way. Agency personnel had a fixation with "Go" songs. The chorus of one proposal, "Go, Party, Go March," received a quick turndown:

> First you start with a grand old G,
> Then you go to a big round O,
> Finally you add the P . . .
> Go, Party, Go . . . Go!

Another, "GOP Rouser," met a similar fate:

> This is the time,
> This is the year,
> The GOP is on the go, go, go.
> We've put the flame in the Grand Old Name,
> The GOP is on the go, go, go.

Then came the chorus:

> Skin that mule (boom, boom),
> Skin that mule (boom, boom),
> Skin that mule and win, win, win.

There were others, but the only one that made it to the bandstand and was actually played during the convention was a chant that simply demanded: "Clear the Aisles, Clear the Aisles, Clear the Aisles." It did not do much good. The aisles remained clogged. But it added to the din and, presumably, to the excitement. It was the agency's suggestion that young women in cheerleader costumes lead the singing of the party songs, but that proposal was quickly vetoed.

Convention business was to be timed so that all events that presumably would reflect favorably on the party would be scheduled during peak television viewing hours. It was the intention to start sessions at 4 P.M. San Francisco time (7 P.M. EDT), with the most important features falling between 6 P.M. and 8 P.M. (9 and 11 P.M. EDT). This schedule was calculated to deliver the largest audience.

That was the theory. In practice, political considerations came first, and the well-laid plans were abandoned for political expediency.

For example, former President Eisenhower had accepted an invitation to speak on the second night, provided his appearance would not come before approval of the party platform. He was adamant on this issue. The evening's schedule was carefully constructed so that all the business to be conducted that night, including approval of the platform, would be completed in time for the former president to begin his presentation at 8:15 PDT. This was later than party officials desired, but Eisenhower was firm that the party's platform must be adopted prior to his taking the rostrum. The report of the committee on resolutions (platform committee) was scheduled for 7:10, with completion expected by 7:55. This would allow 20 minutes for ceremonies connected with presentation of a medal to Mrs. Eisenhower, a short demonstration and an introduction by Representative Charles Halleck of Indiana.

The evening session was scheduled to open at 4 P.M. (7 P.M. EDT). I arrived at the Cow Palace a few minutes after three to check last-minute details. Shortly after my arrival, I was informed by General Counsel Fred Scribner that there had been a change in plans. General Eisenhower would have to go on before consideration of the platform. Before proceeding to call for debate, the document would be read in its entirety, approximately a three-and-one-half-hour marathon.

Guessing at the reason for the abrupt change did not require clairvoyance. Goldwater forces were in control of the convention machinery. Their only opponent with the remotest chance of winning the nomination was Nelson Rockefeller. Word got out that Rockefeller planned to speak in opposition to some planks in the platform. Permitting the New York governor to appear on television during prime time was simply unthinkable. Not only did the Goldwater leadership want to avoid giving him an opportunity to revive any slim chance he might still have of winning the nomination, but they also sought to avoid any questioning of the carefully drafter Goldwater platform. Unless the schedule were changed, Rockefeller's attack on the document would begin squarely in the middle of television prime time.

Permitting Rockefeller access to the largest possible audience had to be thwarted, so Goldwater strategists insisted on a program change. Despite Eisenhower's demand that he speak only after adoption of the platform, Goldwater leaders insisted that the entire platform, from the first word to the last, would be read from the rostrum. That would keep Rockefeller off the rostrum until eastern voters had long since gone to bed, and even on the West Coast the peak viewing hours would have long since passed. It was unlikely that debate could begin until after midnight (3 A.M. EDT).

It was left to me as program director to deal with the former president. We obviously could not keep him waiting in the wings until midnight or later while the dreary process of reading the platform droned on, nor could we expect him to wait patiently during a lengthy debate. It was my responsibility to convince Eisenhower to abandon his position and to speak before the platform had been approved. The former president's son John answered the phone at the Eisenhower suite at the St. Francis Hotel. He was sympathetic, and promised to do his best to convince his father to abandon his position and come to the Cow Palace as soon as he could. He would talk to his father and call back.

There would still, however, be a gap in the schedule that would have to be filled. The easy way out would be to delay the opening gavel. I urged Senator Mark Hatfield, the temporary chairman, to do so. He replied firmly that he intended to start on time.

The first step was to find Senator Thruston Morton, who was to assume the permanent chairmanship. He had told me that his speech on assuming the chair would be very short, but that he had prepared a longer one in the event it might be needed. I urged him to use the long form.

Former University of Oklahoma football coach Bud Wilkinson, Republican candidate for the Senate from Oklahoma, was on the schedule for brief remarks. I remembered that there were 12 young women from Tulsa, members of a political club, wearing uniforms in the red and white of the University of Oklahoma. I sent a message to their leader asking whether she and her group were game to carry on a "Bud Wilkinson for Senate" demonstration. As soon as Wilkinson finished his speech, I told her, the band would play "Oklahoma" for as long as her group had the stamina to carry on singing the song, marching around the auditorium, and waving Wilkinson banners. She agreed to begin a demonstration on my signal. Robert Weede was scheduled to sing the national anthem. I asked band leader Ray Hackett to request that Weede also prepare to fill a 10-to-15-minute period with songs before Eisenhower arrived. While I was negotiating, John Eisenhower called to say his father had agreed to the amended schedule.

The stalling process, although somewhat awkward, seemed to work. The delegates undoubtedly had an overload of "Oklahoma," but the impromptu demonstration filled nearly 15 minutes. Senator Morton's extended remarks consumed more time, and Weede willingly added a short performance.

There was only one hitch. We had failed to get word of the changed schedule to Representative Halleck, who was to introduce Eisenhower. Fortunately, he arrived at the Cow Palace only a few minutes late. We stretched a demonstration for the former president by a few minutes while he stopped in the makeup trailer and then breathlessly made his way to the rostrum.

The whole affair was a glaring example of political expediency triumphing over careful planning. Party managers wanted maximum coverage for those features that portrayed harmony and confidence, and they wanted to bury any evidence of dissent or disharmony. They particularly wanted to avoid permitting prime television time to go to as charismatic an opponent as Nelson Rockefeller.

By the time Eisenhower stepped up to the rostrum, the delegates were in an angry and contentious mood. He poured fuel on the fire with one statement that shook the hall.

"Let us particularly scorn the derisive efforts of those outside our family," he began one sentence before a restive audience that was spoiling for a fight. A majority were Goldwater supporters waiting anxiously for a chance to vent their fury on Nelson Rockefeller when, later in the evening, he would attack the proposed party platform. Then the former president completed the sentence with the provocative phrase that triggered an outburst, "including sensation-seeking columnists and commentators." The phrase struck a chord.[5] The largely Goldwater-oriented audience, reacting to a denunciation of the hated media, stamped their feet, shouted "Ole," and shook their fists at the television booths. It was several minutes before some sense of order was restored. Walter Cronkite was fearful that the angry mob might storm his quarters, from which there could be no escape. Chet Huntley and David Brinkley were similarly unnerved by the unexpected outburst. The former president resumed his speech, and there were no more fireworks until the platform had been read and debate started.

The strategy devised by party leaders had paid off. Nelson Rockefeller would not appear until the early morning hours. By keeping Rockefeller off the platform during prime time, they won another important point. They avoided embarrassment for the party by restricting the audience for the boisterous and enraged demonstrations that greeted the New York governor once he had his chance at the rostrum.

Party leaders had given up their prime-time exposure out of political expediency. On other occasions they lamented that their plans to get national attention for their carefully selected favorites were thwarted by the television networks, which paid little attention to the gimmickry. They grumbled that the tasteless broadcasters were missing a good part of the show. They were switching to other features while the most attractive Republicans were awarding gavels and medals to faithful party members.

The clash between party leaders and television broadcasters is a natural one. Party leaders want maximum exposure for a show they produce. Their goal is to sell the party and their candidates. They look on the convention as free commercial time. The objective of television broadcasters, to the contrary, is to cover a news event. The goals are diametrically opposed. In 1952 television had all the news it could handle. Television viewers were, in effect, looking over the shoulders of delegates as they went about their business. The convention story was one of suspense, drama, and unexpected turns and twists. And it was all genuine. There was no need to pump suspense into thin threads of possible news stories in order to create some artificial excitement.

After some four decades of the uneasy marriage, there are critics clamoring for abolition of the political convention as a useless appendage to the body politic, or at least for a reduction of its importance and scope. They are aiming their fire at the wrong target. The political parties are fully entitled to hold conventions of any length they desire and to behave as outrageously as they see fit. The political system surely profits from the experience of participants in a political convention, just as lawyers profit from a convention of the American Bar Association or Mary Kay salespeople from a meeting with their counterparts from other regions.

It is the television managers who have to decide how they intend to cover political conventions in the future. The convention remains a gigantic spectacle, produced with all the showmanship that the best Hollywood producers can bring to it. But it is similar to the halftime show at the Super Bowl. Does it warrant tying up all three networks, CNN, and C-SPAN to the exclusion of any other programming? The odds are that economics will change the pattern of nearly full-time coverage that has persisted since 1952. There may never again be as profound a change as occurred in 1952, but change will surely continue.

The national political convention has a long and bizarre history. The first recorded convention, Republican, took place in 1831. Democrats met in 1832 to conduct party business, set party policy, write a platform, and nominate candidates. Their candidate for president was Andrew Jackson. Communications were then so primitive that there was virtually no method other than personal contact to conduct party business. The convention reflected the personality of the Democratic Party at that time, as did its nominee for the presidency, the frontiersman from Tennessee. It was noisy, boisterous, rowdy. It reflected the frontier from which the nominee came. It established a pattern for what we now regard as juvenile antics that has prevailed to this day. The antics may not have appeared outrageous on the frontier, but they seem ludicrous in this more sophisticated environment.

In the intervening years the convention has gone from modified Chautauqua show to boisterous rally to circus sideshow and now to Hollywood-produced pageantry. Through the years it has retained all its tribal rites even though society has evolved into something that would have been unrecognizable in the mid-nineteenth century. The frenzied rallies, riotous demonstrations, and passionate oratory of the mid-nineteenth century were not out of place in a nation still bursting at the seams and pushing westward to a new frontier. In the last half of the twentieth century, however, the frenetic antics are clearly forced—frivolous efforts to build excitement out of boredom. Part of the objective is to create a bandwagon atmosphere in the convention hall, but the ticket holders in the hall are secondary. The principal target is the television viewer watching at home, whether it be network television, a local station, or cable.

Conditions in the intervening years have changed dramatically. Transportation and electronic communications tie the nation together. An advanced degree of sophistication has replaced the rough frontier character of the early and mid-nineteenth century, but some of the spirit of the old frontier still prevails. It is reflected in the placards, name cards, chants, shouts, cowbells, whistles, outrageous hats, demonstrations, and unruly behavior on the floor. It is the standard ritual that is repeated convention after convention.

No convention since 1952 has had more than the slightest bit of influence in the selection of presidential candidates. And not since 1956 has a convention actually had any influence on naming a candidate for the vice-presidency. Television has been largely responsible for shifting the focus of the selection process to the primary and the caucus. By covering primaries and caucuses lavishly, the medium succeeded in enticing state party functionaries and candidates alike to devote increased energy, time, and money to winning over the delegates long before they arrived at the convention city. There consequently hasn't been much for delegates to do except let off steam, stir up support for the favored candidate, and quibble about platform details. While, if settling issues is the goal, the convention is about as useful to the body politic as an appendix is to the human body, the quadrennial rites are still celebrated. Much of the form is the same, but there is a significant difference. The target audience is no longer in the convention hall. It is now in the living room, clustered around the television screen. It is a chance that comes along every four years to snitch valuable television time from the gullible networks.

The trend toward producing extravaganzas with little reference to the business at hand has been accelerating since 1956. Show business has replaced political business. Candidates are still chosen and platforms approved, but suspense is a lost commodity. Results are cut and dried, and the convention's sole purpose has become to ratify decisions made weeks earlier. What was once a scene of important public business has become a gigantic party pep rally. And television has become an unwitting but willing tool.

The networks began in the mid-1980s to think better of committing vast resources and valuable time to an event that is newsworthy but in which what kernels there are of genuine news are wrapped in a sea of fluff. They are discovering, however, that they have a bear by the tail. The precedent for full coverage was established in 1952. Breaking with the precedent except for minor change will take courage, a commodity that the networks possess only in limited quantities. There is also the lure of competition. The national political convention is the only protracted and regularly scheduled event in which the networks can compete head to head and test their skills against the other nets. They are also extremely sensitive to political pressures. Party managers, who frequently claim a large measure of political clout, continue to believe that television has a clear obligation to relay their vote-seeking extravaganzas to the entire nation. They are not above using implied threats of legislative or regulatory action to bring any laggards into line. Hence television network options are limited.

That may be changing. Network ratings for convention coverage have been dropping precipitously. Independent stations showing films or sports receive a big bonus in rating points while the networks concentrate on convention business. The Cable News Network and C-SPAN are draining off the real political buffs, and local stations are furnishing reports tailored more closely to the interests of viewers in their home communities.

As the twentieth century comes to a close, the reasons for holding conventions have gone through a constantly changing pattern. With modern communications and transportation, it is no longer necessary to use a national convention to make critical party decisions, including the selection of nominees for high national office. That can be done without calling delegates to a common meeting place. The purpose of the convention has changed, even since 1952, when selecting candidates was the number one item of business.

Even though candidates are now usually selected well before the opening gavel, the convention still provides an opportunity to energize the party, display its virtues, create harmony and unity, kick off a national campaign, and create public interest in the political process. As such, the convention cannot be written off as wholly irrelevant. The public profits from its opportunity to observe party leaders and candidates at close hand even though every conceivable effort is made to present them only in the most favorable light and in a venue frequently more closely resembling a movie set than a meeting hall.

So the question is not whether there should be a convention. The traditional convention is useful for what it is. It is more pertinent to ask whether television should remain frozen in the pattern it established at a time when the convention had quite a different reason for being. Should the networks continue to allocate huge resources—in personnel, money, and facilities—to an event that in reality is a nonevent? Might they not do better to treat a convention as a running news story and permit CNN, C-SPAN, and the local stations to furnish the play-by-play coverage? The question can be answered only by executives in the industry after balancing costs against benefits—benefits both to themselves and to the public at large.

NOTES

1. *Time*, August 27, 1956, p. 54. *Time* goes on to report that Butler told reporters later that it was "absolute sabotage" (on the part of CBS).

2. Ibid.

3. I learned later that there may have been a reason for Stanton's reticence. I was informed by party insiders that he had been consulted regarding whether to produce the film, and had responded affirmatively.

4. The full text of "The Women Speak" is in *Official Report of the Proceedings of the Twenty-sixth Republican National Convention* (Washington, D.C.: Republican National Committee, 1957), pp. 181–88.

5. *Official Report of the Proceedings of the Twenty-Eighth Republican National Convention* (Washington, D.C.: Republican National Committee, 1965), p. 185. The former president stirred up another chorus of boos and angry shouts when he added, "I assure you that these are people who couldn't care less about the good of our party."

7

The Rocky Romance

In the late 1940s and early 1950s, the coverage of politics by televison news was serious business. Political broadcasts were a service for viewers and a useful device for creating an image of responsibility and concern for the public welfare. The possible impact on the Federal Communications Commission and the Congress was not overlooked. Its content was not too unlike an encapsulated version of the front page of a good daily newspaper. The news selection of both the principal network evening news programs (CBS and NBC) was remarkably similar to page 1 of the *New York Times.*[1] The *Times* has never been noted for frivolity.

Those idyllic days are long since gone. The romance between politics and televison may have moved too rapidly. It may have been subjected to an excess of greed from both sides, or perhaps an excess of ardor. Perhaps the change in ownership and management of broadcasting facilities to corporations and corporate managers with less sensitivity to the public interest led to an erosion of high-minded standards, a trend politicians were quick to take advantage of. Whatever the reasons, both partners, broadcasters and politicians, were obviously too quick to exploit each other, and the result has been a rocky relationship that serves their separate interests but one in which the voting public may be the forgotten element.

As a political reporting medium, television's growth from curiosity to household staple in a remarkably short time stemmed from a number of factors. Its methods for covering politics came largely from radio, with a slight infusion from newsreel; its phenomenal growth, from rapidly changing technology and the public's fascination with the fusion of picture and sound.

TV's immediate ancestry, though, lay in radio. Its structure and operating methods were handed down from radio. Its early efforts at political coverage were largely voice reports, sometimes accompanied by motion picture film, sometimes by still pictures, sometimes by maps or charts; but infrequently were they transmitted as sound on film. It was essentially radio with pictures.

As television became more deeply immersed in political reporting, it began to create patterns of its own, but there still remained hints of its radio origins. As late as the mid–1980s, the television networks were operating as divisions of corporations that were founded as radio networks and drew much of their heritage from that medium. The heritage was sufficiently strong that television could establish a distinctive character only as new technologies permitted it to create new programming patterns and its radio-trained personnel began to be replaced by a work force that either grew up with television or was recruited from other communications media.

Television in 1948, as it was described later by Edward R. Murrow, was "just electric light bulbs and wires in a box." Its output was radio with murky pictures and scratchy sound. Its growth was breathtakingly fast, perhaps much too fast. Radio's progress also had been rapid, but news was a late bloomer on radio schedules. Its entertainment programming had attracted mass audiences well before news was much more than a sideshow. It was 1936 before Bob Trout underwent his baptism of fire as a pioneer political reporter at the national conventions. Boake Carter had breathlessly described sordid details of the Lindbergh kidnapping in 1931. Lowell Thomas had become a household name by the middle 1930s. But it was all hit or miss. The news broadcasters were usually independent entrepreneurs, unencumbered by network or station supervision. Under such a loose relationship between news broadcasters and licensees, there was not much room for anything but a casual relationship between radio and politics.

At CBS, however, concern was growing in the late 1930s as to what the role of the broadcaster should be, what standards should govern its news output, what policies should be written to protect the public interest. With war approaching in Europe, there was a growing sense of urgency. Fortunately, the fledgling network was led by a president, William S. Paley, who was concerned about what the medium could and should do. Paley was backed up by two remarkable second-line executives: Edward Klauber, who had been recruited from the *New York Times*, and Paul White, from United Press. The three established principles and policies that gave radio news a solid philosophical base rooted in concern for the public interest.

Television inherited that base, and in the early days succeeded in adapting it to the newer medium. Perhaps, however, the medium grew too rapidly, the onset of new technology came at a pace that could be absorbed physically but not philosophically, competitive patterns changed too abruptly, and both the costs of and income derived from news increased too quickly.

Whatever philosophical base had been established began to erode. There is declining evidence of thoughtful reflection concerning the role of television in broadcasting news and particularly in covering politics. It appears to have been shunted aside in the rush to adapt, keep ratings high, and increase profit margins.

An examination of the evolution of the patterns of news coverage by television networks and stations demonstrates a drift without much sense of purpose other than winning audiences and ratings, and raising profit levels. At the same time it produces clear evidence of the pervasive influence of new communications technology in shaping the news and political coverage delivered by television. In fact, technology may have been the most decisive force in transforming the process of covering politics.

A politically oriented Rip van Winkle who dropped off to sleep the morning after the 1948 national election, slept soundly for four decades, and awoke in the middle of the 1988 election campaign would surely be bewildered.

He could not avoid being baffled by the forests of satellite sending dishes, hordes of television reporters trailed by aides holding portable electronic cameras and built-in videotape recorders, fleets of vans with antenna dishes on their tops and station call letters on sides and rear, and the frantic rush of the media people to confront candidates for statements. He would be equally baffled by the brevity of the 15-second sound bites and the superficiality of the questioning.

The behavior of the candidates would be equally puzzling: their willingness, at times even eagerness, to face television cameras for the brief sound bite; their enthusiasm for live appearances on television news programs; and their careful staging of even the briefest event to produce the most favorable picture for the television camera. He would certainly be struck by their apparent familiarity with television news personalities. That kind of familiarity was once reserved for the leaders of the newspaper pack.

None of this was true in 1948. Television was in its toddling infancy. On election day there were still no more than approximately a half million American homes with television receivers. Stations on the air were struggling to produce enough income to pay their start-up and operating costs, and had no spare funds for costly news coverage. News was considered a luxury to be developed later, if and when profits would sustain it. There was no reservoir of experienced personnel to man the skeleton news departments that had been organized. In short, television was not really a factor in 1948. Its day would come later.

Most Amercians regarded the daily newspaper as their principal source of political news. Campaign managers responded by showing their deference to correspondents for the major dailies and to the nationally syndicated columnists, while tolerating radio reporters.

Radio, particularly the networks, covered the campaign aggressively, but its roster of correspondents was dwarfed in numbers by print reporters. The substance of the coverage furnished by the radio corps corresponded closely to that delivered by newspapers and wire services. When broadcast lines could easily be made available at reasonable cost, they transmitted live 90-second and 2-minute reports from the field for incorporation into regularly scheduled roundup programs. Sometimes they filed telegraphic reports. In effect, their routine was almost indistinguishable from that of their newspaper colleagues: file twice a day, once each for morning and evening editions.

There was very little audio tape-recorded in the field. Tape recorders were cumbersome, and their quality left much to be desired. This was still the era of the purely verbal report, in essence a think piece, delivered by the correspondent, unembellished by recorded quotes and sound effects. It frequently carried analytical overtones.

It was the era of the whistle-stop campaign. The most efficient means of reaching the largest number of potential voters historically had been the passenger train. An engine, passenger cars, and a crew were chartered from railroad companies. Candidates and their entourages of managers, strategists, speech writers, and publicity men shared the train with local political leaders from the areas through which the train would travel and with representatives of the media. The 13- or 14-car train snaked through the countryside for up to two or three weeks at a time, long enough to make a shower the most precious dream of most of the media representatives aboard.

The train stopped on sidings and in freight yards of towns, both large and small. Advance men where charged with delivering an enthusiastic crowd supported by bands, cheerleaders, pom-pom girls, and local dignitaries, all assembled alongside the tracks. When the whistle blew, the crowd knew the train was approaching and would soon stop. So they stood awaiting the "whistle-stop."[2]

The candidate spoke from the rear platform of a prewar-style observation car. As the train pulled to a stop, reporters leaped off, ran along the tracks to the rear platform, and took up their stations as close to the candidate as possible. They then had to be alert to the impending end of the performance so they could sprint back to their assigned cars, in order to board before the train pulled out. Logistical problems would have made recording with the primitive audiotape equipment then available virtually out of the question. It was even more complicated for television. During the few times the whistle-stop tours were scheduled after television became a factor, film crews had to select locations where news was likely to be made, book separate transportation to the chosen site, and prepare to film the event before the train arrived. With their bulky equipment they would never have had time to haul their cameras, sound recorders, tripods, and batteries from midtrain to the rear, set up to record before the speech started, and break down in time to reboard before the train was well on its way.

During the 1948 campaign, as news director of CBS-owned WCCO in Minneapolis and St. Paul, I did brief trips on both the Dewey and Truman trains. I sprinted with the other media representatives to the rear of the train to hear the candidate's brief talks and rushed back with them so as not to get stranded while the train moved on to the next stop. There were no phones aboard trains then, so direct communication with the newsroom was out of the question. The only method available for delivering my reports was to type out a message in a press car on the train and watch for a stop near a station in one of the larger towns so I could run my copy to a telegraph office and hope it would reach the news desk.

On occasion the whistle-stop tour paused long enough in a larger city for more extensive radio reporting. The Truman train, for example, was scheduled to pull into the Minneapolis Union Station and remain there for several hours while the president met with key Minnesota supporters and spoke at a rally at the Minneapolis Auditorium. His staff agreed that he would appear briefly on the rear platform as he was welcomed to the Twin Cities. A broadcaster of the current era would have described the necessary preparations as a nightmare and the costs as outrageous. We had to order broadcast lines from the telephone company; assign technicians to transport microphones, amplifiers, and switching equipment to trackside; connect their equipment to telephone company lines and test the signal quality. Only then could we prepare to describe the train's arrival and the welcoming ceremony, and update the day's political news. Four decades later the job could have been done with a fraction of the effort, and more effectively. Despite all our effort, our role was secondary. The paid political speech from the auditorium was the main event. We were involved in a sideshow.

The episode is representative of radio coverage of political campaigns before the advent of television. Radio had neither the resources nor the desire nor, for that matter, an adequate supply of manpower to deploy the masses of troops that television would later bring to political coverage. We had to buy lines to Union Station because our primitive shortwave unit would not deliver a signal from an underground location. Portable electronic cameras with a shortwave capability or with accompanying videotape recorders could have been at trackside with virtually no advance notice or setup time.

In the 1948 campaign, television was rarely in evidence. Videotape recording was still 9 years in the future; the communications satellite, 15; the fully professional hand-held electronic camera, more than 20. The entire CBS Television news staff totaled only 14 persons as late as the summer of 1951. Television could safely be written off. It simply was not a force in 1948.

The 1952 presidential election began an entirely new adventure in political coverage. Campaign managers had become mesmerized by the power of the television picture. Coverage of the conventions in the summer had galvanized an entire nation. The number of television homes had grown from the half-million level of 1948 to nearly 20 million. Network radio was already beginning to suffer from television competition. Television network news staffs were growing in both numbers and skills, although at CBS the growth in skills was more impressive than the slight increase in numbers. More local stations were beginning to employ minimal staffs and to cover local news. The volume, however, was meager. The time for a standard newscast, either network or local, was still 15 minutes.

Ironically, coverage patterns of television news programs did not deviate much from those of radio. The technology available to television did not permit radical innovation. Film cameras played a part in the field, but film coverage was cumbersome. Cameras were bulky. Picture and sound quality was inferior. Processing was time-consuming and could be done in only a limited number of laboratories. Airplanes traveled at less than half the speed of four decades later. They served fewer communities, and their flights were less frequent.

Television reporters in the field were for the most part radio-oriented. They were accustomed to preparing voice reports comparable with analytical newspaper stories, and they had had only minimal experience, if any, in coordinating their reports with film. CBS was buying its news film from an independent supplier, so it had only a quartet of combination cameramen-film editors on staff, all in New York. Their main assignment was to edit film. Camera chores were incidental. Without staff camera personnel, it was necessary to rely on free-lance camera correspondents and local station crews to supplement film coverage. Some had sound-on-film equipment; others, silent only. The degree of competence varied widely. Exposed negative usually was shipped to New York for processing, causing lengthy delays.

When correspondents reported for television, they reported in essentially the same way they had in 1948. The cumbersome logistics involved in film reports and their unfamiliarity with the medium inhibited them. Jealousy on the part of radio news leadership regarding their use by television restricted their chances to become more familiar. Since all the correspondents on the network staff were carried on the CBS Radio payroll, and were permitted only grudgingly to deliver any service to television, television coverage was largely improvised. Much as they would have preferred a larger role in television, staff correspondents were effectively limited to delivering on-camera "think pieces" rounding up the day's activities. A packaged sound-on-film story was possible only on the limited number of occasions when we had access to film crews and correspondents at the same place at the same time.

The fact that we were purchasing most of our news film from an independent supplier over whom we had little control meant that development of integrated reporter-camera teams was out of the question. We could not rely on affiliated stations. Only a relatively few had built news departments with adequate resources to serve our needs in addition to their own. And even then there was the question of shipping and processing any film they might be able to obtain for us. The net result was that frequently our film stories went one way and the commentary another. We rarely had an integrated film report on which cameraman and reporter worked together as a team.

The problem, however, was not as serious as it might appear. We had a limited outlet for the news we gathered. Our schedule called for one 15-minute news program on Mondays through Fridays. Subtracting time for commercials allowed a little more than 11 minutes to cover the news of the whole world. American politics had to take its place along with the Korean war, crucial elections in Europe, fears of the growing strength of the Soviet Union, and the future of NATO following the departure of General Eisenhower, not to mention the usual quota of floods, fires, tornadoes, and other disasters.

Television coverage of the primaries during the winter and spring, haphazard as it was, had left a solid mark on the process of nominating candidates, created an avalanche of interest in the primary process, and focused surprising attention on television news. Coverage of the conventions had brought an entirely new dimension to political reporting, and simultaneously introduced millions of American citizens to both the conventions and the medium. Day-to-day news coverage, however, while a novelty and a dramatic adjunct to conventional reporting, lacked the logistical support and the specialized reporting skills to leave as profound an impact in 1952 as it would later. Some of the most significant contributions made by television came not through its hard news but through its talk and discussion programs. "Meet the Press" on NBC entered the election year with a running start. Its origin, first on radio and then on television, dates back to the late 1940s. If the candidates failed to appear because of Section 315, the issues did, week after week. CBS's "Man of the Week" opened in midsummer 1951 and was heavily oriented to political discussion.

CBS also offered "Bandwagon" during the winter and spring. The network took a big risk when it invited the major candidates of both major parties to use half an hour of CBS Television prime time as they saw fit. Only one disgruntled noninvitee went to the FCC to protest his exclusion under Section 315. The FCC ordered that the protester, one William Schneider, a book salesman from St. Louis, be granted time equivalent to that offered to Robert Taft, Earl Warren, Averell Harriman, Estes Kefauver, Richard Russell, and others. He won his case, used his time, and had his moment of glory, although he was later regarded as so unimportant by the Republican Party that he failed to get credentials to attend the convention.

As part of its commitment to Westinghouse for convention and election coverage, CBS scheduled "Pick the Winner" once a week in prime time during September and October. Spokesmen for the major party candidates, not the candidates themselves, discussed the issues and argued the cases for their candidates. CBS's fear of becoming ensnared in a Section 315 involvement kept the candidates from appearing to plead their own cases.

Combining the discussion and talk programs with the hard news coverage and the 120 hours-plus devoted to the conventions, television's contribution to national politics in 1952 was significant even though news performance was still primitive. The major change before the next quadrennial nationwide campaign would involve considerably more sophistication in covering the news, better-trained staffs, and improved equipment.

Two significant changes occurred between the 1952 election and the congressional elections of 1954. First, television news at CBS finally received approval to establish its own news film-gathering organization. It would no longer have to be dependent on an outside supplier for whom CBS was only another customer. Hereafter, on those occasions when (and if) correspondents were released from radio assignments to serve television, it would be possible to produce integrated picture, natural sound, and commentary sequences.

The second development occurring in mid–1954 was even more significant. The bitter jealousies and almost total lack of cooperation between radio and television news and public affairs departments encouraged senior management to merge the two—including news, public affairs, and sports—into one corporate department reporting directly to the corporate chairman and president. To the extent that I was selected to head the new department as a corporate vice-president, television had come out the winner. A more persuasive reason, however, probably lay in television's surprising progress. By 1954 the television network had moved substantially ahead of radio in revenues, audience size, and ratings. It seemed only logical that it should become dominant.

For those of us trying to create a superior television news report, the most heartening element was the fact that we could now deploy our troops where they would serve best and in a manner that would make the maximum use of our still limited manpower. We could begin to use the talents of a superior reporting staff that had been restricted from appearances on television except under special circumstances. We immediately undertook a rigorous training schedule to convert radio reporters to the special requirements of television, and hired personnel from the picture magazines, newsreels, still picture services, documentary production units, and wire services to furnish a broader base in developing new television-oriented reporters and editorial staffs.

Winning approval to establish our own news film reporting unit had enabled us to create bureaus in Washington, Chicago, and Los Angeles, and to employ cameramen on a retainer basis in other key areas. A newly established assignment desk coordinated the efforts and blended camera teams with correspondents. The rapid extension of AT&T microwave links permitted additional flexibility. Stories that warranted it could be processed and transmitted from key cities in the field as an alternaive to shipping directly to New York. The growth in size and financial stability of affiliated stations and their expanding news programs provided another source of coverage in addition to adding a backup capability.

The more significant development was the merger of the radio and television news departments. Television would now have correspondents on call without bickering with radio over their use. Their assignments would be coordinated by a central desk representing both radio and television. With the merger, our most critical reporting and editorial problems were well on the way to solution.

Logistics remained the most difficult roadblock. Efforts to commission the design of a lightweight portable professional newsreel camera were not paying off. In Munich, Germany, for example, I tried to induce the Arnold and Richter Company, makers of the respected Arriflex camera, to design and build new units specifically aimed at the television news market. As an inducement I offered to sign an order on the spot for 15 units built generally to our specifications. Dr. Arnold was uninterested. Television apparently seemed a long way off, and the traditional newsreel business was still prospering, but barely so. Obtaining the cameras would have increased portability and quality, both serious deficiencies in the 1950s, but would hardly have been the final answer to keeping up with fast-moving candidates on the campaign trail. Any genuine easing of the logistical problems was far in the future. It depended on technologies still on the drawing boards.

In 1954 we did not even dream of miniaturized electronic cameras with built-in videotape recorders, or of communications satellites that could supplement or replace microwave relays or coaxial cable. Our dreams only went so far as to consider what we might do with a videotape recorder, if we ever had one. And we were in no position to realize that electronic cameras and communications satellites would not be a wholly unmixed blessing. We could not know then that rather than deliver important news rapidly from the most competent reporters, they frequently would become devices for emphasizing style over substance and transmitting trivia.

By 1956 we were much better organized to cover a political campaign. We had correspondents, some of them with some training in television reporting, to send into the field. We had control over their assignments. Patterns had been developed to cut into network lines from a number of larger cities to avoid shipping film to New York. This made more same-day coverage possible.

Demands for both greater volume and more variety were growing. The early evening news still ran only 15 minutes, but a two-hour morning program needed service. Weekend news reviews posed an additional demand. WCBS-TV, the CBS-owned station in New York, whose news schedule was expanding, depended entirely on CBS News for both news and service and production. The station required additional coverage, some of it distinct from that being seen on the network. We also had begun syndicating a news film service to a number of stations, both affiliated and nonaffiliated, further increasing the demands for volume, but fortunately absorbing some of the cost. In short, there was more motivation for intensive coverage than there had been four years earlier or even two years earlier, greater resources to deliver it, and more outlets for the end product.

The report being delivered, however, was largely unchanged. Other than some limited attempts at human-interest or colorful features, the reportage was essentially serious, informative, and analytical. Technology had simplified delivery of individual stories to network origination points, but for pictorial coverage we still had to rely on motion picture film, and film had to be processed and edited before insertion into a broadcast. That was still a slow process. Live coverage was costly and cumbersome, too much so for day-to-day use.

The net result: the content of political coverage, even though efficiencies had been achieved and volume and depth of reporting had increased, looked and sounded about as it had in 1952. New devices for shaking up the old procedures, though, and remodeling television's political reporting were beginning to move from the drawing board to the prototype stage.

There were four technological innovations moving at varying speeds from the scientists' drawing boards to the production line. Each of the four would, in its own way, reshape television's political coverage and transform the relationship between politics and television.

Videotape recording and playback was the first to make its appearance. Electronic tape and film editing would follow a few years later, to be followed in turn by the communications satellite and the portable electronic camera. All four would contribute to enabling television reporting to break loose from the shackles imposed by motion picture film with its inferior quality and protracted processing and editing time, and from the high cost and inflexibility of microwave relays. In short, they would make instant news a reality at a cost that stations as well as networks could afford.

The first of the four to appear on the market was videotape recording. I first learned that Ampex had a prototype ready to demonstrate one day in 1956 when I stopped in my office briefly en route to Columbia Presbyterian Hospital in New York for a back operation. There was a note on my desk asking me to call Bill Lodge, the CBS chief of general engineering. Lodge told me cheerfully that he had good news for me. Ampex had completed assembling a prototype videotape recorder. It had solved the nagging problems that had been plaguing the engineers and delaying introduction of working units. The company, Lodge told me, planned to demonstrate the new device at the CBS affiliates' conference in Chicago the next month

(April). He assured me that within several months we would acquire production units that would be available for news use. I thanked him for the good news and prepared to go to the hospital for the operation. It occurred to me after recovering from the surgery that I might have been able to pay for it out of profits had I called a broker and ordered Ampex stock.

The demonstration at the affiliates' meeting in Chicago in mid-April went off without a hitch. The pictures were sharp and clear, the sound undistorted, and the recording process instantaneous. The one disturbing note was that production units would not be available until winter or spring of 1957, too late for use during the summer political conventions and the fall campaign.

The first innovative use we made of the new device was in sports, not in news. CBS engineers were sufficiently trained in operating the new miracle machine by the time of the running of the Kentucky Derby in May 1957 that I thought we might gamble with an on-the-air experiment. I suggested to our sports director that we tape the running of the Derby, rewind it during the presentation ceremonies honoring the winning owner and trainer, and then rerun the race as soon as the ceremonies were completed. Over some objections from the technical operations department, we scheduled the tape playback. Within 15 minutes after the conclusion of the Derby, we had demonstrated the first "instant replay." It worked without a hitch.

The implications for political coverage were obvious. The political conventions are not unlike a three-ring circus. Videotape would enable us to select the most interesting item for air and store the others for playback later. Use in the field during the campaign would have to await the production of portable units. The bulky machines available in 1957 were practical for studio use only, but by leasing telephone company lines we could transmit remote events to New York for taping and editing.

Electronic editing was slower in coming than we had hoped. We took three of the heavy and cumbersome studio VTRs to Rome during the summer of 1960 to cover the Olympic Games. They were set up in an abandoned motion picture theater we leased at Ciampino Airport. The incoming signals from the various stadia were recorded at Ciampino and edited for air shipment to New York. The editing process, while not as complicated as with film, was no breeze. Cuts had to be made with razor blades and splices with Scotch Tape. It took an entire night to edit the opening ceremony into a one-hour commercial program. The sun was shining brightly and rats were running in the street as we walked up the Via Veneto to our hotel after a night at the VTR machines. Both portable tape units and electronic editing were still several years in the future.

The next electronic miracle to contribute to changing the news coverage process was the hand-held, portable electronic camera. NBC had brought what was almost immediately designated a "peepie-creepie" to the 1952 national conventions, but the 1952 version was little better than a toy. It was almost 20 years before a genuinely professional unit was available. When it came on the market, it quickly began to take a place beside the film camera as the television journalist's primary tool. Before much longer, it had replaced film almost completely. The early version enabled crews in the field to transmit a signal to the central studio recording room or to a van stationed nearby for recording on tape. The next step was the marketing of the fully portable, hand-held videotape recorder. By the early 1980s these miniaturized units were available and quickly gobbled up by both networks and stations. With the addition of electronic editing, television news personnel were fully liberated from the logistical and quality problems of film. Instant news was now a reality.

It took one more electronic miracle to round out the pattern, the communications satellite. The first satellite capable of communicating across the Atlantic Ocean, Early Bird, flew in 1962. Later in that decade the networks were using satellites for long-distance transmission. Much of the Vietnam war coverage reached the United States by satellite. It was in the early-to-mid–1980s, however, that the satellite captured the imaginations of station managers and news directors of television stations in the United States, both large and small. The secret was a substantial increase in the power output of the transponders, the device on the satellite that multiplies the power of the signal received from Earth and beams it back to the ground. The greatly increased power of the signal as it returned to Earth enabled a substantial reduction in the size of the receiving dish and the cost of operating the equipment. An abundance of transponders on the satellites and the relatively low cost of leasing brought satellite use within the reach of even small stations. More than 300 local television stations, more than ten times as many as in 1984, furnished satellite coverage of the 1988 political conventions to their home markets. Scores of local stations also covered the primary elections, using the satellite as the means of carrying the signal back to the home audience.

It is clear that the game is no longer restricted to the heavy hitters. The networks are still the majors, but now anybody can play: amateurs, professionals, and raw recruits, some of whom could not even make a sandlot team. All that is now required is a camera, reservations for time on a satellite, and credentials to cover the event. And there is no proof of competence required to get credentials.

Rather than hold to their standards, standards that had been undergoing damaging erosion for many years, the networks, badgered by the growing presence of the locals and nagging competitive pressure from cable, have all too frequently yielded to the new competition and fallen into a trap. They are playing the local stations' game. The thoughtful, analytical pieces of the 1950s have been largely replaced by froth. The 15-second sound bite is as prevalent on the network as on the local station, even in response to the most complex question. The interview and the debate are programmed to mini-mize the significant, stress the human interest, and emphasize the repeatable punch line. Rather than becoming tools to increase the level of understand-ing, new technologies are being used as devices for promotional stunts. The net result is to diminish the capacity of television to serve as a stimulant to greater understanding of politics and issues, and to frustrate the dreams of election night 1952. The problem is compounded by the speed with which the political handlers pounced on the new tools and the techniques they made possible. Thus the sound bite, born in the television station, quickly became a staple in the political manager's bag of tricks.

Candidates and their managers could not resist the temptation to tailor their performances to this insatiable appetite for short bursts of interesting tidbits. An editorial in the *San Diego Tribune* printed during the 1988 pri-maries was particularly sardonic.

After all, television has become the primary source of news for most Americans. That's why candidates will do almost anything—from riding a bicycle across frozen New Hampshire to milking a cow in Iowa—to get 30 seconds on a network news-cast. It's one reason some modern candidates are better at delivering snappy but superficial one-line answers than at providing detailed explanations of complex issues.[3]

The *Tribune*'s editorial writer went on to point out that "television's influence on the political process is neither good nor bad. It is a commu-nications tool."

And a communications tool is what it is. It has no magic power beyond what it is given by the human beings who control it. Patterns for covering political news were certain to change. It is unfortunate that standards had to slip while the new technologies were coming into common usage. The fault lies with both television personnel who developed the techniques and the political handlers who so promptly adopted them. Both television news personnel and the political community might well ponder Shakespeare's often quoted line from Julius Caesar, "The fault, dear Brutus, is not in our stars, but in ourselves."

NOTES

1. ABC was not a serious competitor in delivering a news service until later in the 1950s.

2. The term "whistle-stop" is said to have originated with railroad men, who referred to the tiny communities where passenger trains stopped only on specific orders as "whistle-stops" because the engineer pulled the whistle cord in order to alert the stationmaster as the train approached.

3. *San Diego Tribune*, March 5, 1988, p. B–3.

8

The Will and Intent to Be Objective

From its earliest days, CBS has prided itself on maintaining strict objectivity in news broadcasts. "Fairness" and "balance" have been watchwords since the middle 1930s, when the network took the first tentative steps toward creating its own news service. There was no mathematical formula for measuring objectivity. The test was simply the "will and intent to be objective." Paul White, its first news director, sternly enforced policies formulated by CBS President William S. Paley, Vice-President Edward Klauber, and White himself.

On the basis of my own experience during the 1950s, however, I have sometimes wondered whether corporate management was always as dedicated to strict adherence to objectivity, fairness, and balance as it demanded that its news personnel be, particularly in relation to coverage of politics. I wondered if corporate leadership might not have yielded from time to time to a temptation to skew coverage of events to support one candidate or the other or to help make a case for one party over another. There were a number of specific occasions in which I was personally involved that defied explanation within the context of our stated policies.

It was out of character, for example, for Chairman Paley to approve the $80,000 required to subsidize construction of a temporary AT&T microwave relay to Abilene, Kansas, to pick up General Eisenhower's campaign kickoff speech on June 5, 1952. Even though NBC ultimately shared the cost, $40,000 was a staggering sum to our resource-starved news department at that early stage in television's development. I was puzzled that we were encouraged to carry the general's speech but were discouraged from insisting on broadcasting the general's press conference the next morning. Of the two, we considered the press conference the more newsworthy. The last-minute reprieve that came two hours before the press conference began permitted us to make the best of the opportunity.

I have no doubt that we should have been in Abilene. The event fully justified the coverage, irrespective of policy and Section 315 problems. Sometimes the newsworthiness of an event justifies bending the rules or taking the risk of finding time for replies from other candidates. But I wondered whether we would have done as much for Senator Taft, Governor Warren, or Harold Stassen. It was widely known that the chairman's brother-in-law and neighbor on Long Island, John Hay (Jock) Whitney, was one of the general's most influencial supporters.

I was even more puzzled by an event more than six years later, in the closing days of the 1958 off-year election campaign. Late in the afternoon of Sunday, October 26, nine days before the November 4 election, CBS President Frank Stanton called me at my home and asked me whether I would be intersted in carrying a live pickup of a cabinet meeting from the White House. He told me that the full cabinet would be present and that the president would preside. It was scheduled for 7 to 8 P.M. the next day, and would be exclusive for CBS.

I perhaps should have asked, "Why now?" but I did not. The prospect of breaking new ground and scoring a first in television coverage of governmental affairs at a high level was too tempting an opportunity to overlook. My answer was "Yes." Stanton told me that Jim Hagerty, the president's press secretary, was in his office, and suggested that I call immediately to confirm our interest. Jim was evidently not surprised at my call. We agreed that I would immediately call Lew Shollenberger, the CBS News executive in charge of special events in the Washington office, and start the production machinery in motion. A call to the broadcast operations department in New York cleared time for the broadcast. The department also notified stations that we would be carrying the cabinet session live at 7 P.M. EST. I also booked air transportation to Washington for the next morning and reserved a hotel room.

From the production point of view, the broadcast of the cabinet meeting was a considerable success. I squeezed into a corner of the cabinet room where I could see both the meeting and a television monitor, and watched it from there. The president took the chair and called on each member in turn. We had tight close-ups of the members as they reported. It was a fascinating glimpse of the top level of the U.S. government in action. From that point of view it justified the effort.

The content, however, was a different story. It was routine, noncontroversial, and could only be described as dull. The reports were perfunctory and devoid of much lively matter. The timing was precise, suggesting that it had been carefully produced by someone in the White House. There was a minimum of easygoing banter and an absence of debate. The selection of the hour for the meeting was also curious. It seemed a bit unusual, but perhaps not entirely coincidental, that the cabinet met in the early evening, when men were more likely to be at home, but early enough so that it would not be necessary to preempt high-budget network programs.

After the program I went with some of the CBS staff to the National Press Club, where I was approached by Jerry Balch of the Associated Press. Balch took me into a quiet corner and asked questions about the origin of the idea to do the broadcast. Where did I learn of the possiblity that we might gain entry to the cabinet room with cameras and microphones? Specifically, who tipped me off? Why did I assume the White House might be inclined to grant permission at this particular time for something that had never before been covered live?

I saw no reason to hold back anything I knew, so I leveled with him. I told him that Stanton had called me and that Paley previously had called Stanton. This was all the AP needed. Apparently the wire service had been curious why the White House was apparently so eager to grant permission to a network—in fact, encouraged it—to carry a cabinet meeting in an unprecedented live broadcast just eight days before a crucial election in which the Republican Party was on the brink of defeat in both houses of Congress. The broadcast did not help much. The Republicans won only 35 percent of the seats in the Senate and a similar percentage in the House.

When I returned to New York, there was a note on my desk asking me to call Stanton. The subject of the call could easily have been anticipated. Paley was not happy that his name had been brought into the affair. It was obvious that, in his view, I should have taken full responsibility. After a few days the story died down, lost in the flood of election news, but my role continued to embarrass me. I could not help wondering whether strict objectivity policies are for news personnel only, or whether corporate management should walk the same narrow line. From a more personal point of view, should I have told Stanton that, in my opinion, carrying the cabinet meeting would be, if not a violation of CBS News policy, at the very least a demonstration of favoritism toward the Republican Party?

Another situation that was personally embarrassing to me arose only eight months later. The producers of our "Face the Nation" program, an interview show in which a prominent figure in national life is interviewed by a panel of Washington media personnel, had booked Senator Hubert Humphrey for an appearance on Sunday, July 19, 1959. Humphrey at this time was considered a front runner for the Democratic presidential nomination but had not formally declared his candidacy. Two of his closest friends and supporters, Governor Orville Freeman of Minnesota and Senator Eugene McCarthy, however, announced on Tuesday, July 14, the formation of a Humphrey for President Committee.

This raised the question whether Humphrey was or was not a candidate.

Did the declaration by two friends that a committee was being formed on his behalf serve automatically, under a strict interpretation of Section 315 of the Federal Communications Act, to place him formally in the running? Or would he become a candidate only after he personally announced a decision to run? Humphrey quickly answered the question from his point of view by giving the "Face the Nation" producers a written declaration stating "I am not a candidate for the presidency." He clearly wanted to keep his options open and remain on the show. While the statement was unequivocal, it did not prevent his announcing later that he would make the run. Members of the production staff were confident that Humphrey's statement precluded any Section 315 problems. The production staff, however, guessed wrong.

Shortly after the Freeman-McCarthy announcement was given nationwide circulation, I had a call from Frank Stanton. He told me that I would have to withdraw the invitation to Humphrey. There was too much risk, he said. If we went ahead with the Humphrey appearance, we took the chance that we might trigger demands from other real or frivolous candidates. Stanton specifically had in mind Lar Daly, a bizarre Chicagoan with little visible backing, who made it a practice of declaring for public office, almost any public office. He sometimes made his campaign appearances wearing a red, white, and blue Uncle Sam suit with the traditional stovepipe hat, and was never known to win more than a handful of votes.

Daly, however, had a become a pesky annoyance to broadcasters. During the primary campaign for the Chicago mayoralty the previous February, he had petitioned the FCC, requesting that station WBBM-TV in Chicago, the CBS-owned outlet in that city, grant him time equal to that given by WBBM-TV to Mayor Richard J. Daley. Daley was a candidate for reelection. On one occasion he had been shown in news broadcasts on the station in his official role, welcoming the president of Argentina to Chicago, and on another occasion, formally opening the city's Community Fund drive. The commission decided by a 4 to 3 vote to grant Daly's request.

I knew that Stanton was campaigning vigorously for elimination of Section 315 and that a bill modifying the section was being debated in Congress at that very moment. Withdrawing the Humphrey invitation would constitute a dramatic demonstration of the folly embodied in the clause and presumably could be a valuable tool for building congressional support. I suggested to him, however, that he might make an even more dramatic appeal for abrogation of the offending clause by letting the Humphrey invitation stand and preparing to grant equal time to Lar Daly. I suggested that, to my mind, there could not be a more effective method for exposing the ludicrous unreality of Section 315 than to welcome Daly to the show, provided he would show up in his Uncle Sam suit. Daly's appearance, I added, would inevitably attract a torrent of media coverage across the entire nation. Section 315 would be exposed to ridicule from coast to coast. Congress would surely see the folly of retaining a regulation that was so manifestly fatuous. Stanton was unmoved. He said he did not want CBS exposed to the ridicule that was certain to follow a Lar Daly appearance. Of course, we had no assurance that Daly would actually ask for the time.

I could not help suspecting that CBS News was being used as a pawn in a campaign to rid broadcasters of the onerous burden of granting equal time to any number of frivolous candidates for public office. This was hardly representative of the objectivity that we were compelled to enforce when dealing with matters that did not directly affect the interests of senior management.

At this point I had no alternative, so I called Senator McCarthy to inform him that we were withdrawing the invitation to his colleague from Minnesota. I also called Douglass Cater, then a Washington correspondent for *Reporter* magazine, who had been invited to serve on the panel of interviewers, to tell him that we were looking for a new guest. I think to this day that we misused a great opportunity to show up the folly inherent in Section 315. The ultimate irony is that NBC, two hours after our invitation was withdrawn, called Humphrey and invited him to appear on the "Today" show, which he did on Friday, July 17. In the course of that interview Humphrey referred to the CBS contretemps: "I couldn't help feeling that maybe I was getting a little high-pressure lobbying here yesterday."[1]

There is no evidence that Lar Daly ever asked NBC for equal time.

Another major equal-time controversy flared up a few days before the 1960 Democratic National Convention. Once more I was puzzled at the CBS attitude. The position adopted by CBS was again diametrically opposed to positions taken by ABC and NBC, and again there was a question, at least in my mind, as to whether CBS was acting purely on the basis of legalities or whether there may have been a deeper motive in the background. The issue was not, in strict terms, a Section 315 matter but one involving fairness, balance, and objectivity. It is true it involved equal time, but not "equal time" within the definition spelled out in Section 315. In that respect it was not a legal matter subject to regulatory action but a matter to be settled by an internal decision based on company policy. Normally this would have been a news division decision that probably would be made after consultation with senior corporate management, but again Stanton preempted me. There was no question the matter was politically hot. It directly involved some of the biggest names and most important figures in the Democratic party. The stature of the party leaders involved made it a matter of major media concern.

Former President Harry Truman had been given a half-hour on both CBS and NBC on Saturday, July 2, in which he made a number of derogatory remarks about John F. Kennedy. Kennedy supporters immediately demanded equal time, citing Section 315. Their case was a weak one, since Section 315 applied only to candidates for public office. Truman was not a candidate. Fairness, however, was a different question. Since Truman had attacked Kennedy, a policy of strict adherence to the corporation's fairness policy might have justified finding time for Kennedy's reply.

The Kennedy demand became a critical issue on Sunday morning, July 3. While the controversy was building, I boarded a plane for Los Angeles in order to be on the scene to oversee final preparations for the convention that was to open on Monday, July 11. The issue still had not escalated into a major confrontation as the plane took off. When I arrived in Los Angeles, I went directly to the Sports Arena. Installation of the sophisticated electronic equipment needed to cover the convention was virtually complete, and I was anxious to check progress. By this time the Truman-Kennedy issue had reached the boiling point. I was sure that Frank Stanton was fully aware of the whole story and would have to approve any grant of equal time, so my first step was to call him.

My intention was to recommend that we grant Kennedy's request and be prepared to make equivalent time available to other candidates at a later date if necessary. It seemed improbable, however, that other candidates for the office could make a very persuasive case, in view of the fact that Truman attacked only Kennedy. Unless Kennedy were to attack another candidate, there seemed little reason to believe that the granting of time for further answers would be required.

Stanton was unmoved. He urged that we sit tight and make no offer. He added that he expected to have further information in a couple of days that would bear on the Truman-Kennedy affair. We could make our decision then.

On July 5 I called again, and was surprised to hear him say that if we waited another day or two, Lyndon Johnson would probably announce for the presidency. We could then schedule time for both JFK and LBJ. This struck me as odd. Johnson was not at that moment a candidate, and there had been no evidence at the time of the Truman speech that he would be. Furthermore, LBJ had not been attacked in the Truman speech, so there was little justification for granting him time. I wondered, without saying it, whether we might be skewing our response to favor LBJ. I knew that the Johnson family owned, in Mrs. Johnson's name, a highly successful CBS Television network affiliate in Austin, Texas, and that he and Stanton met often. It was easy to speculate that the corporation might sometimes consider its own objectives as taking precedence over policy. The policy, it appeared, might be for the news division, but not always for the corporation. LBJ did announce. He and JFK got their time.

While fairness is involved in both news broadcasts and appearances on the air by candidates for public office, it is relatively easy to make judgments on requests for time to reply, either under Section 315 or as a matter of fairness. The FCC will sometimes take the matter out of the broadcaster's hands if it feels action is mandatory. In the case of requests for time, the answer is either yes or no. The petitioner either gets the time or he does not.

Maintaining objectivity in news programs is far more complicated. Many of the experienced correspondents on the CBS News staff had served in overseas posts, mostly for radio. Foreign correspondents in broadcasting cannot be subjected to the same editorial discipline that governs reporters for print. Their normal output is 90-second analytical pieces that round up a story or a number of related developments in their areas of concern. The general nature of the piece is discussed in advance with the editor/producer of the program in New York, but from that point on, the correspondent is on his own. There is no opportunity for the copy editor to use his blue pencil. Since the copy is largely analytical in nature, it necessarily reflects the attitude of the correspondent, and in that respect frequently is something less than wholly objective. When the correspondent is transferred from the foreign scene to cover a presidential campaign, he is still in the field and remote from the copy editor's pencil. Within the constraints imposed by his own respect for objectivity, he is more or less free to express his own attitudes. During the 1950s, only correspondents in Washington and New York were subjected to the editorial blue pencil. Only at those two points did we have editors available to whom correspondents submitted their copy. Others were on their own. We could insist on attention to policy and we could complain after the fact, but there was no way we could enforce compliance at long distance.

Edward R. Murrow was a special case. His experience as a reporter had been entirely overseas during the buildup to war and during the war itself. He was a man of intense sensitivities as to what he regarded as injustice or persecution. To him, broadcasting failed in its mission unless it called attention to injustices and pleaded for the righting of wrongs. As a personal friend of the chairman and a member of the corporate board of directors, he had a degree of freedom to crusade for causes in which he firmly believed, a freedom not available to other correspondents.

"See It Now," the half-hour news documentary program that opened its run in November 1951, furnished Murrow and his coproducer, Fred Friendly, with a forum. It was the period of the most vicious blacklisting by an assortment of extreme right-wingers and of reckless character assassination by Senator Joseph McCarthy. Murrow and Friendly used the mechanism of "See It Now" to attack injustice and restore some sense of rationality to a badly torn American society. Their programs were not blatantly opinionated. But there could be no doubt after watching the programs that they regarded the cases of Annie Lee Moss and Lieutenant Milo Radulovitch as evidence of brutal persecution of innocent American citizens in the fury of the paranoid witch hunt.

Then they attacked the senator himself. Their target was the chief inquisitor of the "Red scare" inquisition. Few previously had dared stand up to the scowling senator, who counterattacked with a vengeance. Even the White House had refrained from incurring the senator's wrath. Murrow and Friendly, though, gathered ammunition and waited for the moment to strike. Their approach was hardly objective, but they let McCarthy condemn himself. They used the senator's own excesses to condemn him and permitted him to do it in his own words. There was no evidence of any "on the one hand and on the other hand" approach. The result was devastating and hardly balanced. In the interest of some level of fairness, they offered the senator a half-hour to reply. It is a matter of history that the "See It Now" program on March 9, 1954, gave the senator the push that started him on the path toward his quick downfall. It is difficult, though, to find in that program evidence of strict enforcement of CBS News policy.

It could be purely coincidental that Chairman Paley, only a little more than two months later, on May 25, 1954, redefined CBS objectivity policies, but it is unlikely. The reaction to "See It Now" was too strong. Too many reservations about its hard-hitting tactics were being expressed. Members of the company's board of directors voiced concern that Murrow was violating policy. There was something bordering on hysteria within the right-wing press.

The National Association of Broadcasters had named Paley as its Broadcaster of the Year for 1954, and scheduled the presentation of the award as a feature of its convention in Chicago at the end of May. It was a made-to-order opportunity to redefine and reiterate CBS policy toward broadcasting the news. The audience was an important one, one that would guarantee his remarks wide exposure.

The speech was hard and it was tough. There were no weasel words. "In news programs," Paley said, "there is to be no opinion or slanting. The news reporting must be straight and objective." He went on, "In news analysis there is to be elucidation, illumination, and explanation of the facts and situations, but without bias or editorialization."[2] Then came what seems to be a direct reference to the "See It Now" situation. "In other types of information programs, such as the feature or the documentary produced by us," he insisted, "the expression of opinion might properly take place. When it does take place, it should be by the decision of the management or through delegation of authority to a member of the staff producing a particular program." In the case of "See It Now," there had been no such delegation of authority, nor had there been a decision of management supporting an editorial point of view. There was not much question that those of us in executive positions dealing with news were being ordered to enforce strict regulations regarding objectivity.

Six weeks later I was asked to add radio to my television duties, and take over the management of a new corporate department of news and public affairs embracing both the radio and television networks, with the title of corporate vice-president. The first injunction handed me was to read the Paley speech and enforce its mandates.

By the time I was settled into my new office, we were in the midst of another political campaign, the off-year elections of 1954. In 1952 no one in higher authority had paid much attention to television news. There was an occasional criticism of inferior picture quality in our film output. Frank Stanton had come to Chicago once between the two political conventions in 1952. Otherwise we were on our own. It was evident in 1954, however, that we would be under constant corporate executive surveillance and that objectivity would be a critical standard against which we would be measured.

It was still impossible to enforce strict standards on reporters in the field. Television offered problems infinitely more complicated than radio, particularly with respect to film stories. There simply was no way to check scripts before a film story was ready to go on the air. The television reporter in the field rarely was granted the luxury of having time for reflection and personal editing of his script prior to going on camera. He worked as a member of a team involving cameraman, soundman, and in some cases a producer. While he gathered information, the camera crew set up for filming. Live interviews calling for ad-libbing were frequently involved, thus further complicating the process. There was no time for getting an editor's approval before filming began, and even less freedom to control ad-libs.

The only recourse was careful editing in the cutting room after production was completed, but editing film does not allow the freedom to shorten sentences, eliminate offending phrases, and shift emphases that is possible with words on paper. Too frequently the words and picture are so closely related that deleting any portion of the content is not possible without discarding the entire piece. The fact that many of the cameramen we used were free-lancers complicated the problem. We could hardly expect full compliance from outsiders who performed for us only occasionally.

We did the next best thing. We kept detailed records of all appearances on the air. If one party had two minutes, we tried to maintain balance by giving the opposition two minutes. At the end of the campaign, we totaled the time given to each. The results showed almost a dead heat.

This, of course, is no measure of objectivity. It is not even a measure of balance. It is simply a measurement of time on the air. It is conceivable that all the time given to one party might reflect favorably on that party and all the time given to the opposition might reflect negatively. It may also distort by giving undue attention to the most outrageous and unfounded charges. But it was the best we could do with the resources then available. An examination of the copy as opposed to a pure numerical analysis suggests that our discipline was strong enough to avoid bias or slanting.

One solution to the question of maintaining objectivity in reporting politics on television began to evolve around an entirely different set of circumstances. The net result might involve reducing the number of violations of standards of objectivity, but at a devastating price. As technology began to simplify the reporting and transmission process, and television-trained reporters began to replace the radio- and newspaper-trained personnel who staffed the first television newsrooms, the reporting became more bland, stories were shorter, and the analytical pieces of the early period gave way to short features, in many cases no more than trivia. There was also less time, and therefore less opportunity, to insert personal opinion or to reflect personal attitudes. The trend was more pronounced in the stations than in the networks, but the networks contributed their bit to debasing the currency. As the content became more bland, the temptation to pontificate declined even if there had been time for it.

There was, however, an ever present danger. Many of the new recruits in the stations, selected more for voice and appearance than for journalistic experience and judgment, began in ever increasing numbers to follow political campaigns. Some 300 stations were represented at the 1988 conventions. The possiblity for turning television into a local soapbox could not be overlooked. Fortunately, the standard 15-second sound bite does not allow much opportunity for blatant opinionating. In that sense technology may save viewers from evidence of bias and editors from the burden of enforcing strict standards of objectivity.

The public suffers from the change. Few of the stars of the earlier period, trained as analysts as well as reporters, remain to lend their expertise. Even though they were inclined to scoff at strict objectivity rules and flout the blue pencil if they could get away with it, they brought a kind of judgment and leadership that is now in shorter supply. And the caliber of the replacements is frequently several cuts lower, particularly at the local stations.

I am still curious, however, whether senior management is justified in imposing rigid objectivity standards on its working-level personnel while possibly using its broadcast schedule to achieve its own sometimes more selfish ends. Or perhaps the incidents recounted here were an aberration of the 1950s.

NOTES

1. Richard F. Shephard, "Humphrey Scores Equal-Time Curbs," *New York Times*, July 18, 1959. In *The Mass Media and Politics*, ed. James F. Fixx (New York: Arno Press, 1972), p. 263.

2. William S. Paley, "The Road to Responsibility," CBS archives, New York, 1954. I have a personal copy of the speech in my files.

9

An Eight-Year Campaign Pays Off

WBBM-TV, the CBS-owned station in Chicago, had never experienced anything like the mob scene that engulfed its studio 1 a few minutes after 9:30 P.M. on Monday, September 26, 1960. Nearly 400 accredited reporters and photographers from newspapers, wire services, broadcasting stations and networks, newsreels, and magazines, some of them from foreign countries, swarmed into the studio. They milled about in frenzied efforts to see for themselves the site of the confrontation that had just ended between the two major party candidates for the presidency of the United States, Vice-President Richard M. Nixon, Republican, and Senator John F. Kennedy, Democrat. The event they had witnessed was the culmination of an eight-year campaign led by President Frank Stanton of CBS to modify a government regulation that had denied use of broadcast facilities by candidates for public office during a political campaign.

They inspected the light gray set that formed the background for the debaters, the austere Danish chairs on which the two candidates sat while awaiting their respective turns to speak, and the slender lecterns from which they spoke. Facing the stage were chairs that had been occupied by reporters who questioned the candidates.

They also collared members of the staffs of the two candidates who remained in the studio, and CBS personnel who had been involved in producing the history-making broadcast. The candidates had left almost as soon as the debate chairman, Howard K. Smith of CBS, had finished giving the cue that formally pronounced the event finished.

The WBBM facility, a converted roller skating rink near the lake shore north and east of Chicago's Loop, had been humming with frantic activity since Sunday morning. The set for the program, designed and constructed in New York, had been shipped to Chicago for installation in studio 1. By noon Sunday, stagehands, lighting and sound technicians, set dressers, and cameramen were beginning the tedious process of seeing to it that everything would be in order for the event the next night. Producer/director Don Hewitt was on the scene checking lighting, testing camera angles, positioning and repositioning chairs, desks and lecterns. The set turned out to be too light a shade of gray, so it was repainted to darken it a little. New picture tubes were installed in the cameras, which were then balanced to avoid distortion and to assure a uniform picture.

Preparations resumed Monday morning. The repainted set was still not quite right, so a scrim was hung in front of it to soften its effect. CBS President Frank Stanton was at one time photographed on hands and knees, using his folding pocket shears to trim loose threads on the carpet that covered the stage. Vice-President Nixon's television advisers, who had been concerned about the lightness of the gray of the set, pronounced themselves satisfied once the scrim had been set in place. They asked, however, that two small lights be placed on the floor in front of the lectern from which the vice-president would speak. They were placed there to minimize the effect of dark areas under Nixon's eyes. Nixon's advisers also asked that the space between the positions the two candidates would occupy on the stage be widened a bit and that a desk be placed in front of chairman Howard Smith, who would be seated between them. The intention was to increase the degree of separation between the two.

Representatives of the media began to stream into the studio complex at about six P.M. They were ushered directly to studio 4, which had been fitted out as a press room. About an hour later, the most powerful collection of broadcast executives ever gathered into so small a space took up positions in a corridor to the rear of studio 1. They were lined up single file to greet the two debaters as their limousines brought them directly into the corridor through wide doors. In the group were Chairmen Paley of CBS, Leonard Goldenson of ABC, Robert Sarnoff of RCA (parent of NBC), and William J. McNight of Minnesota Mining and Manufacturing (parent of the Mutual Broadcasting System). Also in the line were Presidents Stanton of CBS, Oliver Treyz of ABC, Robert Kintner of NBC, and Robert Hurleigh of MBS. The list was complete; every chief executive officer and every chief operating officer of each of the American networks was in line to shake the hands of the presidential candidates.

Vice-President Nixon was first to arrive. He struck a knee sharply against a car door as he exited his limousine and was seen to wince. He had been hospitalized only a few days earlier for a leg ailment. He recovered quickly and went through the line, shaking hands with the waiting executives. The ceremony completed, he went on to the studio to familiarize himself with the facilities and to try out the positions he would take once the debate started. As he sat in his chair and stood at the lectern, technicians tested camera angles, lighting, and sound.

Nixon was still on the set about 15 minutes later when Kennedy's limousine deposited the Democratic candidate at the head of the receiving line. When the ceremonial greetings were completed, Kennedy proceeded to the studio, only a few steps away, shook hands with the vice-president, and began his familiarizing procedure. A limited number of pool photographers were given access to the studio for a short time to picture the two candidates on the set and to record last-minute preparations.

While the photographers were at work, I found myself standing next to the vice-president. We had a rather labored three- or four-minute conversation made up mostly of small talk that was later to haunt me. I discovered after the conclusion of the debate that microphones had been left on, and my whole conversation with the vice-president had been fed into the press room, to the amusement of 380 reporters.

Following the photo opportunity, the two candidates retired to their respective waiting rooms and the four broadcast reporters who were to question them as part of the presentation took up their positions in chairs at floor level, facing the stage. I went to the rear of the studio to take up the role that Don Hewitt had asked me to fill, that of timekeeper. My function was relatively simple. I had a monitor, three stop clocks, and a microphone in front of me. I was to time each speaker, total the minutes each had used, and on cue, prior to the final reound of the debate, announce the exact number of minutes and seconds remaining for each speaker. The verbatim report of the debate records that toward the end of the broadcast an "unidentified voice" was heard responding to chairman Smith's question regarding the time available for summaries. "This will allow three minutes and twenty seconds for the summary by each candidate."[1]

I had confidently expected that the vice-president would quickly demonstrate his killer instincts. I was sure that he would open with a vigorous attack, but I sat at my table in the studio stunned by the mildness of his approach. At some later stage, I thought, he will surely take the offensive and rip into his younger and less experienced opponent with all the fury of which he is capable. But it never came. I had not thought, as I talked to him before the debate, that he looked or sounded ill, but the contrast between the two candidates as I saw them on the stage was striking, and it was even more so on the screen. Kennedy was tanned, vigorous, confident; Nixon pale, tired, and perspiring. Analysts who studied the texts later concluded that if the contest had been a collegiate debate, Nixon would have won on points, but on television he looked like a loser. A majority of radio listeners also felt that Nixon had the better of the contest, but it was television that commanded the overwhelmingly largest share of the audience, some 75 million persons (contrasted with approximately one-fourth of that number for radio).[2]

The general mood in studio 1 after the horde of media representatives had been admitted was spirited. There was relief on the part of the network personnel, who had seen a highly speculative venture come to fruition, and intense curiosity and unalloyed enthusiasm from the media reporters, for whom this had been an unforgettable event. There was speculation as to what may have caused the vice-president to appear so dispirited, but the main topic of conversation was the effect the debate might have on the political process and on future campaigns. A WBBM-TV camera crew pushed its way through the mob scene, asking media people what they thought the future might hold. Most answered that in the future debates would be standard operating procedure in presidential campaigns. When they came to me, I replied that in the future no major party candidate for the presidency would be able to reject an invitation to debate. In view of the spectacular success of this first presidential campaign debate, I told the interviewer, public opinion would force candidates to participate whether they liked the idea or not.

How wrong I was. It was 16 years before major party candidates for the presidency could again be induced to face each other before television cameras. Incumbent President Gerald Ford agreed in 1976 to meet challenger Jimmy Carter in two direct confrontations arranged not by the networks but by the League of Women Voters. Lyndon Johnson in 1964 was not going to step into the ring with Barry Goldwater, and Richard Nixon had learned his lesson. He wanted no part of debate in 1968 or 1972.

While the postdebate mood in studio 1 was generally favorable, some of the more aggressive reporters were beginning to sniff out some disturbing questions, most of them regarding Nixon's appearance and health. Was Nixon really as pale and uncomfortable as he looked on the screen? Or might there have been some aspect of the production that exaggerated his apparent discomfort? Some Nixon supporters suggested sabotage on the part of CBS. They complained about the lighting, about Nixon's makeup, and about the gray tone of the set. One critic argued that the studio cameras had not been properly balanced. The attacks were sufficiently harsh that we were forced to put considerable effort into preparing accurate and exhaustive responses.

The makeup question was easy to answer. We had brought to Chicago the star of our makeup department, Frances Arvold, and offered her services to both candidates. Both refused. Kennedy wore no make up. Nixon's own television adviser, Everett Hart, applied an over-the-counter product called "Lazy Shave" to conceal the vice president's heavy beard.

The camera problem was not lack of balance. It was, rather, that the cameras were too accurate. New tubes had been installed by CBS technicians the day before the debate. They were sharp and precise, and delivered clearer pictures than older tubes could have. This was unfortunate for Nixon. The cameras exaggerated his paleness and heavy beard, but it was a break for Kennedy, who looked robust and healthy. As the cameras had exaggerated Nixon's apparent ill health, they likewise enhanced Kennedy's rugged vitality. In subsequent meetings the vice-president accepted the services of makeup experts. Nixon had also made an unfortunate choice of a suit. He wore a light gray that blended into the background and, if anything, exaggerated his pale appearance.

The remaining three debates in the series went off with relatively few hitches. The second meeting, scheduled to take place in Cleveland, was shifted to Washington when NBC determined that its studio facilities in the Ohio city were inadequate. There was a minor skirmish about bringing notes into the studio. Nixon had stipulated in accepting the invitation to debate that the confrontations were to be conducted without resorting to notes of any kind. Kennedy had entered the studio in Washington with a sheaf of papers, to which Nixon objected. Kennedy in turn complained about the studio temperature in Washington. The thermostat had been set low at the request of Nixon personnel in order to reduce the vice-president's tendency to perspire heavily.

The third meeting furnished television with another chance to demonstrate its capability for electronic legerdemain. Nixon was campaigning on the West Coast, Kennedy in the East. Both were operating on schedules so tight that neither had the time to travel to a central point. ABC solved the problem by assigning three studios to the event, two in Los Angeles and one in New York. Nixon spoke from one of the Los Angeles studios, and the media panel was in another. Kennedy was in New York. Use of a split screen enabled viewers on occasion to see both candidates simultaneously. In the 1980s multipoint pickups with split-screen display are commonplace. In 1960 they were regarded as miraculous.

The fourth debate concluded uneventfully. Critics thought it was dull and repetitive. The public apparently had lost some of its enthusiasm for the novelty value of the first three. The candidates and their managers, though, immediately began negotiating for a fifth debate. Actually, the jockeying between the candidate's advisers had begun before debate number four.

From the very outset the Democrats were upset at terminating the series as early as October 21. They wanted one more go at the vice-president several days closer to the November 8 election. The Nixon team, on the other hand, wanted to avoid a confrontation later than October 21, but was reluctant to appear uncompromising. Three prominent Democratic senators—Warren Magnuson of Washington, Mike Monroney of Oklahoma, and John Pastore of Rhode Island—fired the first salvo for extending the series when they sent telegrams to the network presidents on October 8. They asked for a fifth debate on or around November 2. Frank Stanton answered for CBS on October 10 that the network would make time and facilities available, provided the two candidates could agree on time and place.

Kennedy took the telegram at face value and on October 10 accepted what he referred to as an "invitation." The joint network committee, composed of John Daly of ABC, William McAndrew of NBC, Joseph Keating of Mutual, and me, sent wires to Fred Scribner, representing the Nixon campaign, and Leonard Reinsch, Kennedy's chief negotiator, on October 12, informing them that "the networks are ready to discuss any modification of the current agreements'. . . " but insisting that it was up to them to arrive at "substantial agreement . . . as to dates and times or expansion of remaining appearances as soon as possible."

I don't think any one of the four of us thought the fifth debate or an extension of the fourth would ever happen. The Nixon side was too firmly committed to concluding all joint appearances no later than October 21. Our posture had to be one, however, of giving the candidates' representatives every opportunity to reach an agreement even though we thought it was a most unlikely eventuality. The time consumed in meetings, telephone calls, and drafting telegrams and memoranda was beginning to wear on all of us, particularly when we had an election to cover and an election night to prepare for.

There was a brief respite for a few days following the October 12 telegram. On October 18, though, it all started again. Reinsch fired the first shot. He called to say that he would try to work with Scribner toward postponing the fourth debate so that it could be rescheduled at a time closer to the election. I could guess how enthusiastically the Nixon camp would view this proposal. Knowing of the Republican reluctance to tamper with the dates, I called Scribner, who, as one might expect, did not want to approve postponement. That was no surprise. What did surprise me was that he suggested adding on an hour from 11 P.M. to midnight and calling it a "fifth debate."

The next call was to Reinsch, who was not thrilled about the suggestion. His instructions obviously were to tempt Nixon to face Kennedy again closer to the election date. He told me that he would "okay the second hour" if the Republicans wanted it, but that it would be impractical. The stations, according to Reinsch, a station manager himself, would be reluctant to carry the extra hour. He added that one hour was sufficient, and urged the network committee to meet and make a specific recommendation, thus removing the onus from the Democrats and placing it squarely on the networks.

Telephone calls went on incessantly all day October 19 without any resolution of the problem. Scribner and Reinsch finally agreed to come to New York for a meeting at the Metropolitan Club on Thursday, October 20, just one day before the final debate. The session was as unproductive as the telephone calls and telegrams of the past few days had been. Scribner was still fascinated by the notion that we might open microphones on street corners in three or four cities to permit average citizens to query the two candidates. This might have been technically possible if we had started planning it a week earlier, but it simply could not be done in the 24 hours remaining. There was also talk of bringing in the vice-presidential candidates for the second hour, but there was no time for rearranging their schedules to make them available.

The meeting broke up with the added-hour suggestion abandoned but the prospect for a fifth debate still alive, even though there was no indication that the Republicans really wanted it, or would even agree to it when the proposal came to a "go, no-go" vote.

A flurry of telephone calls over the next few days failed to yield any solutions to the impasse. Toward the end of the week, however, there were signs of motion. By Friday morning, October 28, prospects had turned so promising that Daly, McAndrew, and I met in my office at 12:45 P.M. to make specific production plans in case Reinsch and Scribner could resolve their differences, which by now seemed to be a definite possibility. CBS would assume production responsibility, and Philadelphia seemed the most likely site. I called Washington to start the machinery in motion to develop security clearance procedures and to print the necessary security tickets and badges, and called Philadelphia to alert the CBS-owned station there, WCAU-TV, that they might be in the eye of a big storm by Monday night, October 31. Only three days remained to get ready.

Reinsch had called just before McAndrew and Daly arrived to read me a telegram he had sent to Scribner. The text hardly seemed designed to elicit friendly cooperation. It was critical of Republican foot-dragging and included what in effect was an ultimatum. It seemed, however, notwithstanding the harsh language, to reflect confidence that there would indeed be a fifth debate. It spelled out a detailed format. It was evident that Scribner and Reinsch had cooperated on drafting a tentative agreement relating to format and production plans.

Vice-presidential candidates, under the proposed plan, would appear during the first ten minutes, after which Kennedy and Nixon would divide the rest of the time between them. The presidential candidates would respond to questions from a panel of newsmen, as in debates two and three. Scribner apparently still favored a two-hour duration. Reinsch preferred one hour but would go to two if pushed.

Before McAndrew and Daly had left my office, Scribner responded to my call requesting his reaction to the Reinsch telegram. He guardedly agreed with Reinsch's optimism regarding the fifth debate and suggested a meeting in Washington on Saturday. He thought the two sides were close enough to agreement to justify it. At 3:05 P.M. I reached Reinsch in Washington. He and Scribner were in a meeting ironing out final details. I said that McAndrew, Daly, and I would be at CBS Washington headquarters the next morning, prepared to meet at a time and place of their choosing. He replied that he would call back later that evening to confirm. By 11 P.M. there had been no confirming call from Reinsch, but there was a call from Lew Shollenberger in our Washington office. He had just learned that

Reinsch and Scribner were still conferring. It was evident, he said, that there had been some major disagreement. Since Reinsch had not called to confirm a meeting, he assumed that there would be none. He was not willing to predict whether the disagreement that was delaying a decision would jeopardize the Monday night event.

Daly, assuming that the proposed meeting had been canceled, was no longer within telephone reach. I called McAndrew to tell him that grounds for optimism were limited. I suggested, though, that we give Reinsch a couple more hours before canceling the Washington trip. By 1 A.M. there was still no call from Reinsch. We now had to ask ourselves, since so short a time remained before the projected debate, whether we could afford to wait for Reinsch and Scribner to call, or whether we should go to Washington to be on hand if they arrived at an agreement. We needed to be on the scene if there were actually to be a debate, so I called McAndrew. I suggested that even though there was obviously some serious hitch in the negotiations, we should meet at LaGuardia airport for an 8 o'clock flight. We would then be on the scene in case Scribner and Reinsch could resolve whatever differences were separating them. If the debate were in fact to go on, we would have only a little more than 48 hours to mount a very complicated television program. Being on the scene in Washington would give us a little added time to get planning under way.

We arrived at the CBS offices in Washington by 10 A.M. and informed both Reinsch's and Scribner's offices that we would make ourselves available at any time or place. At 11 A.M. I called Reinsch. His office said he would call back in 15 or 20 minutes. By 11:30 there had been no word from Reinsch, but Scribner called to read me the text of a telegram he was sending to Reinsch. The text was harsh. He complained about a telegram Kennedy had sent to Nixon on Thursday and the one we had received from Reinsch on Friday. Both, Scribner charged, revealed details of negotiations that were to have been kept secret until final agreement had been reached. "The action . . . ," he wrote, ". . . convinces me that Senator Kennedy does not desire a fifth debate. I have no intention," he concluded, "of negotiating under the threat of an ultimatum."

There was still no word from Reinsch. The last time we had heard from him was in the telegram that Scribner referred to, the one that had arrived while we were meeting the previous afternoon. There was one sentence in that message that we might, if we had been more alert, have interpreted as foreshadowing deep trouble. "Apparently Nixon," Reinsch had written, "is not willing to meet Senator Kennedy again face to face in the final stages of this campaign." It seemed apparent that Scribner had reacted with more hostility than we had assumed. Deadlock now seemed quite possible. Did either side really want the debate? In any event, the optimism of the previous afternoon, if it had been genuine, had quickly evaporated.

At 12:30 P.M., since we were unable to reach Reinsch, I tried Scribner again, with no luck. At 1 P.M., not having heard further from either party, we decided that it was futile to wait longer. We left messages with the Scribner and Reinsch offices that we were leaving Washington at 3:45 P.M. and would receive calls only until then. No calls came, so we boarded a plane for New York. As we suspected, neither side really wanted a fifth debate, but neither wanted to accept the responsibility for scuttling it. Neither McAndrew nor I was surprised by the turn of events, nor were our respective networks. Preparing for another complicated event in a little more than 48 hours would have imposed a crushing burden on everyone involved.

Negotiations leading up to the "great debates" were almost as frustrating and much more protracted than the brief skirmish concerning the ill-fated fifth confrontation. The first suggestion that candidates of the majority parties for the presidency appear in formal televised debates came from a former correspondent for the *Detroit News* who had been appointed to the Senate to fill an unexpired term. Blair Moody, appearing on CBS Television's "People's Platform" on July 27, 1952, urged "CBS or NBC or someone else to put on a series of debates between General Eisenhower and Governor Stevenson."

CBS President Frank Stanton rose to the bait. He wrote Senator Moody on August 6, endorsing the suggestion but calling attention to the restrictive influence of Section 315. He urged Senator Moody to support the deletion of the offending clause so that networks would not be forced to make time and facilities available to a host of fringe candidates in addition to the major contenders.

Nothing happened in 1952. The whole idea of debate seemed remote. One of General Eisenhower's advisers, Ben Duffy of BBDO, had flatly turned down a tentative feeler from Frank Stanton regarding the general's possible participation, and Section 315 could not have been modified in time for any confrontations during that campaign. Stanton returned to the attack in 1955 when he urged CBS Television affiliates to support repeal. Even if they had been successful, debates in 1956 seemed most unlikely. Eisenhower did not appear to be disposed to enhance the prestige of his rival, Governor Stevenson, by appearing on the same platform with him. His advisers were unlikely to exert pressure on Congress to permit any confrontation with the governor.

The 1960 campaign was entirely different. There was no incumbent in the race, no sitting president to conclude that debate could serve only to add prestige to his rival. Hopes for a more favorable climate for repeal of Section 315 were buoyed by a series of bizarre applications of Section 315 in 1956 and by the Lar Daly episode in 1959. Both 1956 decisions involved President Eisenhower. It had been the practice at CBS to make a three-minute period available to the president each autumn to open the national Community Fund drive. In 1956 we decided to shorten the popular Ed

Sullivan show by the three minutes required to accommodate the president's public service message. The CBS legal staff, however, was concerned that since this was an election year, the 17 other candidates for the office might request equal time. A query was sent to the FCC. The commission replied promptly that the three-minute message would indeed fall within the area described in Section 315, and opportunity for reply would have to be offered to any candidate requesting it. Rather than wait for demands for time, all 17 candidates were queried before the president's appearance was finally booked. Sixteen replied that they would not request the time. Only Henry Krajewski of the New Jersey American Third Party insisted on strict conformity to the regulation. We went ahead and scheduled Eisenhower's appearance.

An episode as ludicrous as an Abbott and Costello "Who's on First?" routine enlivened the last few days before the election. Israel and the Arabs were at war. France and the United Kingdom had stepped in on the Israeli side. International tensions were running extremely high. The whole situation was so potentially explosive that there was grave risk even for the United States. President Eisenhower asked for network time on October 31, just one week before the election, to make a short statement to the nation. His request was quickly granted. The statement reflecting the position of the Eisenhower administration was unavoidably controversial.

The next morning Eisenhower's Democratic opppponent, Adlai Stevenson, asked for equal time. So did four minor party candidates. CBS immediately asked the FCC for a ruling. The commission replied that the issue was so complicated that it could not make a quick ruling. Only four days remained before the election. That left CBS in a quandary. Should the network play it safe and grant the time? Or gamble that the FCC would decide the equal time rule should not be applied in this case? CBS decided to grant Stevenson's request. The Republicans then demanded time for the president to answer Stevenson. At that point it seemed to be a story with no end. Unless the commission suddenly gave up all semblance of consistency, the president would have to be given time to reply to Stevenson. And this could go on ad infinitum.

By Monday afternoon, the day before the election, the commission had finally made up its mind. It decided that Section 315 was not applicable. But this put the networks in a worse bind. Their grant of time to Governor Stevenson now made it mandatory that the president be given the equal time requested by the Republican Party. The decision was handed down less than 14 hours before polls would open in some eastern states. But the time had to be offered. Fortunately for the networks, the president was too busy to use the time. Abbott and Costello would have loved the routine. The whole episode made Section 315 and the commission's application of it appear ludicrous. It would still be many months, however, before there would be action to modify or repeal the clause.

The Lar Daly episode in 1959, in which the little-known candidate in the Uncle Sam suit demanded time to reply to Mayor Richard Daley's appearances on Chicago local news broadcasts, finally stimulated action in Congress. The application of the rule to news coverage virtually excluded broadcasters from covering on news programs any appearances during a campaign by candidates performing the normal duties of their offices. Congress apparently recognized the absurdity of the situation and passed legislation exempting regularly scheduled news broadcasts, on-the-spot news interviews, and incidental appearances on news documentaries from application of the rule. The amending legislation was written into law in September 1959. It said nothing, however, about debate. As the 1960 campaign opened, debate was still on the proscribed list unless networks were willing to run the risk of finding time for up to 18 candidates of a variety of splinter parties.

In late 1959, both CBS and NBC began hard-hitting campaigns for legislation that would permit the networks to schedule debates during the 1960 campaign. There was an extra urgency this time. The quiz show scandals that had shocked the nation and damaged the credibility of the networks in the fall of 1959 provided a new incentive for scheduling programs that would restore public respect. Debates between presidential candidates would fit the bill admirably. Prospects for bringing both major party candidates into direct confrontation would be much more favorable than in 1956. There would be no sitting president in the race. Both candidates might desire the exposure that debate would furnish.

This time, too, Congress seemed more favorably inclined toward affirmative action. The almost comic 1956 episodes and the Lar Daly case had exposed the absurdities inherent in application of Section 315. Legislation being considered in the Senate as S. J. 207 was not intended to eliminate the equal-time provision but to suspend it for the 1960 campaign, as it would pertain only to debate. It would, in a sense, be an experiment. That helped to soften opposition. The Senate passed the bill on June 27. The House had not yet acted at the time the two national parties convened in July, the Democrats in Los Angeles and the Republicans in Chicago, but it was assumed that action would come before the campaign got under way in earnest at the beginning of September.

Ironically, it was not Stanton but Robert Sarnoff, chairman of RCA, who got in the first blow. I was in the CBS newsroom at the International Amphitheater, the convention site, on the night of July 27 when I was handed a wire service news story. The convention had recessed for the night after nominating Richard Nixon for the presidency. The news story reported that Sarnoff had sent a telegram to Nixon inviting him to appear in a series of debates with his Democratic opponent. I handed the item to Kidder Meade, the vice-president for corporate relations who had been functioning as Stanton's public relations aide in coordinating efforts to win repeal. It was too late to match the Sarnoff letter, but it was clear warning to move fast the next morning. The Stanton invitations were dispatched early the next day. In the meantime, Nixon aides were leaking word that the vice-president was prepared to accept the invitations.

The first formal acceptance came from Senator Kennedy on July 29. Nixon followed two days later. The quick response seemed to seal the matter. There would be debates. As the CBS officer who would be assigned the responsibility of representing the corporation in the negotiations, I was not so sure. Getting agreement in principle was one thing. Working out specific details in a series of hard negotiations, I thought, might be much more difficult. There were going to be too many opportunities for one candidate or the other to back out as the result of a disagreement over some apparently trivial detail.

Legislation suspending Section 315 had not yet passed the House in early August, and time was short if debates were actually going to be scheduled. Assuming that the bill would soon be enacted into law, I took the initiative for calling the first meeting of networks and representatives of candidates. We convened in a suite in the Waldorf Astoria Hotel in New York on August 9. Vice-President Nixon was represented by Leonard Hall, chairman of the Republican National Committee; Fred Scribner, the party's general counsel; Herbert Klein, the vice-president's press secretary; Ted Rogers, a television adviser; and Carroll Newton, a political campaign specialist at BBDO. Leonard Reinsch was the sole Kennedy representative. William McAndrew, president of NBC News, who was on vacation, was represented by Lester Bernstein; John Daly represented ABC; Joseph Keating was there for Mutual; and I represented CBS.

It was obvious from the outset that arriving at an agreement was not going to be easy. Sarnoff and Stanton had each offered a carefully hedged eight hours of time to each of the candidates, provided the Section 315 suspension were approved. The representatives of the candidates opened the meeting by requesting further information regarding the offers of free time. It was obvious that the prospect of tying down three or four hours on major networks without having to go to the campaign treasury to pay for it was an enticing possibility. It did not take clairvoyance to recognize that they were aiming to hold plans for the confrontations hostage to the possibility of free time. Those of us on the network side carefully explained that the offers made by Stanton and Sarnoff depended on acceptance of the invitation for at least four debates. After the debates were approved, the candidates would be invited to participate in regularly scheduled network discussion programs. We placed heavy stress on the words "regularly scheduled." The time was not available, we explained patiently, to the candidates to use as they saw fit. Only after making our point abundantly clear were we able to settle down to discussion of debate.

The meeting turned out to be productive. At its conclusion we issued a joint communiqué agreeing that debates were desirable. Representatives of the two candidates would examine schedules and "determine the number of such joint appearances that may be feasible and at what places and at what times they can meet together." It was also noted that any specific decisions depended on favorable action by the House on S. J. 207. No date was set for a follow-up meeting. It would take two or three weeks for the candidates' advisers to complete scheduling campaign travel. Without detailed itineraries, it was virtually impossible to set specific dates and places for the joint appearances. The House would also have to approve the Section 315 suspension before we could be certain that our efforts would not be futile. The delay was fine for me, because I was booked to leave for Rome on August 17 to oversee preparations for covering the 1960 Olympics, for which CBS had exclusive rights in the United States.

I returned from Rome on August 28 to learn that the House had passed S. J. 207 a few days earlier and that a follow-up to the August 9 meeting had been scheduled to take place in a suite in the Mayflower Hotel in Washington on August 31. On arrival in the low-ceilinged suite on the hotel's mezzanine, I discovered that the composition of the group was somewhat changed. Reinsch was now accompanied by Ted Sorenson, later a member of the White House staff and a close adviser to President Kennedy. Leonard Hall and Carroll Newton had dropped from the Nixon ranks but Scribner, Klein, and Rogers were present. McAndrew had replaced Bernstein for NBC, Daly was present for ABC, and Steven McCormick was representing Mutual.

The session opened almost exactly as the August 9 meeting had. Scribner and Reinsch were again asking how the free hours were to be allocated. As at our first meeting, we explained patiently that any grant of additional hours would be predicated (a) on reaching agreement concerning at least four debates and (b) having it understood that any additional hours would be made available in programs that were part of our regular schedule and over which we had editorial and production control. It took some time before our adversaries apparently decided that we could not be budged from our firm position. After approximately an hour of futile discussion, Scribner asked the network representatives to leave the room for a few minutes but to stay close enough to be available to return on call.

As the four of us stood in the corridor waiting to be recalled, we wondered whether we had overplayed our hand, whether we might come back to be told that if there were no free time, there would be no debates. If that came to pass, I was concerned as to how Frank Stanton, who had worked for eight years to bring the debates to fruition, would react. We did not have long to fret. After approximately 15 minutes, we were summoned back into the room. Scribner withdrew a sheet of paper from a file. Working from the notes in his hand, he began to outline a procedure for arranging and producing four debates. Apparently we had won the first skirmish.

This did not mean that the battle was over. It was evident, though, that the biggest hurdle had been surmounted. We had agremeent in principle, approved by both candidates, that they would debate. The rival camps had gone so far as to agree on dates and places for four debates and on the subjects that would be discussed in each.

We could find no fault with the proposed schedule. The first debate would take place in Chicago on September 26; the second, originating on both coasts, on October 13; and the final one in New York on October 21. A fourth joint appearance was proposed for October 8, but both parties were squeamish about locking in that date because ABC had a football game booked for 5 P.M. that day. A runover into debate time could cause untold embarrassment. Football fans could become violent if a close game were cut off in the concluding minutes. Conversely, it would be difficult to explain to millions of less rabid football enthusiasts that a presidential debate is being delayed to permit viewers to watch the final minutes of a football game. With only this single question still unresolved, the proposed schedule was approved. Agreement on the topics for discussion in the first and last debates came with no argument. Domestic policy would be the subject of the opening encounter; foreign policy, of the final.

Agreement on a format was more troublesome. For the first and last of the encounters, the candidates' representatives proposed that the program open with 8-to-10-minute statements from each candidate, followed by 30 to 34 minutes of questioning by a panel of reporters, and winding up with 2-to3-minute summations. The second program would consist wholly of questioning by a media panel. If it was decided to risk the football runover and go ahead with the October 8 encounter, it, too, would be based exclusively on a question-and-answer format. The inclusion of a panel of reporters and the press conference format was troublesome to the network representatives. All four of us were committed to insisting on genuine debate. The addition of the media panels, we felt, would constitute an intrusion. But we had to ask ourselves how strongly we could make our case. If we remained absolutely committed to traditional debate, would we jeopardize the whole plan? We finally knuckled under. It seemed more important to assure that the debates take place, even if we did not fully approve of the format, than to risk scuttling the whole venture.

There were a number of other points on which we felt we had to give in. We thought, for example, that a highly respected national leader, such as a university president or a prominent jurist, should serve as chairman. Reinsch and Scribner insisted that it be a television journalist. Their argument was that a journalist would be less inclined to favor one candidate or the other. Even a highly respected public figure, they felt, would inevitably carry his prejudices with him. A respected journalist, to the contrary, would be more inclined to nonpartisanship. We gave in. Since the decision reflected favorably on our personnel, we did it with some enthusiasm.

Another issue was less easy to solve. The negotiators for the candidates insisted that there be print reporters on the panels. We insisted on broadcast personnel only. After prolonged discussion we reached a shaky compromise. The panels in the first and fourth confrontations would be drawn only from the broadcasting networks. The second and third panels would be composed of two representatives from print and two from broadcasting. That decision settled one aspect of the controversy, but there was still one sticky point remaining. They insisted that we select the print personnel. We resisted. We refused to risk taking the blame from the print media for making the selections. There was too much rivalry between print and broadcast journalism to think we would not be subjected to outraged criticism from publications whose personnel failed to be selected. We argued that picking the print reporters was a job for the press secretaries of the two candidates. We thought, as we left, that we had won our point, but it was actually not until almost two weeks later, when I met in San Francisco with Herb Klein, that the issue was settled in accord with our wishes. Klein and Pierre Salinger, representing Senator Kennedy, would each select one print journalist from among those traveling with the candidate for each of the two debates.

In retrospect, these seem to be trivial points of contention. None seems to be of sufficient significance to justify bitter and protracted argument. As representatives of the networks, we were living with constant fear that an impasse on any issue might offer an excuse for one of the candidates to withdraw. We were committed to bringing them together, and in our judgment it was better to yield on some relatively minor point than to jeopardize the entire series.

There were other less significant but nagging problems that continued to demand time and attention, but only one was of major concern. A number of special interest groups pressured hard to have representatives of their organizations included on the panels. Neither political party wanted to take a stand on the issue. They did not want to offend any group that might possibly deliver votes, no matter how small its constituency, so it was left up to us to reject their demands. We felt it essential that the panelists be interrogators, not special pleaders. We felt that if special interest groups were represented on the panels, the interrogation process would degenerate into arguments between panelists and candidates. We were able to hold our ground. We were certain that the candidates were thankful that we did.

What eventually appeared on the air was a hybrid. It was certainly not debate in the formal sense of the word. But we did succeed in getting two candidates onto the same screen at the same time, the first time it had ever happened in American history. More than 100 million Americans saw some part of the four debates. A substantial number told pollsters that the debates had contributed significantly toward helping them make up their minds on how to vote.

The first debate, in Chicago on September 26, was considered so significant that it was commemorated at an anniversary dinner 25 years later in the same studio 1 at WBBM-TV. Leonard Reinsch and Herb Klein were there, as were Don Hewitt, who produced and directed the program, and Lou Dorfsman, who designed the set. Of the network negotiators, I was the only one present. Both ABC and CBS recognized the anniversary by devoting special segments of talk programs to interviews with participants in the protracted negotiating and planning process.

Long after the suspension of Section 315 for the duration of the 1960 campaign had been written into law, Congress finally amended the law to permit presidential debates within certain prescribed rules. The legislation was approved in time for the scheduling of presidential debates in 1976, after a lapse of 16 years. The networks, however, played no role. The enabling legislation specified that arrangements would have to be made, and the debate programs produced, by organizations other than the networks. The League of Women Voters accepted the challenge and became the producing agency in the next four presidential elections.

President Eisenhower's press secretary, James Hagerty, turned out to be dead wrong when he told CBS's Lew Shollenberger after the conclusion of the 1960 series, "You can bet your bottom dollar that no incumbent president will ever engage in any such debate or joint appearance in the future."[3] It is true that there was a 16-year hiatus, but history also records that President Gerald Ford debated with his democratic opponent, Jimmy Carter, in 1976; President Jimmy Carter with candidate Ronald Reagan in 1980; President Ronald Reagan with candidate Walter Mondale in 1984; and Vice-President George Bush with Michael Dukakis in 1988. Perhaps my view of the future was at least moderately more accurate when, after the first debate in 1960, I boldly insisted that no candidate in the future would be able to turn down an invitation to debate. I did not count on the intransigence of Lyndon Johnson and Richard Nixon, or perhaps I was mesmerized by the euphoric atmosphere in studio 1 at WBBM-TV when I made that glib comment to a WBBM-TV reporter. Even though debate has now become a standard feature of the presidential campaign, I am not sure I would be quite as confident today, even in view of the willingness of Ford and Reagan, as sitting presidents, to confront their opponents on the debate platform. We discovered in 1960 that there are too many points at which disagreement might scuttle the whole plan to bet very heavily on continuation of presidential debates every four years.

NOTES

1. The full text of all four debates has been printed in a number of volumes dealing with the series. The quotation cited here is in the CBS transcript that I have in my files. The manner in which history can sometimes become garbled is illustrated

in the volume *The Great Debates*, ed. Sidney Kraus (Bloomington: Indiana University Press, 1962). In a chapter titled "Production Diary of the Great Debates," written by Herbert A. Seltz and Richard Yoakum, there is the following statement on page 90: "Mickelson was in the studio, and there was only one hitch in the plan. There was no way to tell moderator Smith how much time was left, and Mickelson shouted it to him when Smith asked for time, which may have been the only unplanned moment in the entire four debates. . . . " Since the microphone on my desk went live on cue, it did not take much shouting to get the message to Smith (and to the listeners and viewers).

2. The "great debates" had been researched as thoroughly as any program ever broadcast on television. *The Great Debates* includes several chapters analyzing the size of the audience, audience reaction, and effects. The data I have used were compiled by the CBS Television audience research department.

3. Memo from James Hagerty to Lewis Shollenberger, dated December 23, 1960. Copy in my files.

10

The Numbers Game

Correspondent James Reston of the *New York Times* created his own oracle at Delphi in the early 1950s. He named it Uniquac. For a change of pace in his regular column, he frequently sought Uniquac's counsel concerning weighty governmental problems. Uniquac responded to his serious questions regarding public policy with tongue-in-cheek replies that made eminently good sense. They were usually delivered with a touch of sardonic humor.

Uniquac was not wholly a figment of Reston's imagination. It was created out of CBS's use in covering the 1952 election of a computer called Univac, made by Remington Rand's Eckert-Mauchly division in Philadelphia. It was one of the few computers in being at that time, and as such was still a novelty. Reston's attention was called to Univac by its performance in projecting probable voting results in CBS's election night coverage on November 4, 1952. Projections from Univac on the presidential race were broadcast at regular intervals, starting at a little past 9 P.M. EST, while polls were still open in the Pacific time zone.

Reston was clearly chiding CBS, but the chiding was gentle. He was obviously fascinated by the introduction of the new technology for the purpose of adding interest to the reporting of returns. Uniquac was a convenient device for commenting on serious public affairs with tongue in cheek.

The use of Univac by CBS came about almost by chance. Election coverage plans had been pretty well completed when, during early August, three months prior to the election, one of the staff members in the CBS Television news department, Paul Levitan, returned from lunch in a state of high excitement. He burst into my office with stars in his eyes. He had just finished lunching with a public relations representative of Remington Rand. His excitement was generated by an offer he had received to supplement our broadcasting of election night returns by using a device that would enable us to predict the outcome of the election at an early hour, while polls were still open in many states. The device, called Univac, he was assured, could produce accurate projections, provided we could deliver the essential raw material to create a data base and a competent programmer could be found to use our data base to write a program. It was up to us to deliver the raw material. If we could, in the short time remaining, gather sufficient pertinent statistical information from previous elections to create a solid data base, we would have the basic component for a dramatic innovation. All that would be needed then would be to feed a steady flow of returns to the computer on election night.

If the parts meshed properly and the program was properly written, we could in all probability announce the winner of the presidential race while our competitors were still floundering in a sea of unsorted data. The novelty value of using Univac was certain to attract attention from both viewers and the print media. "Computer" was hardly a household word at that time. The Univac whose use we had been offered was a very early model and one of very few data processors in existence at that time.

I knew just enough about computers to know that they could perform mathematical miracles. I was also aware of the promotional shot in the arm that the use of the device would give to our coverage. It was a highly promotable tool and might give us the additional top spin that we needed to build our ratings to a level that would permit us to fight it out on even ground with the (at that time) far larger NBC.

The only Univac unit in existence then was at the Eckert-Mauchly factory in North Philadelphia. Not much could be gained by looking at a computer. There was little that could be seen, but since the experts who knew the machine's capabilities and understood the intricacies involved in writing programs were in Philadelphia, it was obvious that a Philadelphia trip was in order, and soon. In a few days we were on a train headed for the Eckert-Mauchly facility. The machine was a monster, a mass of electronic vacuum tubes interconnected by miles of copper wire and cooled by noisy fans. Its rate of speed and storage capacity were at a level comparable with a desktop PC today, but its bulk was enormous. This was before transistors, integrated circuits, and miniaturization.

A mathematician from the University of Pennsylvania, Max Woodbury, was on hand to discuss Univac's capabilities with us. Woodbury was one of a handful of American scientists who had acquired experience in computer programming. He was available to write the election night program if we wished him to do so. The challenge to us was to unearth enough raw material to enable him to create a reasonable base from which to make projections.

We had briefed Charles Collingwood of the correspondent staff that we would like to use him as Univac's interlocutor. Collingwood arrived late at the factory. He was immediately ushered to the console consisting of a keyboard and a Teletype printer that delivered hard-copy printouts of the computer's messages. The printer instantly began to tap out the message "Collingwood, you are late. Where have you been?" Collingwood and the machine established instant rapport. That simplified one of our problems. It was essential that the correspondent assigned to the feature have a sympathetic attitude toward the experiment.

If we were going to use Univac, we had to decide quickly how we would treat it. We could take it seriously and offer election projections as serious news reports. If we did so, we would run the risk of being ridiculed for preferring the output of a machine to that of the human mind. Even worse, if the machine balked or its output was patently in error, we could be subjected to unmerciful criticism. We could go a step further and make it the centerpiece of our coverage. That would greatly increase the risk and make us a laughingstock if for any reason it failed. Or we could slough it off as a gimmick and risk the loss of any benefit it might deliver.

We decided to humanize it, to treat it gently and semihumorously but at the same time give full attention to the data it would produce. That would minimize the risk and would also appease an audience that we speculated might not yet be ready for overly rich doses of high technology. We believed in it, not as a supernatural phenomenon but as a mathematical and statistical aid. We realized that it could accomplish more in seconds than our battery of manual counters could do in hours and, if we delivered the right data to Max Woodbury, could in fact give us reliable data for calling the election earlier than one had ever been called before. Furthermore, in Collingwood we had just the talent who knew how to use a soft touch without degrading the results. His obvious warm relationship with the machine would help deliver the mood we were seeking.

Our decision was to accept the offer. Remington Rand would furnish the Univac and employ Dr. Woodbury to write the program. We would deliver the raw material that Woodbury needed for his program-writing chore.

Woodbury's assignment was not an easy one. No election data were available in a form directly applicable to computer programming. There was no data storage center from which we could draw. The only data we had directly available were acetate disks of the 1944 and 1948 CBS election coverage. We were fairly certain, though, of being able to acquire access to the half-hourly reports that the Associated Press and the United Press delivered to their clients on election nights in 1944 and 1948. This information was hardly infallible. Massive population shifts involved in the migration to the suburbs following the end of the war and the changing of poll closing times in some states made some of our data suspect. But it was

the best we could do in the three months available. We thought it worth a
try. Woodbury also thought there was a reasonable chance it would work.

I wanted to add another set of data, but time did not permit. If we had
had the time, I wanted to obtain data from a number of carefully selected
precincts and match 1952 results there against the two previous elections.
This additional study would have helped to verify Univac's main projections
and furnish additional data on specific regions. It would also have pointed
the way to more sophisticated uses of computer technology in subsequent
elections. It would have enabled us to analyze regional differences and would
have furnished a base for noting regional and local deviations from previous
years. We made a list of some 40 precincts in key areas from which we
intended to gather data regarding past elections. We then planned to assign
to those districts poll watchers whose assignment would be to call in returns
as soon as they were available. These figures would be matched with previous returns, thus pinpointing the extent of shifts in specific areas. But we
could not do it all the first time around, so we had to be content with the
larger project. This type of election research for broadcast projections became commonplace later, but in 1952 it was a matter of plowing new ground
in a time span that was too brief to allow it.

It turned out that no such detailed data, no matter how useful it might
have been in adding depth to our coverage, was essential to achieving our
main goal: delivering a nationwide projection. By 8:30 P.M. EST, Univac's
initial projection declared that Eisenhower would likely defeat Stevenson
in a landslide. The odds on an Eisenhower victory, according to Univac,
were 100 to 1. The electoral vote, Univac projected, would show 438 for
Eisenhower and 93 for Stevenson. This first Univac forecast was remarkably
accurate. The final electoral vote count showed 442 for Eisenhower and 89
for Stevenson, an error of approximately 0.80 percent.[1]

There was only one hitch. Dr. Woodbury, Univac's programmer, was
suspicious of the results. He had been reading news reports forecasting a
close race and was nervous about making a big mistake. So he decided to
withhold results of the first run and try a second one with some new
correction factors added in. In the process he inadvertently added an extra
zero to Adlai Stevenson's total in New York state. An extra zero may seem
harmless, but it can have a profound impact on election results.

It was 9 o'clock by the time the second projection, including the error
in the Stevenson total, had been transmitted from lower Park Avenue and
arrived at the election studio in Grand Central Station. It showed Eisenhower a probable victor, but no longer by a landslide. Odds in his favor
were listed at 8 to 7.

Fifteen minutes later the mistake had been corrected. Odds were returned
to 100 to 1, and Univac's prediction of the electoral vote almost perfectly
matched the eventual official result. Not only was it uncanny in its accuracy
on the electoral college vote, but it was equally close to the mark on the

overall results. At 8:30 P.M. Univac had projected Eisenhower's probable popular vote total at 32,915,000. The official canvass eventually gave him 33,936,252, an error of a trifle more than 3 percent.[2] It is too easy to credit Univac with this uncanny accuracy. Obviously it was Max Woodbury who was the genius behind Univac's success. It was he who wrote the program. Univac only did the calculations.

Some complaints against computers and projections were heard almost immediately after election night. A few critics were irritated that Univac forecast an Eisenhower victory while voters were still going to the polls in the western states. Others seemed to be suspicious of any mechanical device. Charles Collingwood's gentle and somewhat amused treatment of Univac's output surely helped to soften any major surge of criticism. What negative carping there was, was mild compared with the barrage of outraged complaints that followed the bolder, sometimes presumptuous use of computerized projections in subsequent election years.

We used Univac again in the congressional elections of 1954 and 1958, and the presidential election in 1956. Results of the congressional exercise were disappointing. We found Univac not to be very useful in trying to project the anticipated composition of the House of Representatives and the Senate. Our data bases were too small to yield meaningful results, and there was too much variation in the timing from precinct to precinct of the counting of ballots to provide any uniformity in reporting. We were able, however, to provide solid projections in major races, particularly those for the Senate in the more populous states in the eastern and central time zones. The presidential race of 1956 was a cinch. The data stored from 1952 and the experience gained, coupled with the big Eisenhower majority, made projecting results a snap.

By 1956 we were no longer alone in the computer projection field. NBC had formed an alliance with IBM, and ABC with Burroughs. Shortly after the 1958 election, it became evident that NBC would shift to computers made by its parent corporation, RCA. This gave us an opening that we had been waiting for. In 1952 Univac had the field more or less to itself. By 1958 IBM had become the computer giant. Remington Rand had been relegated to a secondary position. A CBS-IBM relationship was a logical step, and agreement was consummated in short order during the spring of 1959.[3]

In 1952 and 1956 the objectives for using computers were uncomplicated. The sole purpose was to deliver early projections of returns. The election in 1960 provided the first real test of both computers and programmers in reaching for far more complicated results. That year furnished the first demonstration of what the computer could do when coupled with skilled reporting to add breadth and depth to election coverage.

As the primaries got under way, IBM had just introduced its model 7090, the biggest, fastest, and most powerful unit then available, one that exceeded many times over the capability of the 1952 Univac. As was the case with Univac, the 7090 was too large to install in an office. It had been assembled in a specially equipped basement room in the new Time & Life Building in Manhattan. The new high-speed data processor gave us the capability of reaching far beyond the simplistic projection of national returns. It would enable us to undertake new efforts to pry into voters' minds to determine why they voted as they did, and whether there were any voting patterns in evidence that would give us a better picture of the electorate. The Wisconsin primary would provide a good starting point. With guidance from Elmo Roper, the widely-known expert in public opinion polling, we decided to try a special, real-time analysis of the results of the Wisconsin primary in April of that year. We contracted with a pair of widely recognized Columbia University social scientists, Bernard Berelson and William McPhee, to develop a program that would use the speed and power of the 7090 to furnish a profile of voter attitudes and behavior before all the votes had been counted. With Roper's assistance, a program was designed that would provide a running analysis of the behavior of voters with varied ethnic, cultural, financial, and religious backgrounds. If successful, the results would give us a clue regarding voter preferences broken down by occupation, economic status, religious preference, and section of the state in which they resided. The religious question was of particular interest because of Senator Kennedy's Roman Catholic faith and the fact that the nation had never elected a Catholic to the presidency. The project amounted to an attempt to draw a detailed voter profile before the ballot counting was finished.

It can't be said that the program ran smoothly. Berelson and McPhee were reluctant to release data without checking and rechecking it in a traditional academic manner. CBS personnel clamored for the evidence so that it could be released while viewers were still watching.

The results were not earth-shattering, but they did pinpoint the importance of religion as an issue. The data were quite clear in demonstrating that Kennedy ran strongly among Catholic voters, even among members of organized labor who were thought to favor his opponent, Senator Hubert Humphrey. It was anticipated that he would do well among German Catholic farmers in the prosperous Fox River valley. It was surprising, however, that he also ran strongly in the labor-dominated Polish Catholic precincts in and around Milwaukee. Humphrey succeeded in building up strong majorities only in poorer rural areas in northwest Wisconsin adjacent to his home state of Minnesota and populated largely by Protestants, many of them of Norwegian descent. Humphrey's mother was Norwegian.

No one previously had been able to deliver so detailed an analysis so quickly after the polls had been closed. The Kennedy forces, who should have been pleased, were apparently upset that religion had been pinpointed as an issue. Shortly after arriving at my office the next morning, I picked up my phone to answer a call from Robert Kennedy. It was clear that he was furious about our coverage, which I defended. After a few minutes I heard an abrupt "I guess I can't get any satisfaction from you," followed by a click as the instrument was slammed down.[4]

The test in Wisconsin was primitive by later standards, but it gave solid proof that we were on the frontier of employing new methodologies for anlayzing voter behavior patterns while the ballot counting was still in progress.

The 7090 clearly outdid Univac's 1952 performance in delivering an early and accurate forecast shortly after counting of ballots began on election night, November 2, 1960. At 8:12 P.M. EST it forecast that Kennedy would receive 51 percent of the popular vote to Nixon's 49, and 297 electroal votes to Nixon's 240.[5] The final count showed an error of only 0.50 percent. Kennedy received 50.5 percent to Nixon's 49. The actual Kennedy electoral vote turned out to be 303 rather than the 297 forecast, an error of six out of 538.[6] Odds on Kennedy winning were established by the computer projection at 11 to 5. This prediction was made while polls were still open in the mountain and Pacific time zones, and even some in the central zone had not closed. There might have been a temptation to trumpet the results to the nation at this point by announcing "CBS declares that John F. Kennedy will be the next president of the United States." The decision, however, was to report the projection as an early indicator in a contest that probably would ultimately be decided by a razor-thin margin. It was not until midmorning the next day that we were sufficiently confident to declare Kennedy the winner.

The use of the 7090 brought a benefit to the coverage that may have been of considerably greater importance than forecasting the national vote. It enabled us to break more new ground by analyzing in detail voter patterns in smaller election districts. We were now developing the resources that would enable us to do what we had hoped for in 1952 but were prevented from accomplishing by lack of personnel and facilities. The Wisconsin experience had proved that running analyses of returns in specific areas was now within our power. One of the pivotal states in the 1960 election would certainly be Ohio. It was obvious that the contest between Vice-President Nixon and Senator Kennedy would be close. Ohio would be a critically important battleground whose electoral vote count might swing the election either way. Cuyahoga County, dominated by Cleveland, usually reported early and recorded a heavy Democratic majority. It would be easy to be trapped into an assumption of an impending Democratic victory if the early Cuyahoga returns were to be interpreted as indicative of the way the state would vote. With the help of IBM programmers and Elmo Roper, a number of representative Ohio election districts were selected for an especially detailed election night study. Reporters were assigned to phone in returns from these districts as soon as they were available.

As expected, Cuyahoga County piled up an early substantial lead for Democratic candidate Kennedy. It looked very much like a Democratic sweep in the making. Results from the selected precincts, though, told an entirely different story. They warned us that not only was Nixon running strongly in the selected precincts, but perhaps strongly enough to overcome the early Cuyahoga County majority. When all the polling places had closed, our private analysis predicted that Richard Nixon would probably be the winner. Although Nixon subsequently lost the election, after playing catch-up most of the night, he did win Ohio. Our program enabled us to escape a trap.

Imaginative programming and the astonishing speed of the computer in solving mathematical problems had demonstrated in both Wisconsin and Ohio that paper-and-pencil calculations were going the way of the horse and buggy. More sophisticated uses of statistical probability analyses based on the speed and memory of the computer were yet to come, but the IBM 7090 and the programs it was given demonstrated that there was more to be learned from early returns than numerical results. Two years later the analytical process would be given a fancy and promotable new title, Voter Profile Analysis or VPA. VPA had the advantage of faster computers, bigger staffs, much higher budgets, and stronger companywide support, but essentially it only carried the work from Ohio and Wisconsin a step further.

The 1960 election was the last national contest in which reporting of returns was to be characterized by dog-eat-dog competition among wire services, broadcasters, and some of the larger newspapers. Historically, the collection and reporting of election returns had relied primarily on the nationwide reporting and transmission capabilities of the two American wire services, the Associated Press and United Press International. Wire service output, though, had been geared largely to the requirements of their newspaper clients. This might include furnishing the raw material for an extra edition of a morning newspaper, but it was hardly adequate for radio and television. By the 1950s, too, "extras" were a virtually extinct species. Broadcasters needed and demanded constant updating. Their deadlines were not restricted to one or two printed editions. They were constant. They needed returns that would flow in an unending stream. They could not wait for returns designed to meet the needs of a morning paper.

The wire service structure was geared to filing from state election headquarters to regional headquarters and finally to the main east-west trunk. This meant that returns from Idaho, for example, might languish in a regional bureau in Seattle before being relayed on to San Francisco, where there could be another delay before the returns found their way onto the trunk line to New York. This awkward procedure met newspaper needs but rankled network news executives, who chafed at the delays. They wanted returns, and they wanted them quickly.

Paul White, the CBS News chief during the 1940s, discovered a way to circumvent the tedious process. He used news directors from CBS-owned radio stations as regional expediters. The news directors recruited observers to be stationed in wire service bureaus in all the state capitals. The observers called returns to the newsrooms of the CBS-owned stations, which in turn relayed them to network headquarters. The process thus gained valuable minutes by bypassing the slow and sometimes lackadaisical wire service procedure.[7]

By 1960 the vote counting and reporting procedure had turned into a hodgepodge. The networks were competing with each other and with the wire services. Returns were being intermingled indiscriminately. A network might use AP returns in one state, UPI in another, and its own data in a third, whichever was highest and thus was likely to furnish the highest overall count. This is the system we used during five elections at CBS. I rationalized the unscientific behavior by assuming that the direction of the balloting was more important than the specific vote count. If Eisenhower was running ahead of Stevenson in both UPI and Associated Press counts, and the UPI totals were higher, use UPI. Otherwise, AP. The system was dangerous, but luck was with us. No single race was so close that our gamble made any real difference.

By 1962 newspapers began to notice that the broadcast networks were consistently running minutes ahead, and sometimes millions of votes ahead, of the wire services. After the 1964 California primary, in which the AP was still declaring Nelson Rockefeller the winner over Barry Goldwater even after Goldwater had been confirmed as the winner by the networks, the wire services and the three broadcasting networks met to discuss creating a cooperative vote-counting agency. Shortly afterward the National Election Service was born. NES established machinery to furnish a quick running account to all its subscribers, thus also protecting the newspapers, all of which were clients of one or both wire services. The new service was activated in time to furnish its organizing members full service for the fall election of 1964.

With the National Election Service in being, the networks were able to concentrate their efforts on fine tuning their own vote-count projection systems. The quickest results came from exit polls. Network representatives queried voters leaving polling places. They asked a variety of questions concerning attitudes toward election issues and usually slipped in one question about how the respondent had voted. The system was dangerous. There was no certainty that the answers, particularly the one regarding the respondent's vote, accurately reflected the vote actually cast. The sample had to be a random one. There was no way to pick a selected sample. By using exit polls, however, the networks were able to call results with some degree of assurance before the polls had closed in the state at issue.

Public protest regarding the use of computers and projections began to grow rapidly in intensity and volume, in direct proportion to the increased use of exit polls and the boasts of network commentators. Some persons simply did not think it was fair to announce results of an election before all the votes had been counted. The foreshortening of the time required to announce what purported to be definitive results stirred up a raging storm of protest. The first crisis point was reached in August 1964, three months before the presidential election. A bill was introduced in the U. S. Senate that would order the broadcasting networks and other news-gathering agencies to "refrain from broadcasting or distributing predictions based on electronic computations . . . until after the latest official closing time of any polling place."[8] The resolution spurred debate but failed to pass. I could not help but think what a tempest our Univac had spawned during its short exposure 12 years earlier.

The most jarring repercussion came six years later, in 1980. NBC had proudly declared at 8:15 P.M. EST on election night that Ronald Reagan had been elected president of the United States. It was only 5:15 P.M. on the Pacific Coast when the announcement was made, only 6:15 in the mountain states. Defeated candidate Jimmy Carter compounded the problem when he conceded the election to Reagan shortly afterward. There was not any question which way the presidential election was going. Reagan was clearly going to be a big winner. One did not need a Univac or an IBM 7090 to arrive at that conclusion, but losing candidates who had run for lesser offices, particularly in the Pacific time zone, were indignant.

Many of them complained that their supporters gave up when they learned that Reagan had won, and failed to go to their polls. Their losses, they charged, were due at least in part to the early announcement that the presidential contest was settled. Washington state soon took action. Its legislature passed a law restricting exit polls by declaring that no voter could be approached within 300 feet of the polling place. The networks sought to soften complaints by promising not to declare states won or lost on the basis of exit polls, and to withhold projections of winners in any given state until all polls in that state had closed. The Washington state law has since been declared unconstitutional by a U. S. federal court, as have similar statutes in four other states, but the controversy shows no sign of abating.

The networks themselves brought on much of the barrage of protest. They established "decision desks" or "call desks," and proceeded to declare in pompous tones that "Network XYZ declares that candidate X is the winner in the race for the Senate in the state of Z." Beating the opposition became so obsessive a passion that rational judgment lost out to competitive fervor. Much of the problem stemmed from the tone of the pronouncement. It would have been just as easy to say, "On the basis of a careful analysis of the returns now in hand—and they are still by no means complete—it appears likely that candidate X will win." The difference may be slight, but the manner and tone are several degrees milder and reflect none of the adolescent puffery that goes with the sonorous declaration.

Legislation is obviously not the way to solve any problem that may exist. Information does not pay attention to state boundaries or time zones. It may be possible to embargo fruit or vegetables, but no inspector can be stationed at the state line to confiscate information that has been proscribed by state law. Satellites not only carry television and radio signals and telephone calls from coast to coast in a fraction of a second, but they also deliver plates for newspapers. Television networks might be prevented from broadcasting projections made by computers, but only at great risk of eroding the protections guaranteed by the First Amendment. Threats to suspend the licenses held by their affiliates or their owned stations could conceivably scare them into complying, but Congress would have to be concerned with the damage done to the First Amendment by such heavy-handed action. No such leverage could be exerted against newspapers or even cable TV. The First Amendment implications would surely stop Congress in its tracks. If efforts to preserve free media were abandoned by Congress and the courts, and all media were prohibited from publishing projections of election returns, those returns could still move across the country by telephone.

The fact is that projection of election returns based on early and fragmentary voting is not a new phenomenon. It has been going on for as long as the media have been covering elections. It was the introduction of electronic communications media that focused attention on the issue. Editions of any single newpaper were so few that published predictions of election victory or defeat were relatively limited. Radio, however, added an entirely new dimension. Starting as early as the 1920s, stations remained on the air constantly while ballots were being counted. The predictions of radio analysts were frequently made on the basis of fragmentary returns long before polls were closed. Newspapers were a less obvious target. Their limited number of editions reduces the temptation to go out on a limb even though their political experts could have done so with a high degree of accuracy and without the help of computers.

Mistakes, however, are not entirely unknown. The nation has never been permitted to forget the front-page banner headline in the *Chicago Tribune* the morning after the 1948 presidential election. The headline announced "Dewey Beats Truman." This was done despite returns showing that President Truman was leading by a slight margin. CBS went off the air at 3 A.M. the morning after the election, convinced that Dewey had won. Both CBS and the *Tribune* were projecting results without the aid of computers before all the votes had been counted, even though polls had closed before the mistaken conclusion was reached.

Virtually every newspaper in the nation has on its staff a political reporter who is expert at forecasting election results based on fragmentary returns. He does it by using his brain, in which he has stored vast amounts of data from previous elections. Incoming returns stimulate the brain to sort and analyze the stored data and lead to conclusions concerning trends or a possible winner. That is exactly what the computer does, execpt that the computer's storage capacity and its ability to retrieve stored data relieve the human brain of much of the mechanical work.

My own quick and favorable reaction to the offer from Remington Rand for the use of the Univac in 1952 was a by-product of experience gained in Minnesota in 1944 and 1948. In preparing for election night coverage, I had noted that the Democratic-Farmer Labor Party, the product of a merger of the rather feeble Democrats with the stronger Farmer Laborites, was unlikely to win unless it was able to command between 52 and 60 percent of the vote in the state's three largest counties. I thought early returns from these three counties might give us a reliable clue reasonably early on election night to determining the possible outcome of both the presidential and the senatorial contests. In addition to the normal attention to the race for the presidency, in 1948 there was an unusually high degree of interest in the contest for a Senate seat between Mayor Hubert Humphrey of Minneapolis and Senator Joseph Ball, the Republican incumbent.

By studying state election manuals I discovered that over a period covering several elections, the Democratic-Farmer Laborites were reasonably certain to win if they received 52 percent of the votes in Hennepin County, the county of Minneapolis; between 53 and 54 percent in Ramsey County, site of St. Paul, and approximately 57 percent in St. Louis county, including its largest city, Duluth. As a double check I examined records in some election districts along the southern border of the state. There I discovered that in that prosperous agricultural area, Republican totals frequently ran as high as 85 or 90 percent. I assumed that if there were consistent deviations from this pattern at an early hour, we would at least have a reliable indicator of the possible outcome.

The key to making the system work was to collect early returns from the three big counties and the handful of small districts as quickly as possible. The operation, even though it was somewhat haphazard and had no computer support, was a smashing success. Hennepin, Ramsey, and St. Louis counties from the beginning were showing a Democratic vote that consistently ran well above the minimums normally required for victory. In the strongly Republican southern districts, both Truman and Humphrey were running far ahead of the 10 to 15 percent of the electorate that had been the norm for Democratic candidates. With this analysis in hand, it was relatively easy to suggest early in the evening that Minnesota was likely to produce a major upset in the presidential race and that Hubert Humphrey stood an excellent chance of unseating Joe Ball. Abnormally strong Democratic showings in Iowa and South Dakota confirmed that a Democratic tide that had not been anticipated by the national experts was clearly apparent in the Middle West. This was all done without the aid of a computer. A computer would have speeded the process and provided a little more confidence in the mathematical calculations, but otherwise the process would have been identical.

After four decades of television's reliance on computers to enhance election night coverage, the broadcasting of projections is still controversial. It was those pretentious proclamations of victory or defeat while the polls were still open that stimulated the barrage of complaints. Even though it all started with Univac, the problem is not the computer. The computer in itself is simply a number cruncher. If there is a culprit, it is television. Television adopted the computer, focused attention on it, gave it status as a miracle worker, and promoted it as the oracle that predicts how elections will turn out. Its excesses in promoting its computer-assisted feats of forecasting returns stimulated the chorus of complaints. It is those excesses, not the computer itself, that should be the real target of the critics.

The effect might not have been quite as controversial had it not been for the fact that television is intrinsically an entertainment instrument attuned more to show business than to information delivery. Projections of possible winners or the results of exit polls, processed by computers and delivered by nationally acclaimed personalities on the television screen, automatically become components in a television drama. Neither radio or newspapers could ever approach the dramatic impact generated by television. In that sense, the numbers game, with its voter profiles, exit polls, and boastful predictions of victory or loss, is a product of television, aided and abetted by the computer. The computer was destined to become an essential tool of television anyway, but perhaps we gave the critics a head start by introducing Univac as early as 1952.

NOTES

1. *World Almanac* (New York: Pharos Books, 1987), p. 306.
2. Ibid.
3. The new relationship very quickly yielded a significant by-product that was totally unrelated to producing election night programs. The 1960 Winter Olympics were scheduled to be held at Squaw Valley, California, in February. IBM had arranged to furnish a service to the U. S. Olympic Committee that would employ IBM equipment and personnel to time events and compute scores. ABC had already contracted for rights to cover the event on an exclusive basis. During July 1959, Paul Levitan and I traveled to San Francisco en route to San Jose, to meet a number of IBM executives who would be concerned with our election coverage. The plan was to spend a day at the IBM facility in San Jose, where much of the planning for the 1960 election coverage would be done. On the way to San Jose from the San Francisco airport, I asked Gil Ahlborn, who was directing the Winter Olympics project for IBM, what he knew about the rumor that ABC was withdrawing from its contract. He was not certain but thought it was true. He suggested that we go to Squaw Valley the next day and see for ourselves. Within minutes after arriving

at San Jose, Ahlborn had plane reservations for Reno and had booked a rental car for the drive from Reno to Squaw Valley. The organizers would meet with us to talk about a possible contract. The upshot is that CBS ultimately bought the rights to cover the games, and our first cooperative venture with IBM turned out to be not the 1960 election but the Winter Olympics.

4. I was told subsequently that John Kennedy later called Frank Stanton to protest, and Joseph Kennedy placed a call to CBS Board Chariman William S. Paley. Neither Stanton nor Paley ever told me directly that they had received such calls.

5. I have on my desk a computer printout encased in plastic of that first projection.

6. *World Almanac*, p. 306.

7. I learned the White system well in 1944 and 1948. As news director at WCCO in Minneapolis, then owned by CBS, I was assigned Minnesota, the Dakotas, Wyoming, and Montana. My assignment was to recruit personnel to monitor returns in central collecting facilities in the five states, and ask them to relay the data to our office in Minneapolis, where we would collate it. We then fed it on by phone to New York. Similar assignments were being carried out by CBS personnel in other regions so that the entire 48 states were being covered.

8. S.Con. Res. 94, introduced August 12, 1964.

11

The Triumph of Imagery

When New York advertising agency executive Rosser Reeves strode into a private dining room at the 21 Club one night in the summer of 1952, a new era in political campaigning was about to get under way. It was to be an era that would see television rapidly becoming a dominant and frequently controversial influence for winning public support for political candidates. Reeves, a creative specialist at the Ted Bates Agency in New York, an agency noted for hard-sell tactics, arrived with storyboards in hand. He was there to convince members of the Eisenhower for President high command that they should launch a spot commercial campaign on television stations across the country. His aim was to urge the Eisenhower leadership to supplement their traditional campaign methods with a novel approach that had no precedent in presidential elections.

The audience for the Reeves presentation included Walter Williams, the chairman of the Citizens for Eisenhower organization; Sidney Weinberg, an investment banker and treasurer of the campaign organization; two more investment bankers, John Hay Whitney and Ogden White; Walter Thayer, one of Whitney's closest associates; and Robert Mullen, who had been the campaign's public relations adviser. By the time the dinner was over, Reeves had his go-ahead. It was not wholly unexpected. Whitney was the host. He had scheduled the dinner after talking at length with Reeves about the plan. Mullen says that Whitney had "stars in his eyes" as he introduced Reeves and his revolutionary approach to winning the election. His enthusiasm was apparently contagious. Support was unanimous. Once the go-ahead decision was reached, Whitney assumed the responsibility for obtaining the required funding. Reeves himself would write the commercials and oversee production.[1]

In fact, Reeves was not the first person to propose using television spot commercials. Four years earlier, in 1948, E. H. Little, chairman of the board of Colgate Palmolive, had asked the Ted Bates Agency, at which Reeves was an executive, to prepare a schedule of 60-second spots to support the Dewey campaign for the presidency. Some sample spots were produced, but Dewey rejected the proposal. His decision to reject the plan was supported by Batten, Barton, Durstine and Osborn, his agency of record.[2]

Another Eisenhower enthusiast with a communications background, Alfred Hollender, also thought that the general's campaign should not overlook the possibility of developing a spot campaign. Hollender, an advertising executive who had served as a communications officer on Eisenhower's staff during the war, had approached both the general and his brother Milton before Reeves made his presentation at 21, urging them to consider the use of spots to support the coming campaign. Both had been sufficiently intrigued by the suggestion that by the time Reeves unwrapped his storyboards, a favorable climate had already been created.

While political commercials of 60 seconds or less had no precedent on television, spot radio commercials had been employed 16 years earlier in 1936, to support Alf Landon's campaign for the presidency. Advertising agencies had been involved in politics as early as 1916. The George H. Batten Company of Buffalo, New York, a predecessor of BBDO, had placed print advertising in Charles Evans Hughes's campaign for the presidency. Advertising and politics had thus established a nodding acquaintance prior to 1952 but no firm relationship. With the advent of television that would change abruptly.

The Eisenhower spots were simple and direct. Reeves, on a six-week leave from his duties at Ted Bates, wrote them himself, using previous Eisenhower speeches and newspaper articles about the campaign as his source material. The standard format called for an off-camera announcer to open with the line "Eisenhower answers the nation!" An "ordinary citizen" on camera would then ask a question. A typical one read, "Mr. Eisenhower, what about the high cost of living?" The answer from the general, "My wife, Mamie, worries about the same thing. I tell her it's our job to change that on November 4." This rather mild approach to highlighting campaign issues is a far cry from the "attack" and "image" commercials that came into vogue with the Johnson-Goldwater campaign only 12 years later and grew in volume and acerbity from election to election thereafter.[3]

Both CBS and NBC were skittish about accepting the Eisenhower commercials for their owned and operated stations. The Bates Agency tried to place them but failed. Managements of both networks regarded them as undignified, excessively abbreviated, and only a caricature of the candidate's views. BBDO then took over the function from Bates and succeeded in convincing network management to accept the full schedule for their own stations. That step opened the gates to widespread acceptance.[4]

Reeves and General Eisenhower collaborated on 50 one-minute commercials that were placed on stations across the country at a cost of $1.5 million—a substantial sum then, a pittance now. The Democrats were either too idealistic at that point to try their hand at commercial spots or were caught asleep at the switch. Late in the campaign they caught on to the impact of the Eisenhower announcements and produced a limited schedule of their own, but it was a matter of too little and too late. Their total bill by Election Day amounted to only $77,000, a little more than 5 percent of the GOP expenditure.

It is ironic that the recommendation for the use of spot commercials did not come from one of the three agencies—BBDO, Young and Rubicam, and Kudner—that had been engaged to work on the Eisenhower campaign. Even though television was barely four years old, all three boasted extensive experience in both commercial production and political campaigning. It remains a mystery why none of them beat Rosser Reeves and Al Hollender to the punch. It may be that they too were squeamish about mixing techniques used to sell products on behalf of commercial accounts with those used for inducing voters to cast ballots for political candidates. Or perhaps they just did not think of it. Campaign staffs were still thinking in traditional terms. Agencies, too, although they were experimenting with a new technology, were generally applying that new technology to traditional campaign procedures.

It is easier to understand how it would never occur to members of the Eisenhower high command to support their candidate with the same techniques used to sell soap and cereals. They were remarkably alert to television's capacity to win support from the general public. They had demonstrated their skills in organizing the successful drive for the Eisenhower nomination at the convention. They were able to achieve a fascinating mix of fresh faces, youth, interesting and forceful speeches, and effective media relations to win the nomination. There is not even a hint, though, that any member of the high command ever gave any consideration to "commercials." It is hard to visualize the haughty patrician Henry Cabot Lodge, the disciplined General Lucius Clay, or the Wall Street-oriented investment bankers pleading enthusiastically for "I like Ike" spots prior to their eye-opening contact with Rosser Reeves.

To most Americans, television was only a remote dream when Governor Dewey opened his campaign for the presidency in 1948. The Dewey organization engaged in some minimal experimentation with telvision, but the set count was so small that it was hardly worthwhile to undertake any major effort. Dewey's campaign for the New York governorship in 1950, however, was a different story. The half-million receivers in American

homes two years earlier had grown to nearly 7 million. The largest con-
centration was in New York City, but the potential audience available in
upstate New York had reached a level that made it an attractive target.
Stations were on the air and attracting viewers in cities from Albany to
Buffalo. Furthermore, it was possible by then to order up a network extending from New York City through the larger cities across the state all
the way to Buffalo.

Dewey and his advisers, including his innovative press secretary, James
Hagerty, saw a heavily concentrated television campaign as an opportunity
well worth exploring. Ben Duffy, BBDO president, was an avid Dewey
supporter and jumped at the chance to turn his staff loose on the melding
of television and politics. Research showed a critical mass of television
homes in New York state now large enough for television to play a significant role, and BBDO was ready to mobilize its considerable talent to
campaign for the governor's reelection.

The effort was a smashing success. It delivered clear evidence that the
agency had the necessary expertise to play a significant part in the presidential election of 1952 if it were to be invited—which, as it turned out,
almost did not happen. It had the experience needed to plan and produce
speeches, interview programs, and man-in-the-street interview shows, and
to schedule statements by the governor with content attractive to news
programs. Agency personnel were conversant enough with television to
know how to schedule events and statements at a time and place where
they would be most most likely to attract camera crews. But there were
no spot commercials on the agency's agenda, and apparently little or no
thought given to them.[5]

Some agencies had plunged more deeply into the medium than others,
and as a result were better prepared to strike out into the thicket of political
advertising. Both BBDO and Young and Rubicam were pioneers. They
were industry leaders in both product advertising and program production.

Political campaigns historically had relied heavily on public relations and
publicity experts for media contacts and, through media, reaching out to
the public. Television, however, brought a new challenge, one that few
political public relations experts had dealt with except on a perfunctory
basis. The medium was far too complicated and the range of expertise
required too varied to be assigned with any real hope of success to any
single individual on the party payroll, to the staff of a candidate, or even
to a public relations firm.

The advertising agency, on the other hand, was better equipped to deal
with the wide range of campaign problems. Within its ranks it had the
required talents not only to undertake producing and placing advertising
but also to tackle general public relations and publicity assignments. It had
leadership experienced in marketing, account executives to organize both
advertising and public relations efforts, creative personnel including writers

and graphic artists to prepare copy and layout, media experts to place advertising campaigns, and research departments to test their effectiveness. In short, the television-oriented advertising agency was able to mobilize a wealth of talent, many with extensive television experience. BBDO and Young and Rubicam were among the leaders who had ventured into the political arena. Their chief executive officers were political buffs. Both were strongly committed to Eisenhower, so strongly that they were eager to work on the 1952 campaign.

It was only logical that advertising agencies would fill a campaign void. The traditional campaign organizations had neither the time nor the talent to cope with the complications inevitably arising out of the fusion of picture, sound, and motion. The vision of the old-line publicity directors was too limited to think beyond press releases and facilitating coverage by media reporters. There were exceptions. Hagerty is one. Robert Humphreys, who directed publicity for the Republican National Committe in 1952, is another. But effective use of television demanded skills and experiences that the publicity directors and campaign directors had never had the time or oppportunity to acquire.

On the other hand, the advertising agencies had stockpiled talent: account executives, producers, directors, writers, and graphic artists. They had experience in contracting for studios, facilities, cameramen, sound technicians, lighting directors, and makeup artists. Furthermore, they had media specialists to determine how and where best to place ads, and research departments to measure results. The better agencies also had personnel capable of bringing imagination and innovation to bear on planning campaigns to win elections. Even though their sphere was product advertising, not quite the same as soliciting support for a political candidate, it was close enough to attract political parties and candidates. In retrospect, it seems only logical that advertising agencies were pioneers in political campaigning on television. There was no one else available to do the job.

Rosser Reeves and his precedent-breaking spot commercial campaign for General Eisenhower made use of the agency virtually indispensable. Producing spots was complicated enough, but placing them on television stations required the expert services of sophisticated media departments to determine the most effective outlets and to negotiate favorable times and prices. It was imperative to determine where the dollars spent would yield the most votes. As the use of spots skyrocketed in subsequent elections, pressures on media departments rose exponentially. The $1,577,000 spent on commercial spots by both presidential candidates in 1952 was a pittance compared with expenditures in subsequent elections. By 1972 the figure had multiplied by approximately 15 times, to $24.6 million. By 1984 the grand total of approximately $154 million was 100 times as high as in 1952.[6]

Producing and placing television commercials was clearly not the only service advertising agencies performed for candidates. They were still concerned with print advertising, booking paid time for speeches, producing major campaign events for radio and television, and in some cases consulting on campaign strategy, but spots soon absorbed a major part of the effort.

It was obvious to anybody who was observant that there cannot be that rapid an increase in production and exposure without a decline in standards and taste. The straight, low-key, and largely factual Rosser Reeves commercials of 1952 were too good to last. It was inevitable that hard sell would intrude as more agencies and more producers entered the field. With hard sell there would surely be more emphasis on show business and communications pyrotechnics.

Television news in the 1960s, at least at the network level, was still seriously trying to inform without going overboard with showmanship. News programs at the local level, however, were beginning to show signs of softening as television homes increased to near a saturation level and dollars poured into the medium in a gushing torrent. Prospects for a bonanza of profit were so promising and competition for the big payoff so fierce that a high-minded approach would almost inevitably succumb to compromise. The infant industry of 1952 had become a mature adult in little more than a decade, and the rules of the game were changing. More stations, more television homes, more dollars, and more competition for both ratings and dollars put an increasing premium on the search for surefire, crowd-pleasing ingredients. The journalistic standards that had prevailed through the first decade were in danger of eroding.

By 1960 a new phenomenon was beginning to appear on the campaign scene, the political consultant. Political consultants were old hat in California. The Whitaker and Baxter firm had been operating since the middle 1930s. California's old-time progressivism had led to liberal use of the initiative as a process for passing legislation by popular vote, thus bypassing or overruling the legisature. All-out, high-cost campaigns for or against initiatives became commonplace. Since party organizations were only peripherally involved, if at all, citizen groups and committees were formed to support or oppose the initiatives. In many instances major corporations had large stakes in the outcome of the voting and were willing to pour vast sums into the campaigns to protect their interests. Masses of dollars were available to win over voters.

But both supporters and opponents of the propositions on the ballot needed leadership, direction, ideas, and implementation. Clem Whitaker and Leona Baxter saw an opportunity and moved in. They established a firm in San Francisco to advise on strategy, produce and place advertising, handle media relations, organize events, and do anything else required to win approval for or to defeat an initiative. They created a structure that would be a model for scores of consultant firms that would be formed later, many of them as a direct result of the capability of television to persuade voters and of the increasing willingness of news directors to accept outside aid uncritically.

Southern California did not lag far behind the San Francisco Bay area. Murray Chotiner, a Los Angeles lawyer with an avid interest in politics, became a consultant to Richard Nixon. Chotiner had worked with Nixon on campaigns for both the House and Senate, and was a key member of the Nixon for Vice-President team in 1952. In that role he played a significant part in planning for the celebrated "Checkers" speech. Later the Spencer Roberts firm in Los Angeles established a national reputation for representing a broad range of candidates.

The senior partner in a Springfield, Massachusetts, political consultant firm became a key adviser to John F. Kennedy in 1960. Lawrence F. O'Brien who had been in partnership with Joseph Napolitan in a combination real estate and public relations firm, had worked on a number of campaigns in western Massachusetts. In the late 1950s he joined an inner group of advisers supporting John F. Kennedy's 1960 campaign for the presidency. After the election he became postmaster general and later chairman of the Democratic National Committee. His partner continued as a political consultant representing Democratic candidates, including Hubert Humphrey in 1968.

By 1964, producers of political spots for television, both agency personnel and independents, had discovered that the best route to the voter's reflexes is not through his capability to reason but through his emotions, prejudices, and lingering responses to previous experiences. By the end of the 1950s, critics had begun to note that television was brilliantly effective in delivering images and symbols but was frequently striking out when it tried to convey information. The viewer was retaining the picture but quickly forgetting the facts. The impression remained, but the accompanying information was lost. Marshall McLuhan was observing that the "medium is the message." The planners and producers of spot commercials were discovering the importance of the image and the symbol. They were coming to the conclusion that it was futile to try to persuade by delivering facts and appeals to reason. They began to apply new theories to persuasion by television, depending on images rather than facts to convey messages designed to win voter support. This trend created a made-to-order opening for consultants.

Before the 1964 campaign got under way, consultants were beginning to carve out a niche for themselves. Television, they argued, posed problems that only specialists in media manipulation were adept at solving. Advertising agency staffs could boast of high competence in producing commercials, but as political campaign advisers they frequently came up short. They were skilled at selling products but not necessarily effective at manipulating ideas. Political advertising called for winning over minds to ideas, not creating impulses to buy products.

One of the best of the specialists was Tony Schwartz, a master at using symbolism and imagery on the television screen to win points without hard sell. Schwartz had unlocked the secret of molding the viewer's attitudes by appealing not to his intellect but to his emotions and prejudices. He reflected Marshall McLuhan in his description of his approach to the art of producing political commercials. His aim, he said, was to achieve "voter resonance." In so doing, his objective was to appeal to the voter's vast storehouse of attitudes, prejudices, and previous experiences, and to rekindle the many miscellaneous bits of information stored in the recesses of his mind, bits that could be useful in establishing a favorable response to an idea or a candidate or an unfavorable response to an opponent. The function of the political spot producer, in this view, is to penetrate directly to those dormant attitudes and stimulate them to action. The effective spot commercial, in Schwartz's view, should be the stimulus that "taps the resonance" of the individual voter.

Two commercials supporting the Lyndon Johnson candidacy in 1964, both products of Schwartz's fertile imagination, were so strong in their play on emotions that they were withdrawn after one showing. Johnson's opponent, Barry Goldwater, had spoken somewhat recklessly about using nuclear weapons. He had once suggested that the use of the atomic bomb in South Vietnam might hasten the end of the war. Many potential voters had learned of the senator's comments through the heavy play they received in the media, and were deeply concerned.

The first of the questionable spots showed a small girl plucking petals from a daisy. As she plucked the last petal, a nuclear bomb exploded in the background. The implication was so clear that no explanation was necessary. The message was clearly "Vote for Johnson to avoid electing a president who would be careless with the bomb."

The second was more explicit. It showed a small girl happily licking an ice cream cone. A soft and gentle woman's voice explained off camera that people used to explode atomic bombs in the air. The fallout from the bombs, she explained, made some children die. She went on to say that there was a treaty being considered that would prevent all testing in the air. It would confine it to underground sites, but a man who now wants to be president of the United States voted against the treaty when it was up for consideration in the Senate. She identified him as Senator Barry Goldwater. The clicking of a Geiger counter as it detected radiation was faded in at a low level and built to a crescendo as an off-camera voice urged, "Vote for President Johnson on November 3. The stakes are too high for you to stay home."

The Hubert Humphrey campaign four years later used the same technique. One spot opened with a title card with the question "Agnew for Vice-President?" A picture of Agnew remained on the screen for almost the full 60 seconds while an off-camera voice laughed uproariously. The tag line read, "It would be funny if it weren't so serious."

By the middle 1960s, advertising agency executives began to have second thoughts about signing on for political campaigns. Many agencies serving political accounts were becoming disenchanted with the uncertain and sporadic nature of campaign advertising. They were disturbed by the negative character of many of the commercials they saw and thought it demeaning to product advertising. Some expressed concern that voters were getting too much hard sell and not enough information on which to make informed decisions. Others argued that you cannot furnish the voters with the facts and background information required to make informed decisions about candidates for public office in 30 seconds or 60 seconds. It may be possible to sell cereals in so short a time, but candidates and ideas are quite different.

Agencies, however, had other and more persuasive reasons for getting out of the political business. A political campaign requires a prodigious amount of effort concentrated over a relatively short period of time. It devours much of the agency's most creative talent and occupies the valuable time of senior executives. In so doing it robs year-round clients of the talent and services for which they have contracted. An advertising agency is unlike a firehouse. It cannot afford to hire firemen to sit in their quarters and play cribbage while waiting for the alarm to ring. One way to stockpile personnel for a short-term campaign is to rob the existing account groups. In that event long-term clients are short changed. The alternative is to hire from the outside for the political account, but campaign organizations are unlikely to show much enthusiasm for a makeshift account group, especially after selecting the agency in question for its record and reputation. It was fun for Ben Duffy and Sig Larmon in 1952 to turn their talented staffs loose on the Eisenhower campaign. It gave them a chance to participate in a campaign that they regarded as vital to the national interest. The staff disruption was far less burdensome than it would become in later years as the industry matured and competition became fierce.

By the 1960s the thrill of innovation was gone. The challenge was not nearly as attractive. What in 1952 had been innovative was now becoming old hat. The Nixon campaign in 1972 found a stopgap solution. A number of executives from a variety of agencies took leaves of absence and joined to form an ad hoc group to handle the campaign. This prevented major disruption at any one agency but left lesser personnel gaps at a number of agencies.

At this point the Whitaker and Baxter model began to look increasingly like the wave of the future. A full-time, year-round political consulting agency, serving a variety of candidates and causes, some of them outside the United States, would be able to retain at least the nucleus of a full staff on a year-round basis. Many of the consultant firms that were springing up like weeds in a garden were able to deliver political advertising services as well as strategy guidance, thus reducing the need for an advertising agency. And they had another advantage. The old-line advertising agencies could conceive and produce spot commercials but were much less expert at creating situations and events that would encourage new coverage. They could deliver the paid spots but had little experience in the art of getting free exposure. They lacked the talent and experience necessary to anticipate what news directors were looking for. Their skills ran to preparing advertising for "paid media," not to dramatizing the character of their candidate and his views in such a way as to get "free media" exposure on the daily television news broadcasts.

The political consulting agency, whose main thrust extended as much to public relations as to regular advertising, could in some part duplicate the agency's efforts in paid media, but it had also sharpened its skills in creating situations and events that television stations and networks would find it difficult to overlook. The free media exposure frequently yielded more valuable results to the candidate than paid commercials. Free media and paid media, harnessed in tandem, made a powerful team. Imaginatively staged free media events, masquerading as hard news, were a boon to the news director. He had a chance to send his crews out to cover ready-made stories that had visual appeal, human interest, political significance, and controversy, and could be delivered without taxing his staff's imagination. If it all worked well, the consultant would get his payoff. He would have succeeded in implanting in voters' minds the image he had designed, and he had done so without paying for the time.

It is important to note, though, that the television station or network created the environment that the consultant exploited. The broadcaster had established a pattern for news broadcasts and for the items that would fit into them. The consultant delivered material to fit the specifications.

Public relations practitioners and press agents in the 1950s had actively pushed tips, suggestions for items to cover, offers of help in arranging coverage, and reams of press releases. But their efforts were simplistic, light-years removed from the highly sophisticated efforts of the new breed of political consultants. The efforts were straightforward. The motive was favorable mention on a news broadcast or an invitation to appear on a discussion program. The term "free media" implied a service infinitely more complex. It implied an effort to create an irresistible setting for a news story that would implant a favorable response in the viewer's mind. Planning for free media required imagination, a clear view of objectives, a sense of drama, an eye for physical setting, and an understanding of how the human thought processes work. It involved coordination with other aspects of the campaign so it could become one facet in a multipronged attack.

Television was not ready for so refined an approach in the 1950s, and the media specialists were not yet ready to deliver it. Prior to 1964, network news was limited to 15 minutes nightly and shorter segments on the morning programs, a relatively limited target for an aggressive free media merchant. Local stations were expanding their news operations rapidly, but the 15-minute early evening program was still the norm rather than the 90-minute and even 120-minute programs that became popular in the late 1960s, following the networks' expansion to the 30-minute format. Until the advent of the longer news program, there was hardly enough time available on the air for the consultant to make a viable business out of aiming at the small target.

By the late 1960s, however, television news was an irresistible target. National television receiver penetration was reaching a near saturation level, and during the winter season the combined early evening network news programs were reaching nearly half the television homes in the nation every night. Local stations were expanding their time for news, adding to staff, and reaching rating levels in their local communities frequently exceeding those of the network programs. They were often less sophisticated than their network counterparts, and consequently less likely to to be skeptical of suggestions from outsiders and less inclined to apply traditional journalistic standards. They were more apt to cover uncritically an event that the network might consider too soft or too biased for consideration.

It was the perfect setup for the smart consultant. No longer would he have to rely solely on sending press releases to the media and hope that they would get some response. He could begin to control all his candidate's activities so as to eliminate any possibility of error, avoid negative impressions, and get the most favorable media response. In the 1972 campaign Richard Nixon virtually never appeared except in the most rigidly controlled situations. He obtained favorable exposure by participating in events that television news felt must be covered. Cameras and microphones, however, never got close enough to pick up any slip of the tongue or awkward movement. The camera was able to record only the moments that the consultants had planned in advance. And, in view of the importance of the event, there really was no alternative for the news organization than to be present and hope that some morsel of real news might escape the tight controls. The consultant exploited the journalistic principle that what the president did was news, no matter if it was simply riding down a Philadelphia street in an armored car out of sight of television cameras.

Shortly after the conclusion of the 1972 campaign, I was asked to write a chapter for a book in which I was to relate my reaction following intensive observation of television coverage. The most striking aspect to me was the futility of Senator George McGovern's efforts to come to grips with an opponent who remained under tight wraps from nomination to election, his every move carefully controlled by his handlers. I wrote then, "The president was as carefully shielded from the political hustle-bustle as if he were flying through the campaign in a hermetically sealed space capsule. The environment was carefully controlled. The course was set by skillfully programmed computer technology."[7] The practice of encasing the candidate in an airtight cocoon did not stop after 1972. The art of candidate packaging has been developing constantly ever since.

The controls that shield a candidate from unwanted exposure can also be turned to arranging for desired display under the most favorable circumstances. There was hardly a public appearance by either major party candidate in the 1988 presidential election that was not planned in the minutest detail. Careful attention was given to selecting meaningful and pictorially interesting backdrops for the planned message. George Bush rode a launch through Boston Harbor to condemn Michael Dukakis's lack of commitment to conservation. A few days later he almost literally wrapped himself in the American flag as he visited a flag factory in Philadelphia. That was the backdrop selected to underscore his complaint that Dukakis had vetoed a bill that would have required Massachusetts schoolchildren to recite the pledge of allegiance at the opening of the school day. Dukakis, in turn, will not soon be forgotten as he was pictured, looking awkward and uncomfortable, riding in a tank and wearing the uniform of a tank driver. His purpose was to illustrate his commitment to national defense. His advisers also flew him almost all the way across the country to find an appropriate setting where he would be able to demonstrate his concern for the environment. They selected fire-ravaged Yellowstone National Park.

The stage settings were selected to create the most striking and effective backdrops for emphasizing the "line of the day," another phrase in the new lexicon of the image makers, one that reflects the effort of consultants to coordinate and simplify each day's campaign effort. Coordinating the line of the day with the proper stage setting is one of the creative functions of the practitioners of the art of political consulting. The line of the day need not be backed up by clear reasoning and exhaustive evidence. The objective is to win the voters' support not by a preponderance of evidence and sound argument but by eliciting favorable emotional response.

Television news is more susceptible to this kind of image making and symbol promotion than it was three decades ago. Gordon Van Sauter, when he was president of the CBS News division during the middle 1980s, encouraged his reporters and producers to look for memorable "moments" to spice up his news broadcasts. Memorable "moments"—many of them can be "sound bites"—are precisely what the image makers try to deliver, and they have acquired considerable skill in creating them. They have probed for and uncovered the soft spots in television news organizations, using the benefit of several years of experience and of methods forged out of trial and error. Television news has generally been a soft target. The dollar stakes have grown so high, the competition so fierce, the hours to fill so expanded, that the station news director and assignment editor are constantly looking for attractive material. The quadrennial national election is so important to the national welfare that no news organization can afford to take it lightly. If the only access to the candidate is through an event the consultant has arranged, the editor has only a limited option to reject it, and virtually none if the event is staged with enough imagination to make it a "must carry" item.

The onrush of new broadcast technology has also had a profound effect on easing the problems of the consultant. Portable electronic cameras with accompanying videotape recording have liberated the consultant from planning all appearances within the drab confines of a studio. Microwave transmission and use of the satellite make coverage of a press conference on a launch in Boston Harbor almost as easy as a studio appearance. The consultant can now plan his backdrops within a geographical range almost as wide as his imagination, with the knowledge that the event covered can be seen within minutes anywhere in the nation.

Notwithstanding the emphasis on free media, paid media is still on a steep upward climb in dollar volume. In a spot commercial the candidate and his managers have total control over the content of the message and its manner of presentation. But free media offers significant advantages in addition to limiting the strain on the campaign budget. The free media item reaches the public in a serious, news-oriented environment, not during a break in a sitcom or a cops-and-robbers drama. A news program offers the ideal environment for a brief sound bite incorporating the line of the day or the theme of the day. It can be attractive to the television assignment editor because it comes disguised as a "photo op" (photo opportunity) in a carefully selected stage setting with an appropriate backdrop. Coverage demands no imagination on the part of the television crew. It has been stage-managed by the consultant. The lexicon of the image campaign reveals the extent to which the campaign has become dominated by media specialists whose main target is television, specifically television news programs.

There is not much room, if any, for interpretation or explanation regarding serious issues, or for questioning the candidate on the logic behind his positions. The brief time allotted to the sound bite does not permit it. There is little evidence that news directors, whether on the local or the network level, prefer greater length. They seem dedicated to the notion that the viewer's attention span is short and a great variety of items must be covered. Long, serious expository pieces justifying complex positions don't grab audiences—not unless the item reeks with human interest. This desire for brevity spares the candidate the burden of having to support a generalization with facts and explanation. He can make his point and keep it colorful, simple, and brief. There is no point, current political campaign theory goes, in wasting time and money on factual and argumentative approaches to issues, particularly if the medium lends itself better to a more subtle approach based on imagery and symbolism. Tony Schwartz demonstrated the wisdom of that theory with his Lyndon Johnson spots in 1964. Even though they were withdrawn after one showing, they had a lingering effect and may have influenced the outcome of the election.

The homogenization process has not been limited to hard news broadcasts. The first presidential "joint appearances" involving Richard Nixon and John Kennedy were not true debates in a strict use of that word. They did, however, provide for opening statements of eight minutes each in the first and last of the confrontations, and each candidate was allowed an additional 3 minutes and 20 seconds for summations. That contrasts with the two-minute and one-minute segments allowed for the candidates to answer reporters' questions in the 1988 joint appearances featuring George Bush and Michael Dukakis. If the candidate did not wish to do so, there was no compulsion for him to answer the question. He could wander off in any direction he chose, responding with vacuous homilies or irrelevant puffery. Little provision was made for follow-up questions from the re-porters. The League of Women Voters was so disillusioned by the format prescribed by the candidates that it withdrew from sponsorship of the second debate.

The debate format, however, gave gainful employment to another rel-atively recent addition to the roster of political campaign experts, the "spin doctors." The candidates were barely able to get off the platform before their respective spin doctors were pleading with media personnel to give their accounts of the event a "spin" favorable to their candidate. In the event of a major blunder by a candidate, the spin doctors would immediately begin a process of "damage control." And the clichés roll on.

It is not only the clichés that are new. The whole process has been remodeled since 1952. It is almost impossible to find an outlet on commercial television news programs that allows for much more depth than the sound bite provides. The exceptions are in public television and in C-SPAN on cable, and some of the network long-form news interview and discussion shows. If the viewer regularly desires more than the fleeting impression he gets from the sound bite, he has little alternative than to go to the Public Broadcasting Service or C-SPAN. Many of commercial television's news programs have permitted themselves to succumb to the service provided by the consultants and the candidates they represent. It is not a matter of covering or not covering the story or event set up by the consultant. Cov-erage is frequently unavoidable. A presidential candidate is news whether he is riding a launch across Boston Harbor or a tank on a military base. Accepting the item uncritically, and without adequate explanation and inter-pretation, is the point at which the voters are badly served.

The pursuit by networks and stations alike of high ratings and the dollars that go along with high viewership created the opening for the consultants and their teams of specialists. The consultants created opportunities for recording attractive sound bites and memorable moments that in turn de-livered viewers. They were newsworthy enough and had a sufficient au-dience appeal that it was easy to use them. The candidates, who want more than anything to get elected, team up with their consultants, and the result is the triumph of imagery over facts, of symbols over character, and of show business over rational argumentation. It remains to be seen whether irreparable damage has been done to the electoral system, whether television has lived up to its early promise or contributed to the collapse of the process of electing candidates qualified to make a democratic system work. Specifically, would the trivialization of the presidential campaign have occurred if there had been no television? Or, conversely, was television a contributor to the degrading process?

NOTES

1. Mullen described the scene to me in a conversation in January 1970. A tape recording of the interview is available in the files of the Wisconsin Historical Library in Madison. Martin Mayer, in *Madison Avenue, U.S.A.* (New York: Harper and Brothers, 1958), pp. 294–96, points out that there was one other significant player in the effort to place commercials on television. Alfred Hollender, a broadcasting station manager and later an advertising agency executive who had met General Eisenhower when he was serving in the radio propaganda effort during the war, had volunteered to work on the campaign. Subsequently, according to Mayer, he had convinced the general and his brother Milton of the value of televised commercials. This had occurred prior to the dinner at 21.

2. Mayer, *Madison Avenue, U.S.A.*, p. 294.

3. Ibid., p. 296.

4. Carroll Newton, one of the political experts at BBDO, accepted the assignment of dissuading network executives from their negative stance. It was felt that if the networks remained inflexible, it would be difficult to convince stations to accept the orders, whereas acceptance by network-owned stations would be a strong endorsement. Newton finally succeeded in winning the approval of both Frank Stanton, CBS president, and Joseph McConnell, NBC's chief executive. He described his efforts to me in a conversation that was taped and is on file at the Wisconsin Historical Library.

5. Descriptions of the 1950 Dewey for Governor campaign by both Carroll Newton of BBDO and Jim Hagerty are available in interviews on audiotape at the Wisconsin Historical Library.

6. Figures supplied by Television Bureau of Advertising in New York and printed in *Broadcasting Magazine*, January 18, 1988, p. 76.

7. "Blurred Image in the Electric Mirror," in *The Politics of Broadcasting 1971–1972*, ed. Marvin Barrett (New York: Thomas Y. Crowell, 1973), p. 165.

12

The Frustrated Dream

The most disappointing aspect of the four decades of the politics–television relationship has been the shattering of the optimism of the 1950s, the subversion of the confident predictions that the nation was on the threshold of a new era in which television would help democracy function with unprecedented efficiency. The exhilaration that permeated CBS studio 51 on election night 1952 has turned into frustration. The promise that television would open up the electoral system, encourage candidates to be more candid with voters, increase the turnout at the polls, and create a more responsive democracy has collapsed in an era dominated by packaged campaigns and avoidance of issues.

Television cannot be charged with full responsibility for the erosion of standards used in appealing to voters, but most of the methods and devices used for projecting those appeals are television-related. The sound bite was born in the television newsroom, not in the fertile brain of a candidate handler. The handlers discovered what television wanted and delivered it to support their own ends. The packaging process was designed to conform to television's requirements. The objective was to create appealing programming for television while simultaneously building insurance that the candidate would avoid any gaffs that would damage his standing in the polls.

Prospects for a television–politics partnership that would measure up to the early expectations looked favorable through the early 1950s. Exploitation of television by political leaders and consultants began slowly but gained momentum once campaign leaderships had discovered the secret of turning the medium toward achieving their ends.

The early response was more one of awe than of opportunism. Even before television had more than dipped a toe into the political waters, national political leaders were beginning to hail it as a miracle worker. Senator William Benton of Connecticut, more than a year before the Republican Party met in Chicago to nominate Dwight Eisenhower as its candidate for the presidency, expressed his admiration for the impact he was sure the upstart medim would demonstrate. "The potentialities of television are so great," he told television critic Jack Gould of the *New York Times*, "they will revolutionize politics." But Benton also offered a note of caution. "The terrifying aspect is the high cost, the expenses of which could well determine election or defeat."[1]

Governor Thomas E. Dewey of New York and Senator Robert Taft of Ohio offered no such caveats. Both had been heavy television users in their successful bids for reelection the previous November. Apparently mesmerized by their easy victories, they were somewhat more optimistic about television's magic qualities than subsequent analyses would support.

"Politically, television is an X-ray," Dewey told Gould. "If a man doesn't know the business of government, he cannot long stand its piercing lights and stark realism. It should make a constructive advance in political campaigning." Taft had even higher praise. Television, he said, "favored the man of sincerity," and eliminated "the false value of the sweetness of the voice and, I think, makes a better medium for the truth."[2]

It seemed perfectly reasonable in 1950 and 1952 to conclude that television "favored the man of sincerity" and that it had eliminated "the false value of the sweetness of the voice." Dewey was not alone in claiming that "Politically, television is an X-ray." Most of us who pioneered the television side of the relationship fervently believed in the myth of the X-ray eye. Percpetions have changed since those early days when television was a new and glamorous toy.

One of the reasons that exploitation of television by political managers developed slowly was the simple fact that television news of the 1950s and early 1960s was still in an adolescent stage. It lacked the time on the air to give much exposure, and the technology required for the vaporous, simplistic campaigns of the 1970s and 1980s. Television had the basic ingredients—sound, picture, and motion projected to a screen in the home—but it still was not producing news programs in the volume that would come later, and the formats did not lend themselves to incorporating brief sound bites. They were still serious in tone, informational rather than entertaining in content, and limited in length. The early evening network news programs were limited to only 15 minutes until the half-hour became standard in 1964. Stations did not begin to expand their news beyond the customary 15-minute pattern until the networks went to the half hour. Then many went quickly to 30 minutes, a full hour, or in some cases to two hours.

The increased time led to a frantic scramble for material to fill the newly available minutes and quarter hours. Coincidentally, station managers began to discover that news programming is not a public service item broadcast only to appease FCC commissioners at license renewal time and to cater to the more serious viewers. They began to discover that there was profit in news programming, profit they had not previously believed existed. This discovery focused attention on news and stimulated spirited competition for rating points that in turn meant dollars in the till. Former news directors, producers, and market research experts saw an opening for lucrative consultancies that would advise stations on methods designed to achieve higher ratings and the profits that followed. On the advice of the newly created consulting firms, news items became shorter, serious reports gave way to human interest, sound bites became a staple, and entertaining the viewers rather than informing them became the norm.

The stage was well set for the political consultant. News departments, both network and local, needed colorful and attractive items to round out their programs and build audiences. They had many hours to fill and voracious appetites for suitable material. The station lives on the proceeds of advertising, and political campaigns furnish a bonanza during the last couple of months before an election. Political managers, noting that the only way to be certain of getting a point across to voters in concise form without suffering editing was the spot commercial, began to buy spots in increasing volume. This meant revenue for the station or network and an outlet for a compaign produced directly to campaign specifications. The themes, dressed up in live settings and given solid news pegs involving the participation of the candidate himself, could then be used as bait to attract news coverage. Free media and paid media worked hand in hand, and television was the outlet.

A political campaign matching widely known candidates is news. It is particularly attractive to a news editor because it has a built-in contest element and participants with star quality. The consultant needs the news department as an outlet for his creative efforts, and the news department needs the political consultant's help in making his candidate available, even though it is only in stage-managed settings. It is not surprising that skillfully crafted sound bites have no difficulty winning exposure. Candidates at the presidential level are, by virtue of their positions, exceptionally newsworthy. The campaign consultant has a single task to perform: get his candidate elected. He has time to think and plan within the relatively narrow scope of his assignment. He is not harried, as is the news director, by the pressures involved in filling broadcast schedules with material calculated to attract viewers and win rating points. He is free to concentrate his considerable talents on planning a single item that will show off his candidate to best advantage. He can concentrate on a topic of his own choosing in a setting that he selects. It is little wonder that the item he conjures up is likely to get maximum exposure.

It is a situation made to order for the consultant and his client. The network or station needs them and the service they deliver. The candidate receives free media exposure under made-to-order conditions. The station or network is able to record a surefire audience-building item with little creative ingenuity required. Radio and print have access to the same item but lack the technological capabilities of picture, motion, and sound to use it most effectively. It is television that is the prime target. The other media are bonuses.

In that sense it is television that is responsible for the most profound changes in campaigning in the latter half of the twentieth century. The campaign has been remade to television specifications. Television created sound bites. Campaign managers exploited them. Television searched out colorful backgrounds for news stories. Campaign organizations made a speciality of meeting their requirements and even exceeding them in their search for dramatic stage settings for making statements or evoking emotional responses and leaving impressions. Television lives by advertising. Candidates satisfied their cravings by buying spots in increasing volume.

In one sense television has been an innocent bystander. It has furnished the studios, cameras, transmission facilities, personnel to man them, an established program schedule, promotional muscle, and an audience, a very large audience. It also has developed the techniques for reaching mass audiences and program formats that have held them. It is little wonder that the medium has become an all-consuming passion of campaign managers. Campaign leaderships were slow to exploit fully television's capabilities in the 1950s and early 1960s, but once the key to its use was discovered, the floodgates were opened. It clearly has been the highest priority target. As such it has exerted more influence on American politics than any other medium. In our political campaigns this is truly the television age.[3]

The results of the uneasy relationship are not very salutary. After four decades in which politics and television have been somewhat uneasy bedfellows, there does not seem to be much clear evidence that elections are any more efficient at selecting the best candidates, that voters are any better informed or more interested, or that candidates are of a higher quality.

The form of political campaigning in the four decades of television has been undergoing astonishing change, and it is equally evident now that the substance has changed along with it. There is more stress on emotional issues that play well on the tube. Long expository statements or detailed arguments in favor of a given position have been largely supplanted by carefully prepared sound bites. Debate is one of those campaign devices that television popularized on a national scale, but the formats have become so restrictive that it is impossible to generate much response from the candidates regarding issues. Presidential candidates are still talking, as they have for decades, about taxes, national defense, foreign affairs, Social Security, farm policies, foreign trade, and the national debt. But in the television era the voter receives less pertinent information, shorter explanations, more labels, and very little interpretation or reasoning on which to base sound judgments. Most of the candidates' responses to issues are delivered in the form of commercial spots and sound bites. Even though the issues are the same, the output from the candidates is not very nourishing, surely less so than before television helped trivialize the process.

The effect on the viewer-voter of this symbiotic relationship does nothing to enhance the voter's capability to chose wisely at the ballot box. The campaign managers and consultants are knowledgeable enough about television to realize that to win voters, they must be concerned with effect rather than meaning, with emotional response rather than factual presentation, with easily digested morsels rather than big bites of heavy dough. The voter is happy because there is no strain on his thinking processes. The candidates have allowed themselves to be mechanized to the extent that they participate easily in the razzle-dazzle of product advertising and enjoy the glamour of being lionized in the news, but not much effort is being devoted to informing the voters on significant issues.

Television is an easy target for the new campaign methodology. It stakes its success on the tyranny of the picture. Most television news editors regard "talking heads" as sure producers of tumbling ratings. And, unhappily, ideas are elusive targets for camera lenses. The camera can show only tangible physical objects, not intangible thoughts. Ed Murrow and Fred Friendly were remarkably successful in conveying important ideas through "little stories," but they had time and resources, and an uncommon wealth of creativity and imagination to devote to their efforts. The net result is that television news broadcasts fail to dig deeply into complicated topics and are easy targets for political consultants who bring features guaranteed to deliver ratings.

It is ironic that the most popular communications device of the century, one that is found in more than 98 percent of American homes and commands more family time than any activity other than sleeping, should not have brought a new era to American politics. In its early days it tried hard enough. In fact, it is still trying. The time, money, and effort devoted to coverage of primary elections and political conventions over and above the intensive coverage of the final two to three months prior to the national election attest to the fact that both networks and stations are trying, but trying apparently is not enough. Too much of the effort is concentrated on entertaining, self-promotion, and striving for ratings. This effort consumes so much attention that not much is left for developing more effective methods for informing the electorate.

The results do not encourage much optimism for the future. The public simply appears less interested than it was in the past. In 1960, 62.8 percent of eligible American voters went to the polls on Election Day, the highest percentage in recent history. By 1976 the percentage had dropped to 53.5, and by 1984 to 53.3. Only 1932 and 1948 registered lower percentages: 52.4 and 51.1 respectively.[4] Nearly everyone who had access to a television receiver watched some part of the national conventions in 1952. In the 1980s, baseball games, game shows, and movies were frequently rating better than the conventions.

There must be a reason, and it cannot be simply a matter of having seen it all before. The novelty has obviously worn off. That can account for some of the decline. It is more likely that the reduced voter interest has been influenced by a variety of factors.

The growing complexity of issues that must be decided by government may drive some potential voters off. Deciding whether to support or oppose the Strategic Defense Initiative or "Star Wars," for example, can be a frustrating experience. It is easier to forget it and let someone else decide. Television might be able to help if it had any competence to explain complex issues in the brief time allotted in news broadcasts, but news executives are, of necessity, dedicated to delivering high ratings. Brief, memorable "moments" are more likely to win the audience than scholarly scientific explanations. Too much time spent trying to explain implications of foreign trade imbalances or proposed tax legislation results only in frustrated viewers.

The entertaining and emotionally charged vignettes that television provides are calculated to entertain and amuse, and even to win sympathy, but they are not likely to arouse voters' passions to the point that they will determinedly march to the polls. Television is more likely to be looked at as a game, a spectator sport, not one for participants. It is conceivably possible for a viewer to get as excited about a serious issue as he does about a Super Bowl or a World Series, but that is a pretty remote possibility; and even if he does, he has little reason to believe that there is a realistic opportunity for him to do anything about it. Election campaign coverage, for the most part, consists of a fleeting series of images that float by on the screen entertainingly but hardly passionately, at least not passionately enough to encourage a sufficient number of voters to go to the polls to make their views known. The images are there to entertain and to create a favorable climate of opinion, but only the most effective are likely to arouse. They lack the inspiration to get the voter to the ballot box. Even the spot commercials are produced to convey strong entertainment values. They are more useful in energizing the committed than in persuading the undecided.

It was once the political parties that assumed the responsibility for seeing to it that voters went to the polls. In the age of television, there is valid doubt whether the party retains much real power. Television may have replaced it. The old ward boss maintained constant personal contact with his constituents. He was their link with government, their advisor on issues. Before the era when entertainment could be brought into the home with a flip of the switch, the ward and county organizations provided diversion at low cost and simultaneously stimulated enthusiasm for both issues and candidates. Now the voter can sit at home, enjoy his game shows and sports events, and get his political information in sugarcoated capsules on the television screen. He no longer needs the political party.

The voter also may be bored by the seemingly endless duration of the campaign. State governments, seeking publicity and increased influence in the selection of national candidates, started their primaries and caucuses earlier and earlier, until Michigan retreated to the year prior to the national election to begin its candidate selection process. Television news follows the entire process. Interest appears to run high during the preliminary jousting in Iowa and New Hampshire but fades as more states come on stream. The national conventions once revived interest in midsummer, but when they became cut and dried, there was no stimulant remaining to resuscitate flagging enthusiasm. Strategically placed rallies or major speeches once pumped new life into a sagging campaign, but even they have faded away. All that remains is a constant bombardment of sound bites and spot commercials flowing in a monotonous pattern with litttle evidence of peaks and valleys. Efforts are made to energize campaigns at the local level through visits by candidates. Even though they are covered by both national and local television, there is little except for the carefully produced and staged sound bites to attract national attention. Polls extract all the suspense, and the potential voter is left with a formless gray mass—hardly an inducement to act.

The media, led by television, have contributed to ennui by removing emphasis from issues and putting it squarely on the horse race. Starting with the first caucuses, the first questions are Who is ahead? and What influence will this victory have on the next primary or caucus? Politics, as a result, becomes a game. The game is relatively simple for television to cover. All it takes is the ability to count and to speculate who will win the next round. Discussion of the issues becomes lost in calculating odds regarding possible winners. Interpretation and analysis have turned from consideration of the dominant issues to guessing which candidate has derived the most favorable public response from his approach to a specific matter of contention. It is probably unfair to pin sole responsiblity on television, but certainly it must bear a large share of the blame. Its appetite for action and brevity, supported by reproduction and transmission equipment that can get an item on the air in minutes and its orientation to show business, have made it peculiarly vulnerable.

The demand for a new type of candidate, presumably dictated by the requirements of television, is largely a myth. It has not been nearly as evident as the evolution in news coverage. Most of the successful candidates look and sound about as they did in the pretelevision era. Franklin Roosevelt, Harry Truman, and Dwight Eisenhower could probably all win election in a late-twentieth-century televised campaign. All three could communicate. All could inspire confidence. All, in the current vernacular, "looked presidential." The question is whether they would have put up with the length of the campaign and with the indignities of being managed by a puppeteer. Or, if one of the three had run during the era of television, would he have demanded a different type of campaign, a campaign in which the candidate spoke his mind, disregarded the advice of his consultant, and stated his positions even without waiting for television cameras and the proper stage setting?

John F. Kennedy was the first genuine television candidate. His campaign was skillfully directed and carefully planned, but not tightly controlled. He and his advisers had confidence in their own political skills and in Kennedy's ability to communicate on television. It is hard to conceive of Lyndon Johnson sitting still for a lecture on campaign techniques from an outside consultant. The first genuine image campaign planned for optimum television exposure was Richard Nixon's presidential campaign in 1968. That effort set the pattern for subsequent runs for the presidency and introduced the tactic of keeping the candidate under wraps except on those occasions when the environment can be rigidly controlled and any slip of the tongue prevented.

There were a number of prospective benefits expected to derive from television. One of the early optimistic predictions held that television would make it possible for the unknown candidate to achieve name recognition in weeks, if not days. It once seemed a realistic possibility. Adlai Stevenson was a virtual unknown when he was nominated by the Democrats in 1952. Television quickly gave him national status as a viable candidate. Unless there is a drastic change in the nominating process, though, it probably will never happen again. Campaigns have become so long and the primary so critical to nomination that the latecomer would face overwhelming negative odds if he tried to inject himself into the race at the last minute. It is virtually impossible that a sudden ground swell for an outsider could detach delegates from their long-standing commitments stemming from victory in the primaries. It is ironic that it is largely television's influence in focusing attention on the primaries that has made nomination of a dark horse virtually unthinkable. There has not been a dark horse candidate since Stevenson who stood a chance of nomination. Television gave the dark horse the opportunity and then stole it from him.

The current primary system, in large part a legacy of television, has forced candidates to plunge all the way into the race without any easy warm-up or stretching exercises. Once they are in the game, they are all the way in. There is no preseason schedule, no Grapefruit League. It is the race for the pennant from the opening announcement. The only escape is to drop out.

The power of the networks to dictate political fashions or to influence them declined rapidly during the 1980s. During the network heyday, from the early 1950s through most of the 1970s, network shares of sets in use during prime time consistently ran in the 90 percent-plus range. By the end of the 1980s they had fallen to the mid-60s, gradually eroded by the rising strength of independent, nonaffiliated stations, by cable, and by the swiftly increasing popularity of video cassettes.

Broadcast news departments in local stations, both affiliates and independents, were flexing the muscles provided by their new electronic equipment: all-electronic cameras and editing gear, short-range microwave relays, and longer-range transmission by satellites. They were discovering that they were no longer dependent on the networks for all but strictly local coverage. Satellite mobile units, owned by individual stations, were being banded together in cooperatives to furnish national and even international coverage competitive with or supplementary to that of the networks. No longer do cooperative pools organized for coverage of major events consist of just three television networks. Now there is a fourth, the Cable News Network. And a fifth, the Public Broadcasting Service, delivers a service more attuned to a smaller audience with a deeper interest in public affairs.

Does the decline of the networks foreshadow more revolutionary changes in political campaign methodology? The answer is "probably not." It was not the networks that brought about the revolution in campaign techniques. It was the introduction of a live medium combining picture, sound, and motion, delivered free of charge and at the speed of light, that initiated the change. Political news and coverage of major political events were distributed by the networks, liberally supported by big budgets, packaged in an environment dominated by attractive entertainment programs, and backed up by massive promotion. All the ingredients required for a quick incursion into covering political campaigns were present. The networks have now crested, but independent stations, cable television, and video cassettes are already taking up the slack. Their capabilities for reaching the viewer are amost identical. Only the technology they use is different. They will continue to program for a visually oriented audience, and candidates and consultants will continue to exploit the opportunities they offer.

We probably cannot hope for a radical transformation of media coverage of political campaigns. An intellectual campaign geared to explanation of governmental policy regarding budgets, taxes, national defense, foreign affairs, and the environment is probably too much to ask from commercial broadcasting. In 1960, during only the third national campaign covered by television, the Survey Research Center at the University of Michigan completed an intensive study of voter attitudes. The result are discouraging reading for anyone hoping that campaign rhetoric will ascend to new heights and that the visual media will be able to contribute to a more sophisticated electorate.

"For a large part of the public," the study found, "political affairs are probably too difficult to comprehend in detail." Even more discouraging is the conclusion that "Very few people seem motivated strongly enough to obtain the information needed to develop a sensitive understanding of decision making in government."[5]

The conclusion would seem to suggest that there is not much that can be done to lead toward that "more informed electorate" that so many speakers and writers point to. Perhaps political issues are simply too complex for the voter. Perhaps the public will not pay much attention to public policy formulation and issues, no matter how attractively and how effectively the media deal with them. In the same study the authors suggest that the voter has a built-in "perceptorium" with a valve that automatically shuts off when he has received an overload of complicated information.[6]

On the other hand, it is possible to conclude from the findings of the Survey Research Center that voters are easy targets for the blandishments of the image merchants. By playing to their natural tendency to avoid the complicated and the difficult to comprehend, television and consultants together may be depreciating the level of understanding and interest, and debasing the electoral process. A new dedication to emphasis on issues, using the uniqe power of the picture tube, might at least bring campaigns back to the level of the 1950s and early 1960s.

It all seemed so easy on election night 1952. At long last the nation had access to a medium that would lead to a nation more interested in politics and more sophisticated regarding electoral issues. The four decades since then have done little to give substance to that dream. We can hope that there still may be the time and the will to turn television and the newer visual media to the dream's fulfillment.

NOTES

1. Quoted by television critic Jack Gould, "Political Leaders Acclaim TV But Warn Against Its Misuse," *New York Times*, June 24, 1951, in James Fixx, *The Mass Media and Politics* (New York: Arno Press, 1972), p. 11. Benton, as one of the founders of the Benton and Bowles advertising agency and a former assistant secretary of state with responsibility for the Voice of America and the international information program, was recognized as one of the nation's leading experts in uses of the media.

2. Quoted by Gould, *New York Times*, June 24, 1951.

3. Gary Braun of the Copley Press reported that "in a state [California] where 10 million people will vote, both campaigns [Democratic and Republican] concede that television was 90 percent of their voter contact" *San Diego Union*, November 7, 1988, p. A–3.

4. *The World Almanac and Book of Facts* (New York: Pharos Books, 1987), p. 305. The careful observer will note that in a previous chapter, quoting from a speech I had made in Austin, Texas, in early 1961, I had placed the voter participation level in the 1960 presidential election at 64.3 percent. That firgure was subsequently revised to the lower 62.8 figure.

5. Angus Campbell, Philip E. Converse, Warren E. Miller, and Donald E. Stoker, *The American Voter* (New York: John Wiley, 1961), p. 543.

6. Campbell et al., *The American Voter*, p. 543.

Bibliography

Alexander, Herbert E., and Brian A. Haggerty. *Financing the 1984 Election.* Lexington, Mass.: Lexington Books/D. C. Heath, 1986.

Barrett, Marvin, ed. *The Politics of Broadcasting.* New York: Thomas Y. Crowell Company, 1973.

Campbell, Angus, Philip E. Converse, Warren E. Miller, and Donald E. Stoker. *The American Voter.* New York: John Wiley and Sons, 1961.

Fixx, James. *The Mass Media and Politics.* New York: Arno Press, 1972.

Glick, Edward M. *The New Methodology: A Study of Political Strategy and Tactics.* Washington, D. C.: American Institute for Political Communication, 1967.

Hyman, Sidney. *The Lives of William Benton.* Chicago: The University of Chicago Press, 1969.

Kraus, Sidney, ed. *The Great Debates.* Bloomington, Ind.: University of Indiana Press, 1962.

Lang, Kurt, and Gladys Engel Lang. *Politics and Television.* Chicago: Quadrangle Books, 1968.

Mayer, Martin. *Madison Avenue, U.S.A.* New York: Harper, 1958.

Reddick, Dewitt C., ed. *The Role of Mass Media in a Democratic Society.* Austin: University of Texas, 1961.

Republican National Committee. "Official Report of the Proceedings of the Twenty-Sixth Republican National Convention." Washington, D. C.: Republican National Committee, 1957.

———. "Official Report of the Proceedings of the Twenty-Eighth Republican National Convention." Washington, D. C.: Republican National Committee, 1961.

Schneider, John G. *The Golden Kazoo.* New York: Holt, Rinehart and Co., 1956.

The World Almanac and Book of Facts 1987. New York: Pharos Books, 1987.

Index

About the Author

SIG MICKELSON is an authentic pioneer in the relationship between politics and television. As director of news and public affairs for CBS Television in 1952, he supervised the network's coverage of that first major effort by television to bring a political campaign to life on the nation's television screens. He also served in that year as chairman of the all-network committee that organized the network coverage pool and maintained liaison with the national parties. He continued to direct network coverage in 1956 as CBS corporate vice-president for news and public affairs and in 1960 as president of the newly created CBS news division. In 1964 he took a leave of absence from Time, Inc., which he had joined in 1961, to serve as program director for the Republican National Convention.

Mickelson joined CBS in 1943 as director of news for CBS-owned WCCO in Minneapolis and St. Paul. He moved to New York in 1949 as director of public affairs for CBS. After leaving Time, Inc., he served as professor of journalism and chairman of the editorial journalism department of the Medill School at Northwestern University in Evanston, Illinois, and as President of RFE/RL, Inc., in Washington, D. C. He is currently VanDeerlin professor of communications at San Diego State University, president of the San Diego Communications Council, and a research fellow at the Hoover Institution.